Marketing in a Nutshell

Key concepts for non-specialists

Mike Meldrum
and
Malcolm McDonald

ELSEVIER

AMSTERDAM ● BOSTON ● HEIDELBERG ● LONDON ● NEW YORK ● OXFORD
PARIS ● SAN DIEGO ● SAN FRANCISCO ● SINGAPORE ● SYDNEY ● TOKYO
Butterworth-Heinemann is an imprint of Elsevier

Butterworth-Heinemann is an imprint of Elsevier
Linacre House, Jordan Hill, Oxford OX2 8DP, UK
30 Corporate Drive, Suite 400, Burlington, MA 01803, USA

First edition 2007

British Library Cataloguing in Publication Data
A catalogue record for this book is available from the British Library

Library of Congress Cataloguing in Publication Data
A catalogue record for this book is available from the Library of Congress

ISBN–13: 978-0-7506-8133-9
ISBN–10: 0-7506-8133-0

For information on all Butterworth-Heinemann publications
visit our web site at http://books.elsevier.com

Typeset by Charon Tec Ltd (A Macmillan Company), Chennai, India
www.charontec.com
Printed and bound in Great Britain

07 08 09 10 11   10 9 8 7 6 5 4 3 2 1

Contents

Foreword   vii

List of Tables   viii

List of Figures   ix

TOWER HAMLETS COLLEGE
Learning Centre
Arbour Square
LONDON E1 0PT
Tel: 020 7510 7568

Part 1   Understanding the Basics of Marketing   1

1   The Discipline of Marketing   3
2   A Market Orientation   7
3   The Marketing Mix   10
4   Marketing: Concept, Function or Process?   15
5   Marketing and Ethics   19
6   World-class Marketing   23

Part 2   Different Types of Marketing   31

7   Marketing Consumer Products   33
8   Marketing Industrial Products   37
9   Marketing Service Products   41
10 Marketing High-tech Products   46
11 Marketing Capital Goods   51
12 Trade Marketing   54
13 Internet Marketing   58
14 Marketing Internationally   63

Part 3   Understanding Customers   67

15 Consumer Buying Behaviour   69
16 Organizational Buying Behaviour   74
17 Market Segmentation   79
18 International Market Segmentation   84

Part 4   Understanding Markets   87

19 Marketing Information and Research   89
20 Preparing a Marketing Research Brief   94
21 Auditing a Market   97
22 Constructing a SWOT   101
23 Competitor Analysis   106

Part 5   Product Management   111

24   Branding   113
25   The Product Lifecycle   117
26   Diffusion of Innovation   122
27   The Ansoff Matrix   126
28   The Boston Matrix   131
29   The Directional Policy Matrix   135
30   Developing New Products   141

Part 6   Key Elements of Positioning   147

31   Pricing Strategies   149
32   Setting a Price   153
33   Sales Promotion   157
34   Advertising   162
35   Public Relations   167
36   Sponsorship   171

Part 7   Marketing Relationships   177

37   Relationship Marketing   179
38   Customer Retention Strategies   184
39   Personal Selling   189
40   Key Account Management: Understanding the Concept   193
41   Key Account Management: Implementing the Concept   198
42   Channel Strategy   202
43   Channel Management   206
44   Customer Service Strategies   210
45   Databases for Marketing   214
46   M(obile) Marketing   220
47   Category Management   226
48   Multi-channel Integration   230
49   Integrated Marketing Communication and Distribution Channels   235

Part 8   Management, Planning and Control   239

50   Managing the Sales Team   241
51   Forecasting Sales   247
52   Marketing Planning   251
53   Barriers to Marketing Planning Implementation   256
54   International Product Planning   261
55   Organizational Structure and Marketing   265
56   Budgeting for Marketing   270
57   Legal Issues in Marketing Communications   274
58   Marketing Due Diligence   278
59   Marketing Metrics   281

Index   285

Marketing in a Nutshell

Foreword

We wrote this book because, like many authors and practitioners before us, it's the book we wanted but couldn't find. Both marketers and other managers alike need quick insights that illuminate marketing topics to help them do their job. To get them, they don't want to study a textbook or hunt the Internet. They want something to hand; something like a pocket book that can quickly convey the essence of a topic, concept or approach.

In trepidation, we have majored on marketing in the title. In spite of the best efforts of marketing academics, professional institutions, and more than a few chief executives, marketing remains an enigma. Many know that the discipline has real value to offer managers across the whole of an organization, but too often that value is never realized.

We hope that this book will help the burgeoning numbers of managers who want to find ways of giving marketing a higher profile in their organizations by making the discipline accessible. The book is therefore compact, easy to use, and full of concise summaries of marketing topics. We trust it will help.

The book could not have been written without the conceptual assistance of a number of people to whom we extend grateful thanks. These include: Tim Dennison (for Topic 46), Malcolm Kirkup, Mark Jenkins, Hugh Wilson (for Topic 48) and Ardi Kolah (for Topics 36 and 57).

However, we don't expect you to read this book! It's not designed for that. Simply choose a topic, find it, and 15 minutes later you'll have the insight you need.

Mike Meldrum and Professor Malcolm McDonald

List of Tables

3.1	Product variables	11
3.2	Pricing variables	11
9.1	Major examples of service industries	41
9.2	Variations in product tangibility	42
14.1	Environment differences when marketing overseas	64
14.2	Key questions in international marketing	66
21.1	Marketing audit checklist	99
23.1	Guide to market competitive position classifications	108
23.2	Alternative business directions	109
23.3	Individual competitor analysis	109
24.1	Bipolar scales for brand positioning	115
25.1	Typical marketing-mix strategies for different lifecycle stages	121
27.1	Kinds of new products and markets	129
29.1	Criteria which might make a market attractive	137
29.2	Factors which might be considered, or which may yield, business strengths	138
29.3	The ten steps involved in producing a DPM	139
31.1	Appeal of a cost approach to pricing	152
31.2	Problems of a cost approach to pricing	152
33.1	Types of sales promotions	159
34.1	Suggested pro-forma for an advertising plan	165
37.1	Tendencies inherent in a transaction approach to marketing	179
38.1	Industries with traditionally high defection rates, where customer retention improvements can have a significant impact	186
39.1	The advantages of personal selling	192
40.1	Key questions for the future of KAM	197
42.1	Major forms of intermediaries	203
45.1	Myths and realities about databases	215
45.2	Problems of reconciling internal and external market audits	216
45.3	Examples of business objectives and segmentation methods	217
45.4	The main components of a market database system	218
46.1	Key questions in choosing mobile marketing	223
50.1	Further quantitative objectives for a sales force	242
50.2	Setting objectives for an individual sales representative	243
53.1	Barriers to the integration of strategic marketing planning	256
54.1	Areas requiring attention in international product planning	264
57.1	Sources of legal information	274

List of Figures

1.1	Marketing as a business process	6
3.1	Channel possibilities for the produce of a market gardener	14
4.1	Marketing as a process	18
5.1	Consumerism's way to better marketing	22
6.1	Ensuring a market orientation	24
6.2	Striving for competitive advantage	24
6.3	Monitoring the environment: key areas	25
6.4	Developing competitor profiles	25
6.5	The process of market segmentation	26
6.6	Identifying strengths and weaknesses	26
6.7	The dynamics of product/market lifecycles	27
6.8	Portfolio of products and markets	28
6.9	Contents of a strategic marketing plan	28
6.10	Core professional curriculum	29
7.1	Priorities for a consumer brand manager	35
8.1	Continuum of industrial marketing	38
9.1	Continuum of tangible–intangible products	42
10.1	The technology lifecycle	49
15.1	Components of a consumer's purchase decision	70
16.1	Organizational buying behaviour model	75
17.1	Example of segmentation of consumer market for replacement tyres	82
17.2	Example of segmentation of market for industrial compressors (£10K–£100K plus)	83
17.3	Typical segmentation grid	83
22.1	Establishing competitive positions using critical success factors	103
22.2	Strengths and weaknesses analysis	103
22.3	Opportunities matrix	104
22.4	Threats matrix	104
23.1	Competitor analysis framework	108
25.1	Standard product lifecycle curve	117
25.2	Phases in the product lifecycle	119
25.3	Alternative product lifecycles	120
26.1	The diffusion of innovation curve	123
27.1	The Ansoff Matrix	126

27.2	An extended product/market matrix	130
28.1	The Boston Matrix	131
28.2	The experience curve	132
28.3	The Boston Matrix – cashflow implications	134
29.1	The Directional Policy Matrix (DPM)	135
29.2	Four strategic categories	139
29.3	Programme guidelines suggested for different positioning on the DPM	140
30.1	New product classification	142
30.2	Cultural blockages to new product initiatives	143
30.3	Risk and new product development	144
32.1	The price continuum	153
36.1	Sponsorship types	171
36.2	Sponsorship management cycle	173
37.1	Expanded marketing mix	180
37.2	The relationship marketing six markets model	182
40.1	Evolutionary nature of KAM relationships	193
40.2	The basic KAM stage	194
40.3	The cooperative KAM stage	195
40.4	The interdependent KAM stage	196
40.5	The integrated KAM stage	197
41.1	Customer satisfaction virtuous circle	199
44.1	Example of customer service trade-off matrix	212
45.1	Information flows in a marketing system	218
46.1	M-market brand enhancement	221
47.1	Category management evolution	229
48.1	Choosing channels – the value curve	231
48.2	Channel-chain analysis: the corporate PC market	233
49.1	Communications strategy	235
49.2	Value chain and associated communications activities	236
52.1	Strategic and tactical marketing plans	254
52.2	Strategic and operational planning cycle	255
55.1	Organizational structure and marketing	266
57.1	Three faces of the law	276
59.1	Map of the marketing domain	282
59.2	The Ansoff Matrix	283
59.3	Critical success factors	284

Part 1
Understanding the Basics
of Marketing

1 The Discipline of Marketing

Marketing has long been recognized as important for the long-term survival and success of organizations, be they commercial or non-profitmaking. Indeed, any analysis of the more successful companies in the world usually confirms the incorporation of sound marketing principles or disciplines within their management processes. In less successful organizations, it is often accepted that marketing is something not done particularly well.

This is not to say that organizations cannot survive without marketing. They can and sometimes do. This will be because they have some natural advantage over competitors such as a patent or a monopoly, or they are operating under conditions of excess demand. In the long run, however, these advantages are rarely sustainable.

Continued success of an organization requires attention to a large number of other activities such as operating efficiency, financial matters and the effectiveness of its logistics. Many of these will have an impact on an organization's relationship with its customers and this makes implementing the discipline of marketing difficult because it implies keeping a large number of 'balls in the air' at once. Underlying this, however, is a set of ideas, principles and concepts that are relatively simple to understand, but which (like most simple things) are quite deep in their meaning. Getting to grips with marketing is thus a two-stage process: first, the development of an understanding of the discipline and its principles and, second, the application of them to individual circumstances.

There are many definitions that try to provide a clear insight into what marketing is all about. One of the best describes marketing as 'the way in which an organization matches its human, financial and physical resources with the wants and needs of its customers'. This is a bit of a mouthful and, on the surface, does not mention any of the things we usually associate with marketing such as advertising, mail shots, loss-leaders, and so on. The definition, however, does focus attention on the crucial elements which the whole organization has to manage correctly – the mechanisms by which a relationship is developed between that organization and its customers so that mutually beneficial exchanges will take place.

At the heart of the relationship is what is offered by an organization: the core product or service, which must match the wants and needs of its target customers. If one company offers a closer match, this will be to the disadvantage of

Organizations can survive without marketing, but seldom for long

their competitors. The process of creating this match, however, is complex. The substance of a matching relationship and the factors which will affect it are at the heart of any understanding of marketing.

The key question this approach generates is thus: 'What will make a potential customer want to enter into an exchange with our organization as opposed to another?' In other words: 'Why will they buy our product, give to our charity or cooperate with our service, given that they have plenty of choice?'

The answer to this question is a long list of different factors, all of which will affect the possibility of achieving such an exchange. Some of these will be under the control of the supplying organization, while others will be beyond their control but can still fundamentally affect their chances of completing the exchange. No matter how good a product is, interest rates, new laws, fashion, etc., can affect its attractiveness to customers. In order to make sense of these factors and to put them into an understandable form, they are usually classified as the marketing mix and the marketing environment. The marketing mix is the offering we control; the environment is the set of uncontrollable variables within which the marketing process takes place.

The marketing mix is usually classified as product, price, promotion, or place – the four Ps:

- *Products* can be varied in terms of quality, size, functionality, range, and so on.
- *Price* can be high or low, can involve a discount or can be affected by credit terms.
- *Promotion* can utilize television advertising, can concentrate on using sales people or can involve branding.
- *Place* includes the channels through which we choose to make a product available plus the service elements involved in delivering the offering, such as after-sales service or delivery lead times.

The importance of the marketing mix is that successful matching depends on customers being aware of the products or services on offer, finding them available and favourably judging the attractiveness of the offering in terms of both price and performance. If one of these is missing or wrong from the customer's point of view, a long-term relationship will be difficult to sustain. Effective marketing management welds these variables into a coordinated whole in the market place in exactly the right combination and positioning for the targeted customer.

The marketing environment is a similarly complex set of factors that can be considered under five distinct headings:

- *Social or cultural factors*   These can include fashion, religious preferences, population trends and other developments such as more working women and an increasing awareness of green issues; all of them will affect people's perception of the appropriateness and value of a product or service.

- *Competition* This exists whenever an organization places an offering in the market place; there will always be some form of substitute somewhere. This may be direct, such as a Ford Focus versus an equivalent Citroen, or it may be indirect such as a holiday versus a home extension. Organizations should never underestimate the power of different sources of competition.
- *Technological change* The pace of this appears to be increasing at an ever-faster rate. It is therefore dangerous to assume that existing products will continue to be demanded by customers. There are many examples of products being superseded by advances in technology elsewhere, for example slide rules, mechanical watches, copper pipes, fax machines, and more recently, CRT televisions and video recorders. Technological developments will determine what is both possible and attractive in all markets.
- *Government activities* These include political, fiscal, environmental, economic and legal activities. All of them will affect what can be done in a particular market. Interest rates will affect the willingness to purchase on credit, deregulation will alter entry barriers to a market and the nature of competition, exhaust emissions requirements will affect the saleability of motor vehicles, and so on. Governments, even if they do nothing, will still be a significant influence on an organization's marketing environment.
- *Institutional changes* These will impact on marketing activities, so it is important to understand the effect of institutions and to predict the consequences of any change. Important examples include the changes that have occurred in food distribution, from small local outlets to large out-of-town supermarkets, the role of the standards institutes, the influence of the press, the rise of consumer associations and the advances in telecommunications networks.

Both consciously and unconsciously, customers are constantly performing a matching exercise between their needs and wants and the products and services they see in the market place. When the match is sufficiently good they will purchase. The methodology for creating a match is the manipulation and management of the marketing mix and the monitoring and evaluation of the environment.

To clarify what marketing is, however, it is necessary to understand that it operates at three levels.

- The first is what might be termed the 'philosophical' level. If the people who control an organization do not believe that striving for superior customer value is critical to long-term customer retention, marketing will never be anything other than a trivial functional department.
- The second level is what is often called the 'strategic' level. Here, many of the disciplines of marketing, such as market analysis and understanding, market segmentation, positioning, product development, and relationship strategies,

Marketing operates at three levels: philosophical, strategic and tactical become major determinants of success, and are clearly essential ingredients of business-unit strategy.

■ Finally, there is the 'tactical' or implementation level of marketing, of which more detailed issues relating to the offer and customer satisfaction are considered.

The discipline of marketing thus covers a wide range of topics and ideas. If depicted as a process, it would have a clear starting point: understanding customers, markets and competitors. Based on this analysis, target markets and customers would be identified and an appropriate strategy and competitive position established. These would be delivered through the marketing mix and then monitored for effectiveness. This is depicted in Figure 1.1.

Figure 1.1   Marketing as a business process

Thought of in this way, the discipline of marketing becomes a core organizational process, and, according to Peter Drucker, something too important to be left to the marketing department. As a consequence, marketing professionals become experts in reading and understanding markets, or specialists in marketing communications. Both are complex specialisms within marketing. The other areas are more general in nature and vital aspects of management, often elsewhere in the organization.

2 A Market Orientation

Many organizations have experienced the introduction of a rallying cry from their senior management to the effect that '. . . we will now become a marketing-led organization. . .'. What they really mean is that they wish to become a *market-driven* organization, not that the marketing department should now lead the business. Turning this statement into reality requires more than just the pronouncement of the principle and the employment of a few people with marketing titles. It requires something much more difficult: the creation of a desire within the entire organization for principles, policies and practices that anticipate and meet the needs of markets. These principles, policies and practices are all core to the discipline of marketing.

To gain a better understanding of the difference between marketing and a market orientation, it is sometimes helpful to think of marketing as occurring in three distinct forms. These can be characterized as: **marketing tasks**; **marketing management**; and a **market orientation**.

The first form, *marketing tasks*, will involve a number of specialized activities requiring a degree of experience and expertise to be performed well. Some of these will be tasks that are normally associated with successful marketing, such as designing brochures, advertising, commissioning market research, and brand management. Other tasks will often still affect marketing success, but will often be the responsibility of managers in other functional areas. These can include calculating volume discounts, stock control, after-sales service activities and product development. Each area will usually be the responsibility of different parts of an organization, but each will affect the nature of relationships with customers and therefore the possibility of new and continued sales.

The second form, *marketing management*, is thus the management of these tasks. If there are a multitude of activities, each of which can affect an organization's success in the market place, then it follows that a degree of management has to be applied to them. In the absence of any management, these tasks will be performed according to the beliefs and preferences of the individuals involved. It does not stretch the imagination to foresee the problems that this might cause. In Topic 1, we referred to this as the 'strategic' level of marketing.

The function of marketing management is to provide coordination by whatever mechanism is appropriate to an organization. The job is to ensure a common direction; an agreement between the various activity centres on what the organization is trying to achieve. The usual outcome of such management would be a set of policies or guidelines for the individuals engaged in performing the various tasks which affect the marketing mix. The overall outcome would be a better degree of organizational integration in relation to its markets.

Such management will occur at different levels within an organization. It will range from the strategic positions adopted or defined by the leaders of any organization, through the specific responsibilities of a marketing director to the various operational activities of the managers and section heads of functional units. At whatever level this management occurs, however, it will still have the same purpose: coordinating and integrating activities to achieve a good match with customer requirements.

A *market orientation* is, then, the third form of marketing found within organizations. It is something which goes beyond marketing tasks and management and is the most intangible aspect of marketing. Orientations are to do with the philosophies, values, attitudes and beliefs of the people working within an organization. In this, they are an aspect of an organization's culture. Orientations are very powerful influences since they will determine what are considered to be legitimate concerns in management action.

The phrase 'we are a market-driven organization' should therefore be a reflection of the organization's culture. It encompasses the way in which priorities are determined and what sort of questions managers and operatives feel they should be asking each other. It also includes the type of management information readily available, the ease with which budgets are obtained for various types of expenditure and the processes by which decisions are made.

The focus of a market orientation is, of course, the customer. More important, however, is a focus on an organization's *relationships* with its customers. Since marketing is about matching resources with the wants and needs of customers, a market orientation exists when all personnel view activities in terms of their likely impact on relationships with customers. Important questions include:

- Why will these customers want to obtain this product from us?
- What impact will this action have on our customers?
- What is happening out there in our markets which will affect our activities?

A market orientation exists when people make sense of their business, justify actions and authorise spending by reference to customers.

Instilling a market orientation within an organization is a difficult job. It is easy to accept that long-term survival depends on creating and keeping customers, whether they are paying customers or otherwise, but it is quite another matter to introduce this philosophy into managerial processes. This is because people are subject to a large number of influences and pressures in their work which will tend to counter the pursuit of marketing principles.

As an example, pressures will derive from people's professional backgrounds where problems are often tackled using different methodologies from those involved in marketing. As an art, rather than as a science, marketing is sometimes difficult for people from engineering and scientific backgrounds since there are few consistent input/output relationships. In addition, most people's work is performed away from the customer interface. When people go to work their direct concerns are with their jobs and their in-trays, not with matching customer needs.

Other orientations which can exist side by side with marketing include: production, design, technology, financial, sales, and social orientations. These are not 'wrong' and are all needed at certain times to a greater or lesser extent. If, for example, a company has profitability problems, it will be important that a financial orientation should emerge as a priority to enable the short-term survival of the business. Alternatively, an organization which relies on product innovation and development for its success in the market place should encourage a technology orientation within its ranks.

The problem with these various types of orientation is obtaining the right balance between them to match the environmental conditions within which the organization operates. Successful organizations are good at matching, not only in terms of the four Ps, but also in terms of the ways in which they manage and set priorities for themselves. In good times, marketing tends to be forgotten and other priorities dominate. Marketing then becomes the way forward in bad times, but by that point is often perceived as a threat to the other traditional values already well-embedded in the organization.

As with other disciplines, a market orientation needs to exist in an organization. It does not have to stem from a marketing department. Indeed, many successful marketing organizations do not have a formal marketing department. It is therefore important that general management are aware of the need for, and are active in the promotion of, a marketing philosophy alongside the other orientations necessary for continued success.

The problem with having different orientations is getting the right balance

3 The Marketing Mix

The marketing mix is the name given to the main *demand-influencing variables* that are available to an organization. This is because when a customer makes a purchase or engages in an exchange, what they are responding to is not just the product, but a whole range of variables which constitute the offer. The classic description of the marketing mix, although something of a simplification, is 'the four Ps'. The four Ps and the fundamental questions associated with them are:

- *Product*
  - What type and range of product or service should we provide?
- *Price*
  - What price should be set for each product or service?
- *Promotion*
  - How do we best communicate with our target customers and persuade them to buy our offer?
- *Place*
  - What channels of distribution and what levels of service are appropriate?

Each of these elements is capable of influencing demand either separately or together with the other marketing mix elements. When considering the marketing mix, it is important to look at some of the general principles underlying decisions about the actual mix that an organization might choose to implement.

Product (including service products)

Although customers and their needs are the focal point of the marketing process, few organizations started with this in mind. Invariably, somebody had a good idea for a product and this became the germ of the business idea.

Not surprisingly, then, many enterprises see the product to be at the heart of their firm's marketing efforts. There may be nothing intrinsically wrong with this attitude, as long as managers can see that their product does not have to remain as a fixed, unchanging entity – a sort of organizational straitjacket. Instead, the company must learn to see its output as flexible, being subject to development and adaptation, just like any other component of the marketing mix. Because the world is never static, an organization should keep asking itself the question: 'Does each product we offer provide relevant and desired benefits for today's customers' needs?'

Some of these benefits can be provided by other elements of the marketing mix, such as availability, after-sales service, and value for money. Aspects of the product which can provide appropriate benefits are shown in Table 3.1.

Table 3.1 Product variables

■ Technical features	■ Packaging
■ Design	■ Compatibility with existing
■ Durability	equipment/services
■ Robustness	■ Degree of customization
■ Innovativeness	■ Flexibility
■ Functional performance	■ Upgrading
■ Noise control	■ Quality
■ Range of sizes, colours, etc.	■ Volumes available
■ Ease of maintenance	■ Safety
■ Pollution hazard reduction	■ Ease of use

Price

Pricing is an area of marketing with a tremendous potential for increasing short-term profits, but unfortunately, if managed badly, can quickly bring a business to its knees. Pricing is both an art and a science. The options open to an organization for using pricing as a flexible 'connector' that helps position a product and match efforts to the needs of the customer are many, as shown in Table 3.2.

Table 3.2 Pricing variables

■ Price point adopted	■ Credit terms
■ Discount structure	■ Stage payments
■ Discount amounts	■ Residual value
■ Special offers	■ Leasing arrangements
■ Sales (end of season, etc.)	■ Financial deals
■ Cost of ownership	■ Psychological elements

Price should reflect a 'package' of benefits

There is a fear amongst many managers that unless they offer the lowest possible price they will not win the order. Whilst this can be true for some businesses, it is rarely the case with market leaders. Take the case of the really successful construction companies which tend to rely on quality, innovation and carefully managed business relationships to win contracts. Other companies without these advantages have to use price to obtain work. As a consequence, their main hopes for profit rest on keeping costs to a minimum and any loopholes in the contract. Such adversarial approaches never seem to last.

As an alternative, take the example of a shopper who prefers to buy goods from a local shop rather than a supermarket or hypermarket where cheaper prices can be obtained. Why? Quite apart from the convenience factor, the shopper knows and values the personal service from a local shop, and is prepared to pay for this.

When a customer buys, he or she purchases a 'package' of benefits and the price should reflect the value of the *total package*. Clearly, price is an important element of the business transaction and, if appropriately chosen, it can not only have a big impact on a company's market positioning, but can also help to differentiate the product or service from those of competitors.

Promotion

The promotional element of the marketing mix is concerned with ways of communicating with customers and potential customers. In practice the promotional element of the marketing mix falls into two broad categories: personal promotion and impersonal promotion.

Personal promotion

This is the role of selling, which is usually accomplished through a sales force or sales assistants. Face-to-face selling has a number of advantages over impersonal methods:

- It is a two-way process which gives the prospective purchaser the opportunity to ask questions about the product.
- The sales message can be tailored to the needs of individual customers.
- The sales person can use in-depth knowledge about the product to identify new customer needs and overcome objections.
- The customer can be prompted to buy by being asked for an order.
- The sales person can negotiate on price, delivery or special requirements.
- Personal relationships with customers can be developed thereby laying the foundations for longer-term business.

However, selling also involves a lot of 'dead' time, such as preparing sales aids, telephoning for appointments, travelling, failing to win an order, administration and research. This makes it a costly business that needs to be regularly monitored to ensure that it provides a good return for the cost and effort that goes into it.

Impersonal promotion

Typically, this area of promotion takes the form of advertising and sales promotion. Advertising is often felt to be the province of only the very large organizations and that it is something best left to the 'experts'. In fact, advertising can be addressed by any competent manager, and can encompass: slots on television; billboards throughout the country; local radio; leaflets; brochures; stories in the newspapers and trade journals; cards on newspaper display boards; advertisements in the local paper, in the Yellow Pages and on local buses; plus gifts such as calendars and pens.

To be managed well, however, advertising needs to be looked upon as an investment, rather than a cost, and like any other investment, it is only going to be any good if it achieves a return. To obtain this, it is important to address the following questions:

- At whom is it aimed? (target customers)
- What is it trying to achieve? (objectives)
- What should it say? (message)
- How should the message be communicated? (medium)
- How will the result be measured? (monitoring)

These questions can only be answered if an organization has a good understanding of its customers and potential customers, what interests them, what motivates them to buy and how messages can reach them.

Although the various advertising media mentioned above vary in terms of their costs and potential for reaching customers, different combinations of message and media will provide a very flexible advertising repertoire that can be tailored to fit most budgets (See Topic 49 Integrated Marketing Communication and Distribution Channels).

Sales promotions

Sales promotions are essentially short-term campaigns to influence customers (perhaps a competitor's customers, or even intermediaries) to buy more of a product or to use it faster. Some companies use promotions to encourage their own sales force to sell more. Generally, promotions take the form of offering a **monetary** incentive, such as a price reduction or a coupon against the next purchase, or **goods**, such as two for the price of one, or **services**, such as free estimates and holidays.

Place

If a market gardener started a business farming organically-grown vegetables, he or she would immediately be faced with several different routes for getting them to the consumer; some direct, and some through intermediaries, as illustrated in Figure 3.1.

This example provides a good illustration of the 'place' element of the marketing mix and how this needs to be integrated with delivery, consignment 'packaging' and the service elements associated with delivery.

Advertising should be regarded as an investment rather than a cost

Figure 3.1   Channel possibilities for the produce of a market gardener

Clearly, the cheapest channel is option (a), where getting the consumer to come along to bear the harvesting costs while receiving no customer service will save the farmer money. But suppose that does not appeal to people in the catchment area, or suppose the farm is in a sparsely populated area? A farm shop (b) would have the advantage of appealing to passing trade as well as to regular customers, but distribution costs are already escalating.

On analysis, each option offers commercial possibilities; equally, each one involves costs. Indeed, within any particular channel, there are areas for cost management. For example, with option (f), the farmer could deliver to the restaurants or could demand that the restaurants arrange collection. In the same way, the essential decision for any supplying organization is to choose those distribution channels which provide a sizeable element of control at a reasonable cost. A supplier might also want to safeguard its interests by using more than one channel to reach different customer segments.

The choice of channel can also help enterprises to differentiate their product. A classic UK example of this was when Avon Cosmetics took their products into the home of the consumer, while the competition continued to trade in department stores and chemists' shops.

When developing policies for the various elements of the marketing mix, it is important to be comprehensive, but also to identify those areas which are significant in the markets in which an organization operates. Thus, some organizations use an expanded marketing mix for managerial and planning purposes. This can involve isolating sales plans, processes, people or customer service for special attention. Whatever the case, the key task of the marketing manager is to ensure that the mix presented to the market place is internally consistent and provides a set of benefits which target-customers will find preferable to the offerings of other organizations.

Topic 4 Marketing: Concept, Function or Process?

It doesn't take long for any business practitioner or student of marketing to recognize that many people are confused about the status, value and role of marketing within organizations. This is mainly due to the focus of the discipline: the satisfaction of customer needs by the organization, which means that marketing activities have implications across the whole of an enterprise.

The problem is compounded by the bad press that marketing has had over the last few years. Headlines such as 'Has Marketing Had Its Day?' and 'P&G Disband Their Marketing Departments' have appeared with uncomfortable regularity. More telling is the fact that one only has to poll a small number of managers within most organizations to find widespread agreement about the low status of their marketing colleagues. Phrases such as 'not sure what they do' and 'waste of time and space' are all too frequently to be heard.

In reality, the problem is not that marketing has outlived its usefulness or is fundamentally flawed in some way, but that there is often a failure to distinguish between the discipline of marketing as a concept, a business function or department, and the business processes the marketing concept implies. To exploit marketing's potential, managers needs to be clear about the distinctions between these three different facets of the discipline.

The basic error has been to assume that all the ideas, analytical tools and approaches contained within the discipline of marketing (and this book) define the job of a marketing department or professional. If they did, then marketing managers would become cross-functional coordinators and drivers of competitive strategy. In the vast majority of organizations, this would be an uphill struggle. It is hard to imagine a business unit's executive board delegating competitive strategy and cross-function coordination to the marketing function. Most managers and strategists see these as key tasks for a business's executive – if they don't do this, what else do they do? It is they who should be running the business; not the marketing function.

Many people are confused about the value of marketing to organizations

The marketing concept

The marketing concept, or concept of marketing, is derived from the realization that organizations only survive if they satisfy customers. Theodor Levitt was one of the first to formalize this idea. In his seminal work, he draws attention to the importance of viewing a business in a way that is appropriate to the markets in which it operates. His classic example was the railroads, which defined themselves as being in the railway business, rather than in the transportation business. 'The railroads did not stop growing because the need for passenger and freight transportation declined. That grew. The railroads are in trouble today not because the need was filled by others (cars, trucks, aeroplanes, even telephones), but because it was not filled by the railroads themselves.' [Levitt T. (July/August 1960). 'Marketing Myopia'. *Harvard Business Review*,]

Levitt contrasted the railroads with companies such as DuPont, which saw their activities in a very different light. Instead of defining themselves in terms of their products, they concentrated on finding 'customer-satisfying' applications for them. They did not abandon the search for technical excellence, but combined it with an awareness of its relevance to market needs.

These examples focus attention on contrary aspects of the business. Seeing oneself as being in the railroad business implies that knowing, understanding and being proficient in running railways is the key to success. If, however, the business is seen as finding the best means of transporting people and freight from one location to another, business management takes on another dimension. The priority then becomes, not running a railway, but providing transport and communication services.

The significance of the marketing concept, then, is that it places duties on managers across the business to think in a certain way, to adopt a certain approach to doing business, and to foster a culture that puts customers at the heart of the organization.

Marketing as an organizational function

The activities in which a marketing department or function engage are distinct and require a well-developed set of professional skills to be performed properly. Its two areas of unique expertise are delivering high-quality and impactful market and customer intelligence, and well-executed marketing communications.

Market and customer intelligence covers a range of topic areas. These include strategic contributions such as defining and segmenting markets, understanding perceptions of value, recommending value propositions to business unit management, identifying gaps in the market, proposing new products, positioning competitors and understanding customer behaviour. The more operational or tactical activities here are concerned with conducting market research, an area where considerable expertise is required, and monitoring the impact of an enterprise's efforts such as customer service assessment.

Marketing communications similarly cover a range of activities, some of which are strategic while others are operational/tactical. The main strategic activity is brand or impression management which covers a range of areas but tends to be communications led. Tactical activities include advertising, public relations, conferencing and direct mail. In addition, new media have created other communications channels which can be used strategically, as in the case of eBay or Amazon, or tactically, as is the case for the vast majority of company websites or pop-up advertisements. Sales promotions are also often part of a marketing department's tactical responsibilities, which can include special offers, coupons, and other forms of merchandising. Also included here might be responsibility for the launch of new products.

Marketing as a process

A business process is a series of actions that will deliver a predetermined outcome. Marketing can therefore be mapped as a process that will deliver value to an organization's customers. The process can be captured in Figure 4.1 and is similar to Figure 1.1, which is used to explain the discipline of marketing in Topic 1 of this book.

The starting point for mapping the discipline as a process is a definition of the market in which an organization wishes to compete and an understanding of how value is perceived by members of that market. Once established, appropriate value propositions can be formulated. Delivering value, however, requires customers to know about the proposition, see it in a favourable light, be able to afford it and be able to source it. Delivering value also necessitates providing appropriate sales and after-sales service and the product or service performing to the expectations set by the market and the provider.

Customer experience and market changes must subsequently be monitored to gain assurance that value continues to be delivered. It is vital for any organization that a supplier's understanding of the market is constantly updated. This 'virtuous circle' is constrained and/or enhanced by an organization's assets, both tangible and intangible.

Concept, function or process

The discipline of marketing, then, is at once a concept, a function and a process. The concept is clear and represents a way of thinking about the purpose and management of an organization. Parts of the discipline, however, form the basis of a professional activity that can be logically contained within a specialist department or departments. Nevertheless, those departments cannot be expected to run the

Marketing can be mapped as a process that delivers value to customers

Figure 4.1 Marketing as a process

business any more than a sales function, engineering division or finance department can. Similarly, they are in a weak position to provide the cross-functional
coordination that the breadth of the discipline implies.

On the other hand, the discipline of marketing and its associated processes do
have a significant contribution to make to the strategic management of an organization. As has been demonstrated many times, business decisions need to be
made in the light of market developments and customer needs. Insight into these
are delivered by good quality, well-founded, market research. All people who
reach a general management level in any organization require these insights plus
the ability to understand and influence the value creation and delivery activities
encompassed within marketing as a process. Unfortunately, and all too regularly,
managers seem to forget the marketing responsibilities of their strategic roles, and
marketing defaults to the 'stuff' of a marketing department. Hopefully, continued
education will make this an increasingly rare condition.

5 Marketing and Ethics

In recent years, dissatisfaction has been expressed by increasingly large numbers of people about a society which seems to have consumption as both its means and its end. In the late 1960s and early 1970s, there was a growing consciousness of the problems that the age of mass consumption brought with it. A new awareness of the alternatives that might be possible, indeed necessary, also became apparent. Such moves were supported by books like Charles Reich's *The Greening of America*, Alvin Toffler's *Future Shock*, and Theodore Roszak's *The Making of a Counter Culture*. The message articulated by these and other writers of the movement was basically a simple one: that people could no longer be thought of as 'consumers', as some aggregate variable in the grand design of market planning. They were individuals intent on doing their own bidding.

Feelings such as these have led to critical examinations of commercial activity of all kinds. As one of the more visible manifestations of such activity, marketing has been singled out for special attention. One criticism frequently brought against marketing is that it plays on people's weaknesses. By insidious means, it is claimed, marketing attempts to persuade consumers that they must drink this brand of alcoholic beverage or use this brand of deodorant; that without them their lives are somehow incomplete. This argument involves the notion of the defenceless consumer.

Viewing marketing in this way tends to exaggerate the influence that the marketer can bring to bear on the market place. It implies that consumers' powers of perception are limited and that their intelligence is minimal. It further suggests that skilful marketing can create needs.

The argument to support this would be that 'Nobody wanted television before it was invented; now it is a highly competitive market. That market must have been created.' This, however, confuses needs and wants. Clearly, nobody wanted television before it was invented; but there has always been a need for home entertainment. Previously, that need had been met by a piano, a book, parlour games, or something of that kind. Now technology has made available a further means of satisfying that basic need for domestic entertainment – television. Many consumers find that television better satisfies their need for home entertainment than did the piano. The arrival of digital and interactive television will bring even more changes in home entertainment.

Marketing is criticized for playing on people's weaknesses

In this example, the contribution of marketing was to identify in as much detail as possible what a customer needed and then to persuade him or her that a specific product or brand would provide the most effective means of satisfying the expressed need. Underlying this view of marketing is the belief that consumers seek satisfactory solutions to their buying problems; first, by acquiring information about available goods and services and their attributes and, eventually, by choosing that product which comes closest to solving their problem.

No matter what 'marketing' is performed, the consumer is still sovereign as long as he or she is free to make choices – either choices between competing products, or the choice not to buy at all. Indeed, it could be argued that by extending the range of choices that the consumer has available, marketing is enhancing consumer sovereignty rather than eroding it. It should be noted, too, that although promotional activity may persuade an individual to buy a product or service for the first time, promotion is unlikely to be the persuasive factor in subsequent purchases, when the consumer is acting from first-hand experience of the product.

Some ethical concerns

Several specific issues have formed the focus of the debate on the ethics of marketing. The main concerns include:

- Marketing's contribution to materialism.
- Rising consumer expectations as a result of marketing pressure.
- The use of advertising to mislead or distort.

It is, therefore, important to consider the arguments involved in these discussions.

Marketing, it has been suggested, helps to feed, and in turn feeds on, the materialistic and acquisitive urges of society. Implicit in such criticism is the value judgement that materialism and acquisitiveness are in themselves undesirable. Supporters would argue that marketing contributes to a general raising of the level of consumer expectations. These expectations are more than simple aspirations: they represent a desire to acquire a specific set of gratifications through the purchase of goods and services. The desire for these gratifications is fuelled by marketing's insistent messages. Further, if the individual lacks the financial resources with which to fulfil these expectations, then this inevitably adds to a greater awareness of differences in society and to dissatisfaction and unrest among those in this situation.

The counter-argument here is that marketing itself does not contribute to rising expectations and thus to differences in society; it merely makes people aware of, and better informed about, the differences that already exist in society. In this respect, it can be claimed that its effects are beneficial, since it supports, even hastens, pressures for redistribution. It can also be argued that materialism is not a recent phenomenon correlated with the advent of mass marketing.

Much of the criticism levelled at marketing is in fact directed at one aspect of it: advertising. Advertising practitioners themselves are fully conscious of these criticisms. These include the ideas that advertising:

- Makes misleading claims about products or services.
- Uses hidden, dangerously powerful techniques of persuasion.
- By encouraging undesirable attitudes, has adverse social effects.
- Works through the exploitation of human inadequacy.

Advertisers themselves would point to the fact that advertising in all its forms is heavily controlled in most Western societies, either by self-imposed codes (such as the British Code of Advertising Practice) or by legislation (such as the Trade Descriptions Acts) and that it cannot by itself achieve sustained patterns of repeat purchase.

The debate about the ethics of marketing also often confuses marketing institutions with the people who work in them. Clearly, there are dishonest business people who engage in activities that are detrimental to their fellow-citizens. However, it seems a grave error to criticize marketing institutions because of the practices of a small number of unethical marketers. It is clear, for example, that there are advertisers who engage in deceptive practices designed to mislead and possibly defraud consumers. Nevertheless, the institution of advertising can be used not only to inform consumers about potentially beneficial new products, such as new energy-saving technologies, but also to promote non-profit community services, such as theatres and state education. This argument can, of course, be applied to all marketing activities.

Consumerism and marketing

Closely connected with the issue of the ethics of marketing is the issue of consumerism. Ironically, consumerism is pro-marketing; it wants the marketing approach to business implemented in a sincere rather than cynical spirit. The cynical implementation, which consumerists claim has been all too widely practised, is no better than high-pressure salesmanship or misleading puffery. The sincere implementation of the marketing approach entails respect for each individual customer served. An interpretation of the consumerist desire is that the sort of relationship found between a manufacturer and a customer in, say, a capital goods market, should be created in consumer markets. In so far as that is both economically feasible and what the consumer really wants, marketers should also want a more satisfactory relationship between organization and customer (see Figure 5.1).

Ironically, consumerism is pro-marketing

Figure 5.1 Consumerism's way to better marketing

The marketing of children's toys provides an example of how customers, consumers and company objectives can all be satisfied by careful business practice. The successful toy companies of today are those which inform parents that their products are not potentially dangerous, not coated with lead paint, and not destroyed the hour after they are first pressed into active service. Fisher-Price is one of the most successful toy manufacturers. Since 1968 it has eschewed child-manipulative promotion, carefully tested its products with children for durability, safety and purposeful play, and charged the prices necessary to make and market 'good' toys. The consequent sales and profit margins have been impressive.

On the other side of the coin, McDonald's, one of the strongest brands in the world in the 1990s and early 2000s, has been forced to make its food offering healthier to comply with changing customer tastes and the demands of consumer lobbyists.

6 World-class Marketing

Research conducted by Cranfield School of Management in the late 1990s with the assistance of some of Europe's best companies, large and small, has produced key indications of how successful companies use marketing to create sustainable competitive advantage.

The challenges such companies address to create this advantage include the pace of change; process thinking; market maturity; the expertise and power of customers; and the internationalization of business. Studying the way these organizations have met these challenges has enabled the identification of 10 guidelines for world-class marketing.

Marketing orientation

Market maturity has had a profound effect on most organizations during the past few years. Typical responses have been financial husbandry, ratio management and downsizing. In companies that are not market-driven this has led to *anorexia industrialosa* (an excessive desire to be leaner and fitter, leading to emaciation and eventually, death).

An alternative response has been attempts to create the 'agile organization' or to manage the business on the basis of the 'balanced scorecard'. In many cases, an over-focus on the systems aspect of these initiatives has led to increased bureaucracy and difficulty in garnering the potential benefits of such moves.

Successful companies might have tried these initiatives but have always come back to the necessity to lift their heads above the parapet and look at their markets and their customers rather than wasting their energy tinkering with their own internal workings. World-class companies believe passionately, from the Board downwards, that creating superior value for clearly defined groups of customers is the best way of creating wealth for all stakeholders. Only then do the initiatives referred to above work; otherwise they become fads. This leads to the first guideline as shown in Figure 6.1: as far as possible, ensure that a strong market orientation exists within your organization.

> - Develop customer orientation in all functions. Ensure that every function understands that they are there to serve the customer, not for their own narrow functional interests.
> - This must be driven from the Board downwards.
> - Where possible, organize in cross-functional teams around customer groups and core processes.
> - Make customers the arbiter of quality.

Figure 6.1 Ensuring a market orientation

Competitive advantage

Successful organizations avoid offering an undifferentiated product or service in too broad a market, and they use any one or any combination of low costs, differentiation or protecting a niche to earn superior positions. Without something different to offer (provided the market requires it), companies will continue to struggle, relying on the inadequacies of their competitors rather than on their own competitive strengths for survival. Advantage within these approaches can come from any of a number of different sources, including technological leadership, superior service, wide distribution coverage, strong positioning or any other value-creating proposition.

World leaders continuously strive to serve customer needs better and more cost-effectively, and work relentlessly towards the differential advantage that this brings. The foundations of this process are summarized in Figure 6.2.

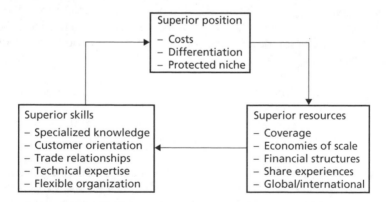

Figure 6.2 Striving for competitive advantage

Environmental scanning

It goes without saying that failure to monitor hostile environmental changes is the most common reason for companies going to the wall. Had anyone at the end of the 1980s predicted that IBM would be losing billions of dollars by the mid-1990s, they would have been derided. But it was IBM's failure to respond to the changes taking place in their markets that caused just such problems. Now, in the 21st century, global giants such as General Motors and Ford are facing similar problems.

Clearly, marketing plays a key role in this process. For successful organizations, this means devoting at least some of the time and resources of key executives to monitoring formally the changes taking place about them. The key areas requiring environmental scanning are summarized in Figure 6.3.

Macro environment	Market/industry environment
• Political/regulatory	• Market size and potential
• Economic	• Customer behaviour
• Technological	• Segmentation
• Societal	• Suppliers
	• Channels
	• Industry practices
	• Industry profitability
Together these imply a formal marketing audit	

Figure 6.3 Monitoring the environment: key areas

Competitor surveillance

Excellent companies know as much about their close competitors as they know about themselves. This implies a structured competitor monitoring process covering the areas noted in Figure 6.4 in order to develop usable profiles. The results of this profiling exercise should be included in the marketing audit.

- Direct competitors
- Potential competitors
- Substitute products
- Forward integration by suppliers
- Backward integration by customers
- Competitors' profitability
- Competitors' strengths and weaknesses

Figure 6.4 Developing competitor profiles

Market segmentation

The ability to recognize groups of customers who share the same or similar needs and offer them appropriate value propositions has always been a major contributor to organizational success. However, the real secret is to change the offer in

Excellent companies know as much about their close competitors as they know about themselves

accordance with changing needs, and not to offer exactly the same product or service to everyone; an indication of a product-orientated organization.

This process of market segmentation is the basis for strategy formation and positioning. Without a good understanding of how needs within a market can vary, and how these variations can be used to identify different market segments, decisions about strategies and positioning become divorced from the markets in which they are supposed to secure competitive advantage. The process of segmentation is summarized in Figure 6.5.

Steps in segmenting a market:

(a)   Understand how your market works (market structure)
(b)   List what is bought (including where, when, how, applications)
(c)   List who buys (demographics, psychographics)
(d)   List why they buy (needs, benefits sought)
(e)   Search for groups with similar needs

The golden rule:
Select a segment and serve it.
Do not straddle segments and sit between them.

Figure 6.5   The process of market segmentation

Strengths and weaknesses analysis

Market maturity, particularly in Western Europe, is a major challenge in most sectors. It is this, more than anything, which has led companies to pay greater attention to market segmentation as a source of continuing growth in profits.

Successful companies usually have a well-established and excellent grasp of the opportunities and threats facing them (derived from the previous three guidelines). The next step is to undertake a SWOT analysis to help understand their relative strengths and weaknesses in each of the segments resulting from the analysis outlined in the previous guideline. The process of identifying strengths and weaknesses is summarized in Figure 6.6.

For each segment in which an organization competes, understand:

• What the 'qualifying' features and benefits are
• What the 'differential' features and benefits are
• How relatively important each of these are
• How well your product or service performs against your competitors' on each of these requirements

Figure 6.6   Identifying strengths and weaknesses

Mirroring market dynamics

Successful organizations use their understanding of their markets and their own positions within those markets to adapt their operations in line with changes as they occur. Some changes will result from the marketing activities of the firms themselves; others will be beyond their control being a consequence of predictable but inexorable trends or unforeseeable events. The combination of these factors creates the dynamics of a product-based market as it evolves from birth through growth and maturity to its eventual decline.

World-class businesses manage their way through this lifecycle so that they are in the best competitive position at each point in the evolutionary process. They build market share before maturity sets in; they try to ensure that they have a cost advantage when it does, and they recognize that different segments will have different lifecycles. Typical responses to the different dynamics of each lifecycle stage are illustrated in Figure 6.7.

Key characteristics	Unique	Product differentiation	Service differentiation	'Commodity'
Marketing message	Explain	Competitive	Brand values	Corporate
Sales	Pioneering	Relative benefits distribution support	Relationship-based	Availability-based
Distribution	Direct selling	Exclusive distribution	Mass distribution	80:20
Price	Very high	High	Medium	Low (consumer controlled)
Competitive intensity	None	Few	Many	Many
Costs	Very high	Medium	Medium/low	Medium/low
Profit	Medium/high	High	Medium/high	Medium/high cost
Management style	Visionary	Strategic	Operational	Cost management

Figure 6.7 The dynamics of product/market lifecycles

Adopt a portfolio management approach

Successful companies recognize that they cannot be all things to all people and that they have greater or lesser strengths in serving each of their various markets. This recognition enables the development of a portfolio approach to determining appropriate objectives and the effective allocation of resources. The portfolio approach is most easily conceived as a matrix as illustrated in Figure 6.8.

World-class business manage their way through product and market life cycles

		Strong	Weak
Market attractiveness	High	2	3
	Low	1	4

Competitive position

Strategies for different boxes in the matrix:
- Box 1 Maintain and manage for sustained earnings
- Box 2 Invest and build for growth
- Box 3 Selectively invest
- Box 4 Manage for cash

Figure 6.8 Portfolio of products and markets

Set Strategic priorities

The previous six guidelines effectively comprise a marketing audit; that is, the basis of a strategic marketing plan. World-class companies usually engage in some form of planning of this nature. However, the best also take great pains to avoid stifling creativity through excessively bureaucratic planning procedures. The strength of a good planning process is that it provides a sound and logical foundation for defining key target markets, sources of differential advantage and intended sources of revenue and profits.

This implies something more sophisticated than forecasts and budgets. Commercial history has demonstrated that any fool can spell out the financial results they wish to achieve. It takes intellect to spell out *how* they are to be achieved. This identification of what needs to be done to achieve logically derived objectives will then highlight the strategic imperatives for the business. Only when such priorities are clear can they be used to create key performance indicators and drive other business processes. The key contents of a good strategic marketing plan are listed in Figure 6.9.

A written strategic marketing plan for 3 years usually contains:

- A mission statement
- A financial summary
- A market overview
- SWOT analyses on key segments
- A portfolio summary
- Assumptions
- Marketing objectives and strategies
- A budget

This strategic plan can then be converted into a detailed one-year plan.

Figure 6.9 Contents of a strategic marketing plan

Be professional

Professional management skills, particularly in marketing, are the hallmark of commercial success. Leadership and entrepreneurial skills, combined with hard-edged marketing skills, will see any company well into the new millennium. Leading companies maintain a corporate optimism because they believe that what they are doing and what they have to offer is worthwhile.

They recognize, however, that the increasingly hostile and dynamic environments within which they work demand professionalism at a number of different levels. It requires the courage to question strategic priorities that do not appear to have been adequately defined or refined. It requires conventional wisdom to be challenged if it appears to be no longer relevant. It requires the discipline to follow the logical processes of strategic analysis and planning rather than jumping at the first good idea that comes along. But at its base, it also requires professional marketing skills and formal training in the underlying concepts, tools and techniques of marketing as a management discipline. The core of this curriculum is outlined in Figure 6.10.

```
• Market research
• Gap analysis
• Market segmentation/positioning
• Product lifecycle analysis
• Portfolio management
• The four Ps
    – Product management
    – Pricing
    – Place (customer service, channel management)
    – Promotion (selling, sales force management,
      advertising, sales promotion)
```

Figure 6.10   Core professional curriculum

Professional management skills, particularly in marketing, are the hallmark of success

Part 2
Different Types of Marketing

Marketing Consumer Products

Consumer products are those which are sold to individuals and then consumed by them, or someone they pass them on to, for the satisfaction they provide. This distinguishes them from industrial products which are purchased for their ability to help make another product. Consumer products are therefore at the head of the value chain and rely on the whole chain performing well for their success. At the same time, those in charge of marketing consumer products also determine the survival of that value chain.

Consumer markets

The key marketing issue for manufacturers or retailers of consumer goods, or providers of consumer services, is that they are faced with large numbers of potential customers. This applies equally to organizations which supply consumer durables such as refrigerators, and consumables, such as grocery products. The main differences between these two categories tend to be:

- Frequency of purchase.
- Absolute cost.
- Degree of involvement.

For these reasons, consumable products are often referred to as 'fast moving consumer goods' (FMCGs) where acceptance or rejection occurs in a relatively short space of time. Consumer durables, such as 'white goods' (freezers, cookers, etc.) or 'brown goods' (furniture, etc.), on the other hand, tend to be infrequent purchases of some significance to a household. Their purchase tends to be a much longer and more considered process, requiring a supplier to adapt their marketing accordingly.

Whatever their category, the fact of very large numbers of potential purchasers presents the suppliers of these products with a significant problem: how to make contact with customers when there are so many people who might be persuaded to buy your products in preference to a competitor's. This problem is compounded when those potential consumers are geographically dispersed or where they represent a small proportion of each community within the market.

Consumer products both head the value chain and rely on it

Main methods for marketing consumer products

Over the years, this difficulty has been addressed in a number of different ways and is an area in which significant innovations have taken place at various times.

Personal selling

The most effective way to develop a sales relationship with a potential customer is for a person to meet with that customer to explore his or her needs and to explain the virtues of the offer to him or her. In most consumer markets, this would involve a sales person calling on individuals and engaging them in the sales process either over the phone or in person. Traditionally, this is known as door-to-door selling. However, employing sales people in this way is a very expensive means of making a sale and, where the value of each sale is relatively small, not very profitable. For this reason, consumer goods sold in this manner tend to be:

- Difficult to sell (i.e. the benefits are hard to explain, e.g. insurance, solar heating or time-shares).
- Highly profitable (i.e. the margin per sale is large, e.g. some vacuum cleaners).
- Commodity items (i.e. where the only differentiating aspect is the sales process, e.g. loft conversions).

Direct mail

In parallel with the increasing sophistication of information technology and databases has come a significant increase in the use of direct mail. This is a cheaper means of placing a product in front of a consumer but enables a direct contact to be made. The increasing ability to target particular types of customer has encouraged many consumer products organizations to explore this route, and the 21st century has seen a proliferation of letters and catalogues arriving through consumers' doors.

The downsides of this method include: a relatively low response rate, progressive disillusionment on the part of consumers who begin to feel deluged with offers, and a loss of any personal contact with suppliers.

Retail outlets

Given the number and dispersal of potential customers, suppliers of many consumer products rely on retailers to distribute and sell their goods and services. This emphasizes the need to select appropriate retail organizations and the requirement for maintaining good relations with them. Indeed, for some grocery products such as a new cook-in sauce, simply being on the right shelf in the right part of the right chain of supermarkets is almost enough to guarantee success for a product line. The power of such retailers has also given rise to a particular type of marketing in the form of trade marketing and a supplier industry providing retail 'own label' products.

Brands

Creating and maintaining a brand for a product or set of products is essentially a way of developing and keeping a relationship with a consumer without the need for personal contact. Strong brands are those that have a personality with which consumers can identify or that evoke a feeling within a consumer that matches their personal values and lifestyle. Consumers are therefore attracted to brands of this nature and will buy them in preference to lesser (commodity) brands or brands that are targeted at a different segment of the market.

Brand values

Brand personality		Product consistency
Image consistency		Appropriate packaging
Media management		Product range
Competitive brands	**Brand**	Monitoring consumer
Positioning	**Manager**	preferences
Promotions		Target customers
Enhancements		Fashion changes
Stimulating sales		Channel management
force support		

Potential conflicts
between brand
and organizational
processes

Figure 7.1   Priorities for a consumer brand manager

Possessing a strong product or company brand name provides their owners with a lot of power in the market place. Manufacturers and service suppliers who own such brands are able to exert considerable influence on retailers in terms of price, shelf location, competitor positioning, merchandising, promotions policy, acceptance of new products and many other areas. Distinct retail brands are similarly able to influence lesser branded suppliers and to gain favourable locations and terms for their outlets.

For these reasons, brands and brand strategy are often at the heart of a supplier of consumer products' marketing strategy. The priorities or focus of attention for marketing managers of such supplier and retail brands are depicted in Figure 7.1.

Value chain management

The highly competitive world of consumer marketing has led many suppliers and retailers to pay closer attention to the value chain at whose head they sit. These

Brands are often central to consumer marketing strategy

organizations have recognized that advantage can be gained by exerting influence across all those who affect their products and their ability to supply. These advantages include: lower cost, higher quality, better availability, product innovation, speed to market, and a host of other important competitive factors.

In some industries, such as automotive manufacture, this management is sometimes delegated to a small group of key suppliers who are expected to influence and coordinate the other suppliers in the chain. In others, such as the computer supply industry, businesses like Dell are working directly with suppliers right down to component level and beyond in seeking efficiency and innovation for competitive advantage.

Micro marketing

Large numbers of potential consumers with similar needs leads many consumer marketing organizations to a mass marketing approach which tries to satisfy the majority of the market with an undiscriminating product, brand or approach as classically practised by Ford, Coca-Cola or McDonald's. Modern consumer marketers are, however, increasingly finding that markets are fragmenting as consumers become more sophisticated, individualistic and demanding.

The result has been a proliferation of new brands, or, in some cases, existing brands being 'stretched' across a number of product variations. A recent example is provided by Neutrogena which is now one of the biggest brands in the personal care portfolio of Johnson & Johnson. Originally, however, the brand was a skin-friendly range of mild glycerine soaps which only diversified into shampoos in 1980. Today the 'mild' associations of the brand have been used to stretch the name, which now covers a wide variety of products ranging from cleansers and moisturizers to haircare products, cosmetics and anti-aging creams.

Another initiative has been efforts to provide 'mass customization'. This involves consumers being able to configure their own product from a series of modular offerings added on to the core product or service. The new 'Mini' car designed and produced by BMW is a good example of this. The base product is devoid of most extras, which will add 50 per cent to the retail price once added, but which allows purchasers to create the car of their choice.

Finding ways of keeping the cost of such practices down and utilizing the growth of new direct consumer channels, such as the Internet, to provide customization in innovative and consumer-friendly ways remain important challenges for future consumer marketers.

Marketing Industrial Products

Whenever an organization consciously applies marketing to the management of its products, be they services, fast-moving consumer goods or industrial products, the fundamental principles of marketing always apply. Any market-orientated organization will seek an understanding of its customers, the markets of which they are a part, the opportunities which exist within that market, the best ways to compete with its rivals, and so on.

In spite of these similarities, most organizations in industrial markets instinctively know that their markets are different and that marketing their products requires a different set of approaches. To operate effectively in industrial markets, it is important to understand what these differences are since they will highlight the areas on which the organization must focus.

Having accepted this, it is also important to note that there is no simple or clear divide between industrial and consumer products and markets. On the product side, some products are sold in the same form to both industrial and consumer markets. Examples of this include bank accounts, motor cars, personal computers and parts for washing machines. In terms of markets, some consumer-goods manufacturers will only sell directly to other businesses i.e. trade sales. As a consequence, industrial marketing cannot be defined simply by the products involved or by the fact that it involves business-to-business selling.

Understanding industrial marketing

The best way to conceptualize industrial marketing is to look at it as a continuum with obvious slow-moving industrial products at one end and fast-moving consumer products at the other (see Figure 8.1). In the middle of the continuum are faster moving industrial products and slower moving consumer products.

The existence of this continuum also illustrates the possibility of the transfer of marketing approaches between these different markets. Whilst the context of their usage and the way in which they are applied may vary, no idea should be ignored because it is thought to be more appropriate to the realm of one market or product than another. Brands, for instance, are usually thought of as most appropriate for consumer products marketing. However, recent efforts by Intel and

Industrial marketing is different from consumer marketing, but the divide is not easily drawn

Figure 8.1 Continuum of industrial marketing

the success of Caterpillar provide contrary examples. Earth-moving equipment is an unlikely candidate for branding. However, Caterpillar have established the stylish yellow-tabbed CAT logo as the symbol of the leading global manufacturer of off-road trucks, tractors and other multi-terrain vehicles. The power of the brand is demonstrated by its easy transfer to a range of high-priced heavy-duty designer boots and associated apparel sold to the general public. The latter, though the smaller of the two businesses by far, trades off its sibling's well-established brand values of rugged, durable and dependable performance.

Issues in industrial marketing

The first issue concerns the way in which an industrial purchaser views a product it is considering purchasing. Industrial products are often thought of as being more **complex** than the equivalent consumer products, which is obviously not always the case. What is different is the attention paid to the details of a product. Even a commodity product, such as sheet steel or a simple component, will be considered in much greater detail by an industrial purchaser. This is because it will be used in more complex ways, or that small variations will have potentially harmful consequences. As an example, the wrong grade of steel will not machine properly and may put cost up and quality down. Similarly, a personal computer with a slightly wrong specification may make previous software purchases obsolete or networking with existing machines impossible.

The implications of such detailed product evaluations are that industrial purchasers have greater **information needs** than consumer purchasers, both before and after a purchase is made. In turn, this implies larger numbers of people being involved in the purchase decision. Consequently, organizations marketing industrial products have to cope with a larger and more diverse **decision-making unit** and a greater degree of **formalization** in the procedures applied to a purchase.

It also implies that a greater degree of **personal contact** between the supplier and buyer will be necessary, since this is the best way of providing complete information. Personal contact is necessary to isolate *who needs to know what* and *at what point in the decision-making process*, in order to improve the chances of a sale, or continued sales.

Apart from costly and infrequently purchased capital goods, the **volumes** bought by an industrial purchaser are also likely to be higher than those bought by individuals or families in a consumer market. The significance of this is the importance of the loss of these volumes to *both* the supplier and the purchaser. If a supplier fails to deliver the right quantity, the purchaser will find it difficult to continue their business. On the other hand, if a purchaser stops buying, this will have a significant impact on the supplier's income. In industrial markets, therefore, there is often a high degree of **interdependence**. Both supplier and purchaser will rely on each other for their continued existence. The loss of one purchaser in a consumer market is not nearly so significant.

This situation is further complicated by the fact that it is difficult in the industrial context to find mass markets. Apart from there being **smaller numbers of customers**, one buying organization is likely to differ significantly from the next in their buying requirements. This means that **segmentation** in industrial markets has to be conducted on a different basis.

A further implication is that the degree of **product variability** required can also be greater. In some cases, a single customer can form an entire segment and can consequently demand a high degree of customization. In others, the consumer variables for segmentation, such as demography, lifestage and lifestyle, need to be replaced by alternatives, such as size, applications and competitive positioning. Such **heterogeneity** is an important factor for the organization marketing industrial products.

In trying to understand, and give some structure to, the markets which industrial suppliers face, it must be recognized that their customers also have customers of their own, who may in turn have customers! Unless the customer is a country's defence ministry, or some similar body, all industrial products will eventually translate into a consumer purchase. This means that the structure of the market in which an industrial organization operates can be complex, with a whole series of intermediaries or 'value adders' between them and the final consumer. Industrial suppliers are thus faced with a situation of **derived demand** for their goods and services. The way they perceive their market and the way in which opportunities are identified and defined can therefore become a very complicated process.

Paradoxically, these factors combine to make **market research** in industrial markets sometimes more problematic, and sometimes easier, than consumer market research. Because of their low numbers, potential customers are likely to be difficult to find, extract information from, and generalize about. One cannot simply stand in shopping centres and stop passers-by or ring at random from the telephone directory. In addition, the influences on demand are likely to be more complex and remote from each organization, making them difficult to interpret. Where an organization has existing customers, however, market research is often easier since the people who hold valuable information and opinions should already be known and are usually quite willing to be approached.

Industrial markets exhibit a high degree of interdependence between buyer and supplier

Industrial marketing and general management

One of the consequences of the complexities which exist in the buyer/seller relationship in industrial markets is that many different functions within the selling organization are required to interact with various aspects of the customer organization. This can include service or maintenance sections, the design team, installation group, training, delivery and finance departments, as well as senior directors and the sales people. While many of these are also points of contact in consumer marketing, these contacts tend to be extensive and of greater significance in industrial markets.

Such complexity has also given rise to a need for key account management. Supply relationships which are significant for both parties can easily falter if left on a simple transactional basis. Key account managers who take a relationship perspective on an organization-wide basis are more likely to ensure that potential problems are avoided.

The management of marketing in industrial organizations, therefore, tends towards a **general management** function with small decisions in one area having a greater impact on the customer and business success. This is not to say that such coordination is inappropriate for consumer markets, but that closer attention to building a marketing approach across the management functions has a higher profile.

In general, then, marketing industrial products is a diverse area which can utilize a number of the approaches developed by consumer marketing organizations. What is important is a recognition of the differences which exist in industrial markets and the implications these hold for the supplying organization. In particular, the way that the relationship between supplier and customer is managed takes on a different perspective, but one which must be well understood and nurtured over time for the achievement of continuing and successful business.

9 Marketing Service Products

Service businesses became an increasingly significant sector of most advanced economies towards the end of the last century, and continue to be a dynamic sector as the 21st century unfolds. It currently provides around 70 per cent of civilian employment in the USA and the UK. Table 9.1 illustrates the potential range of service activities involved. At the same time, there has been an accelerating trend to differentiate what were once considered to be simply 'goods' by highlighting the service elements of the offer. Together with the deregulation experienced by many professional and government services, these factors have forced organizations to consider whether any differences are required when marketing service-based products.

At one level, a negative answer can be justified, since the theory of marketing has universal application. At another, the nature of many service-based products dictates that more emphasis is placed on certain elements of the marketing process. It is, therefore, crucial that marketing organizations understand what these elements are and how they will affect the marketing tasks they face.

Table 9.1 Major examples of service industries

- Retailing, wholesaling and distribution
- Banking, insurance and other financial institutions
- Real estate
- Communications, information and multimedia services
- Health services
- Business, professional and personal services
- Leisure and entertainment
- Education
- Public utilities
- Government services and non-profit service organizations

Defining a service

Defining a service for marketing purposes, however, is not easy. The diversity of organizations involved in services and the tendency to highlight the service elements of an 'offer' for competitive purposes, mean that they are sometimes hard to classify. One important element, however, is the degree of tangibility involved.

Service is an important differentiation factor

Table 9.2, for example, identifies four categories, varying from a 'pure' tangible product to a 'pure' service.

Table 9.2 Variations in product tangibility

■ A pure tangible product	A tangible offer, such as sugar, coal, or tea. No services are bought with the product
■ A tangible product with accompanying services such as commissioning, training, maintenance, etc.	The offer has built-in services to enhance its customer appeal, e.g. computers, machine tools
■ An intangible product with accompanying minor goods	The offer is basically a service, but has a physical element e.g. property surveyors, whose expert inspection is encapsulated in a report. Similarly, airlines offer in-flight meals or entertainment
■ A pure intangible product, where one buys expertise	The offer is a stand-alone service such as psychoanalysis or ski-instruction

Looked at in this way, a continuum of tangible–intangible products emerges as illustrated in Figure 9.1. Point 'a' on the left-hand side of this figure illustrates an offer where there is no service element and the product is highly tangible. At the other end of the spectrum, point 'd' illustrates a product which is entirely a service and is therefore highly intangible. Points 'b' and 'c' show varying mixes. For example, point 'b' illustrates the mix of tangibility for a computer company.

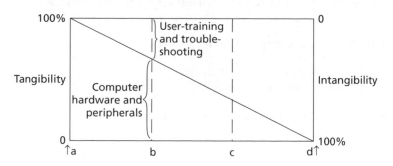

Figure 9.1 Continuum of tangible–intangible products

Computer hardware and peripherals are highly tangible and can be regarded as commodities, whereas the service elements of user-training and troubleshooting are largely intangible.

The intangible nature of a service leads to a number of other differences of significance for marketing. These include the implications that:

■ Services can be easily copied by competitors, since they cannot be patented and specified with drawings.

- Quality cannot be guaranteed since services are not previously produced or 'manufactured' under controlled conditions. Instead, they are produced and delivered at the time of consumption.
- A service cannot be stored on a shelf or taken down and used at a later time. Services are therefore highly perishable.
- People are an intrinsic part of most services and are difficult to separate from the product.
- The true value of a service can only be assessed on consumption. Thus, the purchase of a service involves a high component of trust.
- Services are often very personal in their nature and can involve the customer in their delivery and consumption, as in the case of a golf lesson or making a purchase at IKEA.

An important area in marketing services is, therefore, the **relationship** between the customer and the supplier. The close link between production and consumption, and the personal nature of many service products, emphasize this aspect. Where no personal relationship exists, the contrast between membership-type organizations and 'hands off' or automated services is stark and has led many businesses to seek a means of marketing more concrete affiliations as a substitute. In looking at ways and means of marketing the specific features of service products, the management of the relationship with the customer is, thus, always important.

The nature of a service also makes it hard for the customer to **evaluate** an offer prior to purchase. Unlike a car, it cannot be test-driven; it is difficult to encapsulate in a technical specification, and quality is uncertain. As examples, it is hard for a potential customer to assess a bank before opening an account with them, and a stay in a hotel can only be judged after one has checked out.

Thus, a crucial aspect of marketing services is to provide, as far as is possible, **tangible evidence** of the product quality. This highlights the need for careful attention to the 'product promise', such as the initial points of contact, descriptive literature and the peripherals which provide clues to the product's integrity. It is no coincidence that professional service businesses often have plush reception areas, holiday brochures are a masterpiece of presentation, and spa-based health clubs make a big show of testing the water. The problems associated with service evaluation can also be addressed by focusing on reputation, or by enhancing the value of a service through the provision of extra benefits such as free offers. Here, word of mouth or third-party endorsements become particularly influential. These can come from existing customers, referral markets and media institutions, all of whom can provide powerful testimony to the quality or value of an organization's offering.

Since many services rely heavily on a personal interaction between the service provider and the customer, or depend on individuals exercising judgement when

The relationship between customer and supplier is an important aspect of marketing services

creating the service, considerable **heterogeneity** between purchases becomes possible, so that customer-experiences of the product may vary enormously. Thus, the performance of a waiter or a shop assistant will have a great impact on the way a customer experiences the core benefit they are seeking. Similarly, two customers in the same hotel can have completely different opinions of their visit if one found their towels unlaundered or had their breakfast delivered late. Since the quality of such elements is in the hands of the people performing the service, employees become a vital concern for marketing services effectively. This requires attention to service-modelling to identify people-related 'fail points', as well as taking an interest in recruitment markets to ensure the right calibre of person. The process of **service delivery** thus needs careful specification which should include an identification of the skills necessary to reduce the likelihood of product heterogeneity as a consequence of 'people problems'.

At this point, it should also be noted that both the intangibility and heterogeneity of services mean that **attention to detail** becomes central to marketing effectiveness. This is, first, because it is often small factors that provide clues for the consumer about quality and, second, because such factors can have a major impact on customers' experience of service quality. Details, however, are also that part of the process of delivering the service most influenced by individual employees, thereby giving further weight to the focus on process design and human resource management.

The fact that a service will require the customer's involvement in its creation and delivery enhances the need for efficient management of this customer/provider **interaction**. Since manufacturers are able to check quality prior to delivery, service providers have to find substitutes for this. One solution has been to utilize technology to enhance consistency and improve accessibility, as was achieved by banks when they introduced automated tills or 'banking through the wall' and the introduction of e-tickets by airlines. Another approach has been to focus attention on frontline staff and to 'empower' them to negotiate service delivery to prevent excessive disappointment. Such a situation has worked well with in-store supervisory staff, receptionists and service engineers. A further method has involved better customer management to ensure satisfactory service delivery. Customer management can cover a number of different aspects, from setting appropriate expectations and encouraging customers to signify their satisfaction levels whilst utilizing a service, to getting them to behave in a way which enhances the service. A good example of the latter is the widespread improvement in the queueing technology which now ensures nobody waits longer than necessary in many banks, post offices and railway stations.

For marketing managers the **perishability** of a service places extra emphasis on understanding demand patterns and why such fluctuations exist. However, **matching demand** at all times is rarely possible or, indeed, cost-effective. In the end, the only alternatives are to try to change patterns of demand or to generate increased capacity at peak times. The techniques for managing demand revolve around incentives, such as offering better value and other sales promotion activities to encourage off-peak use, or using pricing mechanisms, such as premiums or discounts. Capacity can be enhanced by using part-time staff, subcontractors and shared facilities, or by carrying overheads in the form of staff, or assets, which are redundant at certain times. Managers, therefore, have to ensure careful coordination to balance the overall offer with the market's preferred pattern of utilization.

Services are sold into a whole range of markets, including industrial, government, not-for-profit, and consumer purchasers. Whilst each market creates its own unique marketing requirements, for services it is the distinct characteristics of the product which provide the major marketing challenges. In particular, it would seem to demand an expanded marketing mix beyond the four Ps of product, price, place and promotion, to include **people**, **processes** and **customer service**. These three additional elements significantly affect the success or otherwise of a service-based offering and will benefit from discrete programmes and action plans being developed for them. The features of service products also underline the importance of third-party markets such as recruitment, referral, influencer and internal markets, plus the overall concept of relationship marketing. Indeed, it has been argued that the recent interest in relationship marketing first grew from developments initiated within service businesses.

Interestin relationship marketing probably stems from the problems of marketing services

Topic Marketing High-tech
10 Products

Technology is becoming an important competitive tool for many organizations in differentiating themselves from other businesses in a marketplace. Where technology is a significant part of the overall market offering, organizations must consider whether its inclusion requires a particular approach or whether the nature of the technology will have little impact on the way in which the product is marketed.

The key distinction is between products which are high-tech for marketing purposes and products which simply involve advanced technology but do not require specific attention to that aspect of the offer. If the situation is the former, then there are a number of marketing issues that require special attention. If it is the latter, then other product and market issues are likely to be more important.

Distinguishing high-tech products

In trying to identify whether or not a product is high-tech for marketing purposes, it must be recognized that few products consist of a single technology. They are more usually a mixture of advanced, new and old technologies which, together, create the substantive product. Thus, automobiles, copiers and cameras utilize a whole range of technologies, but will only be high-tech for marketing purposes if the new or advanced technology they incorporate acts as a focus for customers' evaluation of the product. The first criterion for identifying a product as high-tech is how the customer views the product. Recent successes include digital cameras, iPods and DVD technology, while failures include 3G mobile technology, and face-recognition technology's future is still in doubt.

Whatever the product, purchases involve a risk for the buyer. For high-tech products, the problem is that the **risk** for the purchaser is increased as a result of the uncertainties associated with a new or advanced technology. However, risk does not only exist for the buyer – the supplier will also experience a higher than usual element of risk. This is because both the supplier and the buyer, be they end-users or supply-chain intermediaries, will lack experience of applying, maintaining and using the technology. In turn, this will increase the chances of unforeseen problems arising, such as further cost, supply continuity, unanticipated side effects, or quality problems.

The newness of a technology forming the key feature of a high-tech product will also contribute to marketing issues since the product is unlikely to be an accepted solution, yet, for the problem(s) it has been designed to solve. As such, there is unlikely to be widespread understanding of how a high-tech product can provide benefits for both customer and potential customer organizations. In addition, it is doubtful if there will be support structures in the market that supplying organizations can utilize in their marketing efforts.

A further implication of high-tech or 'state-of-the-art' technology is that supplying organizations will have to employ comparatively large proportions of highly skilled scientific and technical specialists. These will be necessary to obtain the developments needed for new products and to provide the know-how required for manufacture, sales and post-purchase support. This will be particularly important given the absence of external expertise to which such problems can be out-sourced. The downside is that large numbers of technical specialists may encourage a technically (rather than market) oriented organization.

The key features of high-tech products that have implications for marketing are:

- Advanced technology that acts as the focus for product evaluation.
- High degrees of uncertainty on the part of both the supplier and the customer about the technology.
- Products are not yet accepted as a natural solution for the problems they have been designed to address.
- Lack of any associated external infrastructure.
- Likely to have been developed in a highly technical environment.

These do not negate the fundamentals of marketing management such as benefit analysis, segmentation and careful targeting via the marketing mix. They do, however, lead to the critical issues that marketing managers of high-tech products must address.

Critical marketing issues

Technology seduction

Since high-tech products tend to be derived in a technologically orientated organization peopled by large numbers of technical specialists, marketing managers must first be aware of the potential for **technology seduction**. Seduction will involve the internal promotion of a technology which is unwarranted by the market(s) that a business can realistically address. This can lead to either products whose performance exceeds market needs, or investment based on gaining technical improvements rather than market potential. The role of marketing managers is to recognize a case of technology seduction and to avoid becoming seduced themselves by the enthusiasm of others.

High-tech products involve greater risk for buyer and supplier alike

Credibility

As a second issue, if high-tech products are not yet accepted solutions and tend to generate a high level of uncertainty, customers will need to develop a greater degree of trust than might otherwise be the case. An important ingredient for the creation of trust is **credibility**. This can involve both the credibility of the supplying organization and the technology itself. Establishing credibility may require: high-profile demonstrations; the offer of substantial guarantees; wooing 'lead users'; fostering excellent media relations; and so on. Creating or changing people's perceptions, however, can take a long time. This means that high-tech marketing managers need to foresee the potential for credibility problems well in advance to avoid them becoming barriers to entry into new markets or establishing new products in existing ones.

Standards

In technology-based markets, **standards** have always had a significant impact on marketing strategy, but for high technology they can be very important. As an example, conforming to standards can enhance credibility while the absence of standards can increase the uncertainty felt by customers and can leave a supplier without frameworks within which to work. In addition, the creation of a standard which is based on an alternative interpretation of a technology can make an organization's products obsolete. When marketing high-tech products, attention must therefore be paid to:

- Influencing the creation of standards.
- The possibility of becoming 'the standard'.
- Conforming to standards.
- Gaining approval or being certified as meeting a standard, and so on.

Unfortunately, this usually requires a lot of time, money and effort, and will demand careful coordination to gain the maximum marketing benefits.

Technology lifecycles

The 'newness' of a high-tech product and the uncertainty associated with it implies that managers should also place their marketing decisions in the context of the technology's lifecycle (see Figure 10.1). By definition, a high-tech product is at the early stages of its technological (as opposed to market) life. This means that marketing managers have to prepare for the transition from a situation where performance improvements have been hard to achieve to one where improvements become relatively easy to obtain. At the same time, the marketing task will change as risk and uncertainty reduce while technologies move through their lifecycles. This also suggests that marketing should contribute to decisions about which element of performance should be prioritized for development, and how sufficient flexibility can be maintained for future product development.

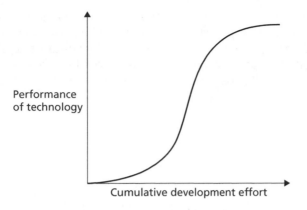

Figure 10.1   The technology lifecycle

Positioning

A further contributor to overcoming the problems associated with high-tech products is good **positioning**. Favourable product evaluation, reduced uncertainty and broadened supplier acceptance can be enhanced by positioning which implies leadership (to support credibility), customer service (to compensate for the lack of general knowledge about the technology), and a clear performance benefit (to make the risk of purchase worthwhile). This could involve positioning the supplier as the technology innovator and service leader and the product's benefits as improved quality, cost savings, or performance levels which were previously impossible.

Infrastructure

Finally, since a critical feature of high-tech products is the lack of associated market and technological **infrastructures**, marketing managers must also find a means of redressing this problem. Where they cannot be redressed externally, a business must seek an in-house solution and bear the associated costs. Alternatively, it will require an enterprise to select markets, and, therefore, product development priorities, where limited infrastructure will have the least impact on commercialization and business development.

Overall, then, like other product-based marketing activities, marketing high-tech products requires a good understanding of their distinctive features and the marketing priorities they imply. If these are ignored, decisions and consequent actions will be taken according to other criteria such as: instinct; short-term considerations; ill-informed assumptions; or significant voices. The role of the manager is to establish the marketing priorities associated with this type of product as an integral part of, and a timely contribution to, the managerial processes of the organization.

The role of the marketing manager is to establish marketing priorities

In addition, and unlike products in established and growing markets, high-tech products require a more proactive approach to the establishment of demand. The sheer newness of the product or its position will necessitate a 'supply-push' approach as opposed to the product being able to ride on the back of 'demand-pull' conditions. Latent demand will need to be sought and activated into purchasing activity.

11 Marketing Capital Goods

As with any product-based approach to marketing, the marketing of capital goods presents suppliers with some special concerns. These are generated by the nature of the products and the circumstances under which they are bought and sold. Capital goods can be pieces of plant and equipment, such as large machines, boilers or storage facilities, or complete systems, such as refineries, telecommunications networks or civil engineering projects.

Customers will similarly be large organizations and may be either private or public sector. Whichever the case, the purchase will be a significant event for the customer in terms of both the amounts of money involved and the benefits which the products will be required to deliver. At the same time, purchaser and supplier risks are also high, requiring a systematic approach to marketing which takes all these factors into consideration.

Consequences for marketing

By their nature, orders for capital goods tend to be few in number, even for the 'faster-moving' capital goods such as machine tools. In addition, their cost makes them very prone to economic fluctuations. Suppliers are thus often faced with a 'feast or famine' situation whereby they either have no orders and are standing around idle, or they are overwhelmed with enquiries and find it difficult to meet delivery or completion schedules.

This is further exacerbated by the fact that each purchase is usually supplied against a different specification. It is unlikely that such large and complex products will be used in the same way, or serve exactly the same purpose, from one customer to another. Such a situation prohibits the creation of finished stock except at a very early stage in the manufacture or construction process.

The risk associated with the supply and purchase of capital goods also creates pressures which militate against the use of innovative technologies or approaches. On the supplier side, the consequence of product failure in terms of financial penalties or loss of reputation can be very high. Similarly, from the customer's point of view, a capital purchase will frequently have strategic, or at least operational, significance and buyers are likely to be anxious to reduce the chances of something going wrong by sticking to proven technologies or methodologies. Where

The purchase of capital goods involves high cost and high risk

innovation does occur, its adoption is therefore likely to be a slow process and the recovery of development costs a long-term activity.

The consequences that such features will have for marketing cover a number of areas. High levels of customization plus the complexity of (particularly) larger products will mean that a product specification will take time to evolve and will typically be the result of much **negotiation** between supplier and customer. This will require suppliers to resource such negotiations and to maintain the ability to understand a customer's perspectives so that they can translate the benefits which customers seek into a product specification. Protracted negotiations and the absence of finished goods stock will create **long order lead-times**, which will also require suppliers to maintain sales relationships over time. Without this, suppliers may risk losing an order through: changes in personnel; loss of interest; situational changes which will alter the product specification; and the activities of competitors.

The size of an order may also require suppliers to **join together**, sometimes as international consortia, to be able to fulfil the requirements of a customer. Managing such relationships in a way which presents customers with a unified face is a distinct skill, but one which is important for the maintenance of relationships with customers. Such relationships, however, will also need to be continued after a sale has been made since capital goods usually involve **lengthy installation** or construction. Although repeat business is not as significant a feature of capital goods marketing as it is for other types of industrial products, client or customer referrals and references *are* an important aspect of selling and good relationships will be needed to ensure that these are forthcoming.

Capital Goods pricing

Since each product is unique, the price of a particular sale will also vary. In addition, since there is much negotiation about each specification, price is often one of the last factors to be considered. The complexity of supply also means that competing bids for a contract often vary significantly between competitors as a result of the way prices are calculated and the different methodologies which can be applied to the fulfilment of a specification.

At the same time, the variations in demand mean that organizations may sometimes adopt a pricing strategy which is closer to **marginal cost pricing**. This may be done to maintain capacity during times of 'famine' in order to prevent the loss of resources which would make them uncompetitive when business becomes more buoyant. Alternatively, during periods of growth, organizations will often seek to recover cost and limit demand, which will tempt them to quote much higher prices.

Prices in capital goods markets, then, have a tendency to fluctuate quite wildly, both between time periods and between different forms of the same product, which makes it difficult to decide how to use price as a competitive weapon. On the other hand, the amounts of money involved and the complexity of the product provide more scope than in other areas for variations on the pricing mix. This can involve:

- Payment terms.
- Payment penalties and bonuses.
- Profit sharing.
- Leasing arrangements.
- Modular pricing.
- The way a price is presented.
- Technology transfer agreements.

Decision-making in the purchase of capital goods

The size and significance of a capital purchase will mean that large numbers of people are likely to combine to form the decision-making unit. Since relationships are an important factor in capital goods sales, contacts, and the ability to keep and develop such relationships, are a critical factor for success, as is the flexibility to have different types of relationships with different people. The significance of capital purchases, however, can mean that governments can also have an interest in the product. Indeed, for some products, governments may even be *the* customer. Thus, there can be a political, as well as a commercial, influence in the decision to buy.

In some instances, such as a defence project, high levels of confidentiality may also be required. In others, such as a large infrastructural civil engineering project, awareness of a country's development plans, the involvement of national suppliers, or some 'tit-for-tat' investment by the supplier or the supplier's government may be a prerequisite for a successful sale. This political aspect, plus the complex nature of the 'buy-centre', may require a lot of 'politics' and building of credibility along a number of different dimensions for an organization to be a viable contender for a piece of business.

Marketing capital goods is, therefore, conducted in a complex market environment. Marketers are faced with long product lifecycles and circumstances that make it difficult to innovate. In contrast, they are also faced with volatile demand and large variations between one purchase and the next. This is further complicated by the need to develop good relationships with customers, but with the likelihood that any relationship will only be temporary since any one customer is only likely to purchase once or, at best, infrequently. This demands that suppliers are able to be flexible in terms of relationships, capacity and the product they supply. It also demands that they take a long-term perspective on several counts, including sales negotiations, product design and development, relationship management, profit planning and funding issues.

The price of capital goods tends to fluctuate wildly

12 Trade Marketing

In the marketing of consumer products and 'fast-moving' industrial goods, much effort is applied to 'pull' activities (i.e. creating demand amongst large numbers of users which will 'pull' products through the supply chain). This is the logic behind most branding strategies, sales calls and promotional activities such as couponing or distributing free samples through the door. An alternative or complementary approach is to apply marketing effort to a 'push' strategy focusing on intermediaries (the trade) and 'pushing' products through the supply chain to the consumer.

The power and influence of these trade intermediaries in western economies has grown significantly over the last 30 years. Indeed, the ability to have your product on the shelves or in the catalogues of these prominent intermediaries is often a key factor to gaining position and advantage in many end-use markets. Focusing marketing effort on these intermediaries, termed trade marketing, has therefore increased in importance for many organizations and has required the development of new approaches to relationship management.

The rise of intermediaries

Factors that have contributed to the increasing importance of trade intermediaries for suppliers of mass-market goods and services can be identified as follows.

Retail power

As has already happened in North America and much of Western Europe, retailing and some aspects of industrial distribution have become dominated by a small number of large organizations such as Wal-Mart, Carrefour and Tesco. Suppliers relying on these intermediaries for sales to end-users can easily be denied access to such markets even if only one intermediary decides not to stock their products. Effective marketing to these intermediaries therefore takes on much greater significance. The strategy can no longer be a reliance on large sales forces placing their products in a wide range of different retailers or distributors in a 'hit or miss' fashion, but one which sustains effective presence in these outlets.

Brand differentiation

In some markets, consumers are finding it increasingly difficult to differentiate between leading brands or suppliers. This is particularly true in markets for mobile telephony or personal computing, but it is also observable in traditional fast-moving consumer areas such as washing powders or tinned foods. The result of this growing brand parity is that consumers more frequently purchase on the basis of availability and price within their chosen 'retail set'.

Market fragmentation

As markets become more competitive and customers grow in sophistication, demands for individualized supply similarly increase. Demand consequently fragments making it less effective to adopt mass-marketing techniques. While this has encouraged organizations such as Heinz and wine importers to experiment with more direct and individualized marketing methods, it has also emphasized the value of reaching out to customers at the point of purchase. This requires trade promotions to encourage preferential stocking and point-of-sale support.

E-commerce

Advances in information technology have meant that suppliers can be in direct contact with an intermediary on a real-time basis. This has enabled retailers and other intermediaries to reduce cost and increase efficiency by effectively delegating inventory responsibilities to a small number of key suppliers. Establishing oneself as one of these key suppliers in the eyes of intermediaries therefore becomes a priority for many manufacturers.

Brand management deficiencies

Brand managers in many organizations are often young and ambitious people trying to leave their mark on a brand's performance. The most effective way of achieving short-term position is often through trade promotions since brand value enhancement in the eyes of the consumer is more difficult and inevitably a longer-term proposition. Trade marketing therefore becomes more valuable to a brand manager's career than brand development.

Trade marketing tactics

Traditionally, tactics for trade marketing have centred on the marketing mix elements of promotion and price. These have taken the form of:

Promotion	Price
■ Incentives to staff of intermediaries	■ Additional discounts
■ Point-of-sale material	■ Supplying to retailer price points
■ Merchandising support	■ Supporting buyer margin targets
■ Cooperative advertising	■ Price promotions such as 'buy two
■ Joint trade-fair representation	and get a third free'

Trade marketing traditionally focused on price and promotion

Trade marketing strategies

As intermediaries have become an increasing focus for marketing activities, so tactical approaches have given way to a more strategic view. At the heart of this is an understanding of how both supplier and intermediary can mutually benefit from a well-managed long-term relationship.

One manifestation of this is product profitability studies which analyse in great detail the way that cost attaches itself to a product both during manufacture and in its distribution and handling within the retail environment. Another is the development of category management whereby a single supplier takes responsibility for a product category such as hair care or chocolate bar confectionery.

Where category management has become widespread, as in the case of the USA, Germany and the UK, suppliers vie with each other to become 'category leaders', leading to significant adjustments in the structure of many suppliers' brand portfolios.

The strategic importance of trade marketing has also led to heavy investment in information technology by many suppliers to enable logistics and communications to proceed as smoothly as possible. Other aspects of the relationship will be enshrined in joint product development plans, the sharing of 'best-practice' information and a long-term view of category development such as the introduction of more organic produce.

The future

The factors which have led to the expansion of trade marketing have also stimulated many suppliers to reassess their relationship with end-users. Whilst some suppliers have concentrated on better marketing relationships with intermediaries, others have sought to strengthen their brand franchise so that retail or product categories will be weakened without the inclusion of their brand. This is quite apparent in a number of areas such as fashionable sportswear, pet foods and some aspects of the soft drinks market. It is also a major part of Intel's long-term strategy and the global 'Intel Inside' campaign.

At the same time, there has been an upsurge of 'direct' provision in many areas, particularly in the financial services arena. The advent of the Internet has dramatically fuelled this trend. Whilst some retailers are also beginning to add this to the range of services they offer, the possibility of direct provision for manufacturers is an attractive proposition. Not only does it imply higher margins but it also reduces their reliance on retailers who may not always approach supply relationships in the true 'spirit of partnership'.

The increase in global retailing and the emergence of 'category killers' are also good and bad news for suppliers. The global expansion of stores such as Toys-'R'-Us,

WalMart and Carrefour means access to much expanded markets and growth in line with the retailers. However, such stores are usually situated out of town and offer focused category goods at heavily discounted prices. Their predatory nature often decimates local retail competition, reducing suppliers' routes to a market, and putting them in a stronger position to demand lower prices from suppliers.

Managing the conflicting demands of these powerful intermediaries, including the need for independence and long-term profitability on the part of a supplier and the continuing possibility for creating a consumer or brand franchise, will be an important determinant of the way trade marketing develops in the future.

The future of trade marketing lies in how the conflicting demands of powerful intermediaries are managed

13 Internet Marketing

The term 'Internet marketing' can best be summarized as:

> *'The effective promotion of goods and services through the medium of an interactive, computerized information channel and the enhancement of existing customer information for the purpose of refining an integrated marketing strategy.'*

The two most important Internet applications are the World Wide Web and electronic mail, or e-mail. These provide the vehicles for the most extreme example of Internet marketing, 'electronic commerce': the sale and purchase of goods and services over the Internet. The long-term future of the Internet is difficult to predict, with some commentators forecasting that it will be replaced by media such as interactive digital television or innovations in mobile telephony. However, success to date would indicate that it is likely to remain a significant medium for the provision of interactive communication of electronic information.

The challenge for suppliers is that many websites attract a continuum of visitors. At one end are passive users seeking a reference site. The challenge is to satisfy these 'browsers' while finding innovative ways of attracting active users to visit the site and get involved in *your* product rather than a competitor's.

As an example, *The Economist* relies on weekly subscriber e-mails to keep their publication in front of computer users on a regular basis. Internet Florists use 'Virtual Bouquets' to encourage visitors and to generate 'pick-ups' from their website by providing users with the opportunity to send a real bouquet as an alternative. The 'AIDA' standard applies to the Internet as much as to any other advertising media. In order to attract and involve users, providers must generate **A**wareness, **I**nterest and **D**esire, culminating in **A**ction, as a result of effective marketing communications.

Internet marketing: principles and considerations

The Internet is an important new way of interacting with customers, but as just one of the channels for interaction, it cannot be considered in isolation. Its potential contribution can be assessed through a model of the role IT adopts in marketing generally. This can be summarized under the following headings.

Integration: know your customer

In order to manage customer relationships, organizations need systems which can manage data throughout the customer purchase-cycle, from initial contact through sales to delivery and post-sales service. Customer data must also be integrated across communication mechanisms to ensure coordination across the multiple channels by which consumer demands can reach the supplier (e.g., by telephone, through a sales person, via written communication, and so on).

Many organizations fail to integrate their websites in this way, simply advertising their products on the Web and making no attempt to gather vital customer information beyond the creation of a database of e-mail addresses. Websites are frequently wasted as an opportunity to obtain, utilize and enhance existing knowledge about customers in the way that Hewlett Packard currently do. They similarly fail to exploit the Web's interactive nature to add value through product configuration, online pricing, information on availability, decision trees and other sales support activities, although many are getting much better at this. Domestic boiler manufacturers and suppliers, for instance, now take consumers through a series of questions to lead them to the correct boiler for their premises.

Interactivity: beyond addressability to dialogue

Truly knowing your customers means effectively closing the loop between the messages sent to them and the messages they send back. In the age of 'addressability', where organizations try to communicate with individual customers through carefully targeted direct mail, 'interactivity' goes one step further. The Web's interactive nature is being used by retailers, such as Waitrose in the UK, to provide customer services such as 'Recipe Search', which allows users to search for a recipe by type (i.e. vegetarian, month, cooking and preparation time, and even including or excluding specified ingredients). The website builds up its customer knowledge, enabling it, for example, to offer personalized promotions as a by-product of the service.

Individualization: mass marketing and microsegmentation

The ability to deal directly with individual members of a mass market from one central source enables personal service through mass customization. Amazon.com, for instance, provides a simple book retail service, but over time began to offer customers information about other books that other readers of similar purchasing patterns have found interesting. Leveraging their data on customers and the interactive potential of the Web, the company can move beyond personalized promotions to the provision of information and product configurations unique to each of their individual customers. Once this is combined with a pricing and delivery/customer service package similarly uniquely configured, the age of mass customization is truly upon us.

Internet marketing enables personal service through mass customization

Independence of location: the death of distance

A bedroom made to order by an Internet design service achieves the individualization of a men's tailors, combined with post-industrial revolution economies of scale. The independence of location allows individualization to be achieved economically on a grand scale. Niche products can serve their target markets even if spread globally.

Being able to reach customers wherever they are may also have the effect of widening consumer choice and extending consumer power. The growth of software 'agents' (who search the Web for specific items at the lowest price) effectively outsources a time-consuming activity whilst levelling prices. One survey found that 22 per cent of US car buyers paid the asking price, against only 9.3 per cent of online buyers. Computer support in the areas of pricing individually tailored services or providing information services has the added benefit of freeing up expensive sales people for the tasks that they are good at: building up individual relationships with key accounts at senior levels.

Intelligence: informed strategy

Better customer data can also improve decisions on marketing strategy. In some cases, segments may also be derived from the data gathered. This again illustrates the importance of data integration, enabling more effective planning and initiatives to serve particular target segments more effectively.

Industry restructuring: redrawing the market map

As organizations redefine themselves to take advantage of IT-enabled marketing, or are replaced by newcomers who operate according to the new rules, some industries are restructuring. In the financial services sector, the Internet is replacing human advice in product specification, as well as basic transactions. As an example, new electronic intermediaries will search for the best live quote from a range of life insurance companies.

Top six considerations

The appropriateness of the Internet for a particular customer interaction will vary according to the characteristics of the market segment. It can be used to advantage where its features match the needs of the customer interaction.

- As long as the Internet is only accessible by a proportion of the population, it is necessary to establish what proportion of the target segment of the market will have access.
- The accessibility provided by the Internet means that those communicating do not need to do so at the same time. Information can be accessed across time

zones without the restrictions of contact in respective national business hours only. It is therefore particularly relevant to geographically dispersed markets and those where the cost of sales visits is prohibitive.

- The Internet offers the benefits of being more interactive than direct mail or broadcast media. Since interaction is with a computer rather than a person, the interactivity is different from that of a telephone or sales visit, making it appropriate for pre-programmed, high-volume, repetitive tasks.
- The Web is mainly a medium of two-dimensional static words and graphics, although use of sound and video is expanding. This has enabled, for example, hotels and conferences to make use of virtual reality technology to demonstrate their services and facilities to Internet browsers. Internet restrictions still make certain products, such as clothes, less appropriate for sale over the Web since, as part of the purchase, the customer may wish to feel the fabric or try an item on.
- The marginal cost of the Internet as a communication tool can be low. However, it is generally false that the cost of advertising is saved, since the size of the Internet still poses the problem of how to get people to the website in the first place. This can be done using online search engines such as Google or Yahoo, or service providers such as AOL.
- User concerns about security and privacy can impede the placement of orders over the Internet. This is likely to bias Internet sales in the direction of relatively low-value items such as books or CDs, and in favour of suppliers with strong, trusted brands. Market research suggests that the dominant factors affecting Internet use remain the traditional concerns: price, convenience, service levels, product availability, and so on. Internet speed and the quality of websites will therefore be just as important as addressing security issues for the growth of the Internet over the coming years.

Future challenges

With the advent of digital and WebTV plus advancements in mobile telephony, one of the major challenges for advertisers is determining how products are going to be promoted most effectively in five years' time. In the 1940s, Procter & Gamble spent more than half its advertising dollars on radio. From 1950 to 1955, the new medium of television went from taking nearly nothing to 80 per cent of the advertising budget. In contrast, only 0.4 per cent of its 1998 $3 billion-a-year advertising budget was spent on the Internet. Unilever, meanwhile, has agreed to invest $20 million in partnerships with America Online and Microsoft to explore ways of Internet advertising.

Part of the problem is that while in the USA radio and television developed as a form of mass-market entertainment with advertising slots incorporated from the start, the Internet evolved mainly as an information resource used by individuals. Advertisements only started to appear on the Internet in the mid-1990s and

Issues of security and privacy still plague the Internet

generally rely on the user to click on the 'banner' to be taken to the advertiser's website.

Digital television and WebTV challenge the Internet's big advantage over traditional television in their potential for interaction, transforming a passive viewer into an active participant, more likely to absorb and respond to the advertiser's message. The key question for advertisers is: how can we maintain a presence in our target customers' minds given the decline in TV as a unique mass medium?

14 Marketing Internationally

International marketing, at its simplest, is the performance of the marketing task across national boundaries. The basic approach, therefore, is no different from domestic marketing and the principles involved remain the same. Thus, a supplier organization has to perform market research, identify a target market, develop appropriate products, adopt a pricing policy, promote sales, and so on. In spite of this, whenever organizations begin to operate outside their domestic markets, many otherwise successful enterprises seem to suffer setbacks to their marketing efforts.

Observation of this phenomenon has led both academics and practitioners to pay increasing attention to the subject of international marketing in an attempt to reduce the problems which seem to arise. When this is done, what emerges is the significance of the *differences* rather than the *similarities* involved when marketing abroad. Within this, it becomes important to recognize that:

- The environment in which international marketing takes place is significantly different in certain areas.
- There is a different dimension of complexity involved in planning the marketing process.
- The control it is possible to exercise over the marketing mix is reduced.

Environment and complexity

It is obvious that there are likely to be major differences in the way that customers behave between different countries. For many organizations, however, although these differences are acknowledged, they are not always investigated or consciously included in the planning processes. There are many examples of simple mistakes that have cost organizations millions of dollars through lost sales, and which have occurred as a result of a lack of rigour in investigating such differences. Some are amusing, such as Toyota's launch of the MR2 in France not realizing that, when spoken in French, the letters and numbers made a rude word. Others are just silly, such as the poor translations often found in technical instructions. Some of these areas of difference are shown in Table 14.1.

In addition, organizations seeking to market internationally also face political, legal and regulatory differences. Thus, they may find that they are required to use a

The focus of international marketing is differences rather than similarities

Table 14.1 Environment differences when marketing overseas

■ Language	■ Business hours
■ Tastes and fashions	■ What is polite and impolite
■ Religion	■ Social priorities
■ Physical environment	■ Literacy levels
(temperature, humidity)	■ Communications infrastructure
■ Power supplies	■ Distribution facilities
■ Security arrangements	■ Methods of transaction
■ Family structure and size	

local partner as a distributor or that prices are controlled by the government. There may also be different technical standards operating in the country and taxation may be applied in a completely different way. The economic practices can lead to complications and may include: tariffs; quotas; exchange controls; non-tariff barriers; customs; unions; and so on. Together with such factors as political volatility, an additional element of complexity and uncertainty is added to the marketing task.

International control

The degrees of freedom an organization has when operating abroad, and the consequent control they can exert over their marketing activities, will be mostly determined by the method chosen for entering a foreign market. The two main forms can be described as simply exporting or, alternatively, actually producing abroad.

Straightforward *exporting* can be either indirect or direct. Indirect exporting is when a third party arranges the documentation, shipping and selling of an organization's goods abroad, and this usually represents the lowest level of commitment to international marketing. As foreign sales grow, however, an organization often begins to make a limited commitment, frequently in the form of taking on the documentation task for itself. It is usually at this stage that overseas agents or distributors are appointed to carry out the selling task abroad, with the result that the business is now a direct exporter, although it is likely that the commitment is still limited to marginal production capacity, with no additional fixed investment.

Recognition of the importance of overseas trading really happens when a limited fixed investment occurs, not just in the form of production capacity, but also in the form of a marketing subsidiary abroad in recognition of the need for a more aggressive marketing approach.

Foreign production can take the form of licensing, contract manufacturing, local assembly or full manufacture, either by joint ventures or wholly-owned subsidiaries. With licensing, the company is hiring out its brand name, technical expertise, patents, trademark, or process rights. The licensee manufactures and markets abroad for the licensor. Whilst this avoids the need for a heavy investment, it can lead to an over-dependence on the licensee, who quickly builds up both manufacturing and marketing expertise. Associated Engineering, the largest engine components manufacturer in the world, and Pilkington Glass are just two examples of organizations with a successful record of licensing abroad.

Contract manufacturing is merely using someone else's production capacity and is usually only possible for technically simple products like some basic foods. It is a useful way of getting round tariff barriers, as well as of gaining experience of a foreign market, without the need for investment in capital and labour. Similar advantages apply to local assembly, which is also a learning device, as well as enabling a company to avoid paying the higher tariffs on assembled products, since bringing in unassembled goods helps local employment. Car manufacturers such as Honda and Toyota have successfully employed this technique to enter attractive foreign markets.

Sometimes, laws forbid 100 per cent foreign ownership of assets, especially in less-developed countries. Many companies, therefore, set up joint ventures, either with a foreign government or with local partners. This is certainly a good way of sharing risk and of gaining experience using local expertise. Its major disadvantage lies in the loss of complete control, and hence freedom of action, especially in the field of marketing.

One-hundred per cent ownership of foreign production plants represents a major commitment to international marketing and should only be done after much research. Most overseas manufacturing occurs as a result of some factor associated with that market. As an example, Nissan and St Gobain have both built manufacturing plants in the USA and the UK because this was the best way to overcome barriers to entry. Likewise, GKN's big stake in the German components industry gave them a market share which could not have been achieved by direct export from the UK as a result of the German need for short delivery lead times.

From this, it will be clear that there is a big difference between the marketing task of a company selling to an overseas intermediary as a final customer, and the task facing the organization that assumes full responsibility for all stages of marketing internationally right through to final user satisfaction. The important point is that each of the options should not be considered as a series of steps to be followed *en route* to becoming a multinational company (in which all opportunities are assessed from the worldwide viewpoint, and in which the terms 'home' and 'foreign' are meaningless), but more as strategic alternatives. And since the method of market entry is the major determinant of the degree of control a company has over its marketing, each of the different options should be carefully considered before a decision is made.

The importance of overseas trading is acknowledged by having a marketing subsidiary abroad

Table 14.2 Key questions in international marketing

- *Whether* to sell abroad. Geographical diversification may be more desirable than product diversification, depending of course on circumstances. However, the decision to sell abroad should not be taken lightly.
- *Where* to sell abroad. This is one of the major decisions for international marketing. Choosing foreign markets on the basis of proximity and similarity is not necessarily the most potentially profitable option to go for.
- *What* to sell abroad and the degree to which products should be altered to suit foreign needs is also one of the major problems of international marketing.
- *How* to sell abroad is concerned, not just with the issue of how to enter a foreign market, but also with the management of 'the four Ps' once a company arrives. It also involves the difficult question of how to coordinate the marketing effort across a number of foreign countries.

Overall, then, international marketing involves a number of issues which make decision-making a difficult task. Merely recognizing the differences and the complexities, however, is not enough. Policies must be debated in the context of the critical questions which need to be addressed when considering marketing internationally (see Table 14.2).

Part 3
Understanding Customers

15 Consumer Buying Behaviour

As well as understanding a market in terms of trends, competitors, segments, and so on, organizations supplying products or services also need to have an appreciation of the way customers **think** when coming to a specific purchase decision and how they **behave** when making a purchase. Understanding thinking is, however, not easy as it is hidden from view; it is a bit of a 'Black Box', so we can only ever look for clues as to what's going on in someone's head. Behaviour is easier to observe and a better basis for analysing customers. In addition, an understanding of how behaviour varies between different groups of customers enables businesses to ascertain the ways in which markets can be segmented. Without this knowledge, suppliers will find it difficult to choose between the alternative elements of the marketing mix to construct a value proposition that will find favour with those customers it has decided to target.

Components of a purchase decision

The basic process can be described as an interaction between a number of external factors and a buyer's 'Black Box', which will, in turn, determine how a buyer responds to those circumstances. The outcomes of this are the different components of a purchase decision (see Figure 15.1).

External factors

The external factors that may affect a potential buyer consist of the marketing mix offered by a supplier plus various environmental issues such as:

- The economic situation.
- Technological developments.
- The media.
- Political and legal influences.
- Cultural differences.
- Competitor marketing mixes.

The 'Black Box'

A buyer's 'Black Box' is really a combination of internal factors, consisting of the stages through which an individual passes on the way to a purchase decision, plus

Figure 15.1 Components of a consumer's purchase decision

the various personal characteristics any individual will possess. These will be a combination of cultural influences; social context, such as social groups, or family values; psychological make-up; and personal circumstances. Personal circumstances will include socio-economic position, lifecycle stage, lifestyle, access to credit facilities, and so on. Psychological profiles are more complicated and will involve factors such as an individual's motivations, perceptions, values and attitudes.

The buyer's response

The outcome of a purchase decision will consist of:

- The type of product chosen.
- The particular brand or supplier picked from the range of choices within a product type.
- The retail or dealer channel used.
- Issues such as the timing of the purchase or the volumes bought.

Together, these create a very complex situation about which to make marketing decisions. They also present supplying organizations with some fundamental options. As an example, it is reckoned that only 15 per cent of West Europeans who could benefit from a hearing aid actually use one. This is thought to result from a number of influences including, amongst others:

- Self-image.
- The social stigma associated with incapacity.

- Non-recognition of the onset of deafness.
- Ignorance of the range of aids available.
- The high cost of hearing aids.

For hearing-aid manufacturers, the choices this leads to are:

- Trying to alert people to the need.
- Changing attitudes.
- Concentrating on those who are actively seeking a hearing aid.

Each alternative has its drawbacks and does not exclude action in other areas. The choices, however, do illustrate the problems inherent in making sense of, and responding to, a consumer's propensity to purchase.

Personal involvement

In understanding consumers' buying behaviour, it is also usual to distinguish between **high involvement** and **low involvement** purchases. The degree to which purchasers will find themselves spending time, effort and thought on a purchase will depend on the frequency of the purchase, plus the level of perceived **risk** they experience. Feelings of risk will be driven by four main 'need' areas:

- The importance of the function the product performs for them.
- The proportion of disposable income it requires.
- The emotions aroused by the product.
- The extent to which the product reflects their self-image, or causes others to view them in a certain light.

Thus, for a young executive with high aspirations, but with income constraints due to a large mortgage, the purchase of a new 'smart-phone' might be influenced by:

- Its functionality in areas such as battery life, screen visibility, range of information sources, data transferability, and so on.
- Feelings of importance or success.
- The cost of a good/reliable product.
- The significance of the brand.
- The way others would view possession of such a device.

Under these circumstances, the purchaser is likely to be concerned to make the 'right' decision and engage in some highly complex purchase behaviour.

If the purchaser were a young person in full-time education, behaviour is likely to be less complex and driven more by appearance, price or availability, rather than by weightier issues of functionality and social impact. Likewise, in the purchase of items such as paper clips, organizational involvement (as manifested by the

The decision-making process follows typical stages

purchaser's personal involvement) is likely to be extremely low and the decision process, therefore, less complex.

The decision-making process

The process by which the final decision is made during a purchase tends to follow a number of stages. The extent to which each stage is included will depend on the nature of the purchase and the complexity implied. Fundamental to all purchases is **need recognition** or **arousal**, which may come in the natural course of events, or which may require effort on the part of a supplying organization. The latter will be especially true for new products or product categories with low market penetration.

Once a need has been acknowledged, people will either start an **information search** or, in the case of low-involvement habitual purchases, move straight to a purchase. If seeking variety, this latter purchase might involve a cursory review of alternative brands. The information search may be informal and take the form of becoming open to information about the product type, or it may be active and involve talking to friends, collecting sales literature, consulting reports and experts, or actually visiting outlets to try out different offerings. This can be described as a **cognitive** stage in which beliefs and knowledge are developed about the range of alternatives available. Suppliers without high market shares, therefore, have to work hard if they wish to be included in the list from which a final choice is made.

The next stage in this process will be some form of **evaluation**, during which a cus-tomer is likely to develop a liking or preference for a particular brand or small group of brands. At some point, a customer will become **convinced** of the value of a par-ticular offering, at which moment they can be characterized as having a **purchase intention**. This is known as an **affective** stage, during which potential buyers develop an emotional response to different offerings, which will be a reflection of their cultural, social, personal and psychological make-up. It will also be a reflection of the influences exerted by the different aspects of the market environment and the ways products have been positioned in the market by their suppliers.

Purchase intention, however, can still be altered by the **intervention** of others or by some unanticipated factor. If a buyer's intentions conflict with the attitudes of peer groups or some strong social/cultural values, they will have to work hard to maintain their intention, but could easily be persuaded not to buy if their emo-tional convictions are not well-grounded. Thus, an Italian male who had decided to buy a French car might find his conviction crumbling in the face of strong nationalistic views combined with others' attitudes that such cars were designed for more 'effeminate' drivers.

Unanticipated factors might include the arrival of new information, a change in priorities, or a change in personal circumstances. For the supplier, the implications are that clarity is of vital importance in positioning and communications, and that they should plan to reduce the impact of unanticipated factors, especially those not within their control. These could range from availability, ease of contacting a supplier, point-of-sale information, or the actions of a sales person. For high-risk purchases, customers will be more vulnerable to such deflection as a result of their heightened anxiety.

Once a purchase has been made, the final stage in the process is the customers' **post-purchase perceptions** of their acquisition. High-involvement purchases, where a choice has been made between several carefully considered alternatives, often lead to feelings of discomfort, or **cognitive dissonance**, since they will be well aware of the advantages of other offerings and the possible existence of disadvantages. Dissonance will be magnified by:

- The extent to which perceived performance is below pre-purchase expectations.
- Receiving fewer validating messages through communication such as advertising.
- Any shortfalls in after-sales service.

Customers will naturally seek to reduce their dissonance, either by confirming the wisdom of their choice or through seeking some form of redress such as instant upgrade or refund, publicizing their misfortune, or taking legal action. Whatever the result, it will have a significant impact on repeat purchase decisions if the outcome is felt to be unsatisfactory.

Together, these factors combine to make consumers' buying behaviour a complex process, and consequently difficult to research and predict. Apart from the models used above, there are a number of other models, more or less mathematically based, which seek to explain the formation of preferences in different ways. Thus, there is no clear picture, or universal theory, which encapsulates all aspects of consumer behaviour. What *is* clear, however, is the need to develop the best possible understanding of the dynamics and variations of the ways that customers approach a purchase. The more this is understood, the easier it is to see how continued sales could be jeopardized without constant attention to the careful manipulation of the marketing mix.

Consumer buying behaviour is a complex process and is difficult to predict

Organizational Buying
16 Behaviour

When a business wishes to sell its products to other organizations rather than to individuals, it faces a rather more complex marketing situation. This complexity is a result of the number of people involved in the decision to purchase, the situation in which those people operate and the activities which, together, form the stages of the decision-making process.

These processes are not entirely dissimilar to those followed by consumer purchasers, but tend to be characterized in different ways as a result of the contexts in which an organization buys. For example, organizations have more formalized purchasing procedures as a consequence of the need to monitor and control purchasing activities, and they will often appraise a product in more technical terms because of the impact that a wrong purchase may have on the organization's operations.

Organizational buying stages

The major stages, or 'buy phases', of an organizational purchase are usually listed as:

- Problem recognition.
- General need determination.
- Supply specification.
- Identification of suppliers.
- Solicitation of proposals.
- Evaluation and selection of a supplier/suppliers.
- Establishment of order routines.
- Performance review.

These stages will not necessarily be followed sequentially and not every stage will be included for all purchases. In general, though, they indicate the way in which an organization will approach a purchasing problem, but will involve different people and processes at alternative stages and in different situational contexts. The interaction of these factors will determine the information required by a purchaser and the purchase outcome (see Figure 16.1).

Buy phase		DMU composition (buying centre)		Buy class
Problem recognition General need determination Supply specification Identification of suppliers Solicitation of proposals Select supplier(s) Establish order routines Performance evaluation	×	Initiators Gatekeepers Influencers Deciders Buyers	×	New buy Modified re-buy Straight re-buy

Different information requirements

Purchase outcome

Figure 16.1 Organizational buying behaviour model

Organizational buyer situations

To help to unravel the complexities of such purchasing, it is useful to isolate the situations in which purchases generally are made. These are frequently referred to as 'buy classes' and cover: **new buys**; **modified re-buys**; and **straight re-buys**.

New buy

When purchasing for the first time or making a complete reappraisal of a particular requirement, there will be little experience in the organization of purchasing that type of product. As a consequence, the organization and the individuals within it will experience high levels of uncertainty and risk, which are likely to produce a number of behaviours less in evidence when purchasing within the other two 'buy classes'.

Behaviours that will be of particular interest to potential suppliers will be associated with the need to reduce perceived risk. Buyers are likely to attempt risk reduction by requiring much more information about a purchase, not just in terms of the product itself, but also the ability of the supplier to meet specifications, quality levels and supply continuity requirements. In addition, they will tend to seek outside opinions and recommendations about both the products and suppliers. This can incorporate the use of paid advisers such as product experts and consultants, the collection of assessments and appraisals in technical journals, talking to existing users or customers of particular suppliers and the use of other referees such as bankers and credit reference agencies. Risk reduction is also likely to be sought

Suppliers are particularly interested in behaviours associated with risk reduction

through visits to suppliers' premises, inserting penalty clauses in the terms of the contract and by soliciting quotes or offers from a large number of potential suppliers to ensure that they have not missed the least risky purchase. In some industries, **pre-qualification** is used to ensure the suitability of suppliers.

As a consequence, purchase decisions often take a long time and will probably be taken at a fairly high level in the organization. In addition, individuals will try to reduce their own vulnerability by involving a wider range of people in the decision and passing responsibility upwards, thereby spreading the risk. A further response will be a tendency to purchase from the market leaders, or the higher priced suppliers, since these will be perceived as lower risk solutions.

Modified re-buys

Modified re-buys will occur when a purchasing organization becomes dissatisfied with existing suppliers, or modifies its requirements in some way. Since the organization will already have experience of sourcing the product, less risk will be perceived by higher management and the decision is likely to involve fewer people and focus on those at lower levels in the business. Those at the lower levels, however, are likely to experience greater personal risk in the absence of the involvement of their superiors. The main risk factor is the possibility of changing to an unknown supplier. The purchaser will then probably require 'out-suppliers' to demonstrate a significant advantage to break the inertia of an existing relationship.

Straight re-buys

Straight re-buys refer to purchasing on a routine re-order basis with little risk being perceived by the purchaser. Individuals will either select a product of their choice from the offerings of 'approved suppliers' or will place orders in strict adherence to company-established specifications and relationships. Where choice can exist, it will be exercised by either the user or the purchasing department. As long as 'in-suppliers' maintain both product and service quality, this is a difficult situation for 'out-suppliers' to penetrate. One drawback for the purchaser in this respect can be that price loses its visibility in the purchase process, which helps explain why annual purchase reviews are often institutionalized as part of supply-chain management processes.

The organizational decision-making unit

The risk associated with a purchase, plus the complex way in which the product will be viewed and used, means that a number of people will have the opportunity to influence the outcome of a purchase decision. As indicated, the greater the risk, the more people likely to be involved, with as many as 40 for an expensive, first-time, purchase. Together, these constitute a decision-making unit (DMU), or 'buying centre', with individual members playing one or a number of different roles. Whilst there have been several approaches proposed for classifying these roles, there is general agreement that they will cover:

- **Initiators**, who will first propose a purchase and who could be anyone from the chief executive to an operational employee, depending on the nature of the product.
- **Policy-makers**, who will set the overall context for a purchase, or who may even initiate a purchase; policies could refer to dual sourcing, just-in-time manufacturing, preferring domestically produced products, quality requirements, and so on.
- **Users**, who will actually consume the product or service as part of their job. Where such people have expert knowledge, they can significantly influence the choice of supplier. For less risky purchases, they may also have significant influence, both positive and negative.
- **Other influencers**, who may include: technical experts; the media; referral markets; financial personnel; the organization's own customers; and so on. Exactly who influencers are will vary from one organization to another, but the notion is important to spur suppliers to view any purchasing relationship in its wider context.
- **Deciders**, who will have the power to approve or veto a purchase decision and who will ultimately reconcile conflicting opinions within the DMU. They often rely on the presentational power of the people requesting the acquisition, but may also be driven by personal preference.
- **Gatekeepers**, through whom information is passed into the organization. These can sit at many points in a business and can range from receptionists and secretaries to purchasing officials, product experts and general technocrats.

Since sales people or account managers are usually the most significant external influence on organizational purchasing, it is vitally important for them to work with the appropriate gatekeepers within the organization. Once 'in', they then have to recognize the different information needs that each member of the DMU will have and the general orientations or perspectives they bring to the decision-making process. As examples: users will be concerned about ease of use, consistency and continuity of supply; influencers such as finance people will be concerned with cost, while influencers such as design engineers will more likely be interested in quality; and deciders such as the chief executive may be concerned with reputation or status. As an example of different needs, one French supplier to hospitals segmented the market by age of purchasing officer, since those with low levels of experience required much more support to be able to satisfy the information requirements of the various hospital administrators involved in the decision.

An outline of the complex interactions of the organizational purchasing process is shown in Figure 16.1.

It is clear that organizations do not, in themselves, exhibit behaviour. It is the collective interactions between individuals from supplier and buyer organizations

Suppliers must recognize the different information needs of DMU members

that are at the heart of the process, plus the buyer's interactions with their external environment. These will include: the state of the economy, regulatory changes, technology advances, competition and social developments, plus the culture and structure of the organization itself. Often, internal politics and the nature of the personalities involved will be as much a determinant of a purchase decision as anything else.

Organizational buyer behaviour, then, emphasizes the notions of relationship marketing and the need to understand both the organization as a whole and the buying styles of the individuals within the buying organization. A continuing trend is the 'outsourcing' of requirements by establishing supplier partners. Within this, many organizations now prefer total solutions or systems purchasing where suppliers provide 'turnkey solutions' either on their own or as a prime contractor. In addition, purchasing is progressively becoming a professional activity incorporating the concept of supply chain management. Together, these are promoting the tendency for organizational buyers to become more demanding and even more complex in their behaviour, which in turn leads to a greater requirement to understand organizational buying behaviour.

Topic

17 Market Segmentation

Some organizations view marketing as a process which tries to persuade a faceless mass of customers to see things their way. Such an approach misinterprets totally what marketing is all about. Ultimately, to survive and prosper in business in the long-run, organizations have to satisfy the needs of customers. Central to this need-satisfying process is what in marketing is known as 'market segmentation'.

The process relating to market segmentation is based on a continuous dialogue with specific groups of customers (market segments), whose needs are understood in depth, and for whom specific offerings that have a differential advantage over the offers of competitors are developed. Only when this has been done should an organization consider the array of communication and other marketing communications possibilities they have at their disposal. Market segmentation, then, is a process that identifies different requirements in the people who buy, and as such is the key to successful marketing.

Market segmentation, however, remains the most difficult and elusive of marketing skills, being both complex and multifaceted. At its heart are a number of judgements or insights that an organization makes about it customers, which rely on the skill, experience and creativity of the individuals involved. Too often, managers see markets as a series of fixed segments that are described in terms of the products they use: the family car segment, the *Guardian* newspaper readers or soft cheese eaters. While these are useful ways of referring to a segment, they can disguise the reasons behind a particular product preference and suppliers can lose sight of customer needs.

Starting the process

Although no two customers are the same, except in very special circumstances, it is not commercially viable to make exclusive products for single customers. Organizations thus need to find commonalities between customers so that they can group them in a way that enables them to deal with such groups in a cost-effective way. Thus, the principal criteria for identifying a commercially useful segment are that:

- Segments have to be large enough to make it worthwhile developing products or services especially for them.

Market segmentation is a difficult and elusive skill

- Segments must be sufficiently different from other segments to warrant creating something different for them.
- There has to be some way of identifying members of a segment so that they can be communicated with in a cost-effective way.

There are basically four steps in performing a market segmentation analysis:

- Analysis of customer responses, preferences or behaviour.
- Analysis of customer characteristics or attributes.
- Analysis of benefits sought.
- Clustering of groups with similar needs.

Analysis of customer behaviour

This is essentially the manifestation of the way customers actually behave in the market place. In respect of *what* is bought, suppliers should look for buying behaviour in terms of: the physical characteristics of products; how they are used; where they are bought; how they are bought; the price paid; and so on. This can indicate whether there are any groups of products, outlets, or price categories of potential interest to a supplier (i.e. where the opportunities and problems might be). These natural groupings, whilst obvious, do at least provide clues as to what is happening in the market since they represent the different purchase combinations that actually take place. Collectively, they are known as microsegments.

Analysis of customer attributes

Supplying organizations also need to know **who** these customers in the microsegments are so that they can communicate with them. In this respect **demographic** descriptors have always been found to be the most useful method. For consumer markets, important variables include: age; sex; stage in the family lifecycle; and socio-economic groupings which describe people by their social status in life as defined by their jobs. It is easy to understand how demographics can be related to purchase behaviour, since people have specific needs at certain times in their lives. There is also a useful relationship between readership habits, viewing patterns, and socio-economic groupings which is very helpful in deciding what media to use to communicate with customers. Additionally, analyses such as a classification of regional neighbourhood groups (ACORN), which classifies all households according to 40 variables drawn from population census data, can be particularly useful for retail businesses in terms of outlet location or direct marketing. In the UK, ACORN classifies neighbourhoods into 54 types with similar characteristics that are closely related to specific consumption patterns for different categories of goods and services.

For industrial markets, standard industrial classification (SIC) categories, number of employees, turnover, production processes, and so on, are also examples of demographic descriptors.

Analysis of benefits sought

The third step is to try to understand *why* customers behave in these ways, so that suppliers will then be in a better position to sell to them. In this respect, it will be important to look at what *benefits* customers derive from their purchases. These benefits will obviously be closely related to customers' attitudes, perceptions and preferences. This needs to be done for each microsegment.

Clustering of groups

The fourth step is to search for clusters or groups of microsegments with similar needs. Whilst this can be done manually, it is preferable to use a computerized clustering package such as Market Segment Master®, as there can often be as many as a hundred microsegments identified during the preliminary segmentation process. (**Note**: Details of Market Segment Master® can be obtained from Professor Malcolm McDonald at Cranfield School of Management, Cranfield, Bedford MK43 0AL, England.)

Figure 17.1 provides a good example of actual consumer segmentation in the replacement tyre market, from which it can be seen how segmentation criteria can be used to identify discrete segments.

Exactly the same principles can be followed in respect of industrial markets. An example of the segmentation of a particular industrial market based on purchase behaviour is shown in Figure 17.2.

Figure 17.3 illustrates the end objective; a way of classifying purchasers that enables alternative value propositions to be formulated. If these can be translated into typical members or caricatures that can be displayed for all members of an organization to become familiar with, it can help ensure appropriate customer responses. For example, one of the contributors to the success of Tesco supermarkets in the late 1990s and early 2000s has been that most employees, including the shelf-stackers and checkout staff, can all tell you the type of customer their store has been designed to serve and they have a good appreciation of their shopping needs.

The objectives of market segmentation are:

- To help to determine and to focus the direction of marketing resources through the analysis and understanding of trends and buyer behaviour.
- To help to determine realistic and achievable marketing objectives.
- To create a basis for developing sustainable competitive advantage.

The objective of market segmentation is competitive advantage

Priority / Segment	Brand	Outlet	Price	Characteristics and behaviour
Prestige buyer	High priority	Medium priority	Low priority	Mainly men who tend to be brand and retailer loyal. Predisposed to high brands and does little investigation before a purchase.
Comfortable conservative	Medium priority	High priority	Low priority	Mixed sexes. Females tend to be more dependent on the retailer for advice and recommendations. As a consequence, tend to have long-term relationships with outlets.
Value shopper	High priority	Low priority	Medium priority	Although having price as a priority, these buyers are also very brand oriented and are drawn towards the higher profile makes of tyre. Do considerably more research and are well informed when they make a purchase. Very low retail loyalty.
Pretender	Medium priority	Low priority	High priority	Starts with a desire for a major brand, but ends up purchasing on price. Do a lot of information gathering but have very limited brand or retailer loyalty.
Trusting patron	Low priority	High priority	Medium priority	Similar to the comfortable conservative but more female dominated. Are therefore very outlet-loyal with virtually no brand loyalty and little pre-purchase information gathering.
Bargain hunter	Low priority	Low priority	High priority	Almost totally price oriented, dominated by younger drivers who delay tyre replacement as long as possible. Tend to buy re-treads.

Figure 17.1 Example of segmentation of consumer market for replacement tyres
Adapted from Doole I. and Lowe R. (2004) *International Marketing Strategy*, Thomson Learning EMEA

Segmentation of the market for industrial compressors (£10K–£100K plus)

- Segment One: Single sourcers (30%)
  – Take distributor service engineer's advice and put proposed product and amount in next year's budget; loyal to distributor.

- Segment Two: Competitive tenderers (51%)
  – Asks distributor service engineer for proposal – sources 1–3 tenders; uses tenders to negotiate with existing distributor.

- Segment Three: In-house processors (19%)
  – Own service engineer creates specification – sources 3–5 tenders; uses tenders to pressure existing distributor.

Figure 17.2 Example of segmentation of market for industrial compressors (£10K–£100K plus)

Benefits sought	Demographics	When used	Psychographics	Brands favoured	Features required	Segments
						Segment One
						Segment Two
						Segment Three
						Segment Four

Figure 17.3 Typical segmentation grid

Segmentation enables alternative value propositions to be formed

International Market Segmentation

The purpose of any segmentation exercise is to identify groups of purchasers who are sufficiently large, different and reachable to make them worthwhile for the investment of marketing effort. The isolation of a new segment whose needs are poorly served by existing suppliers can provide an opportunity to gain significant competitive advantage. Unfortunately, segmentation models in international marketing tend to consist of geographical groups, such as Western Europe, Eastern Europe, North America, ASEAN, Australasia, and so on. Such groupings, however, are of very limited value as actionable marketing propositions, since they bear little relationship to actual consumption or usage patterns.

Using Europe as an illustration, there are typically three discrete groupings that are often used as a basis for differentiating between segments: European Union (EU); European Free Trade Association (EFTA); and Eastern Europe. Within Eastern Europe, however, there are at least three subgroups: the 'strong' group (the former Czechoslovakia and Hungary); the 'middle' group (Poland, Bulgaria, Romania and the former Yugoslavia), and the 'poor' group (the former Soviet republics). Even within the European Union, there are significant differences arising from natural phenomena. For example, Scandinavia has short summers and long winters; Greece, Portugal, Italy and Spain have long summers and short winters; The Netherlands has low plains; and Austria has mountains.

Similarly, the per capita gross domestic product of Switzerland is seven times that of Portugal and, at the same time, there are significant communication and distribution differences. As examples: there is virtually no domestic television in Norway, whereas in Italy, television has very high levels of penetration; retail channel concentration is very dense in Northern Europe, whereas there is a preponderance of small, independent outlets in Southern Europe; there are also significant cultural and linguistic differences, and so on. If, therefore, geography is to be relevant, it is more sensible to think in terms of the Anglo-Saxon North; the Latin South; North-East France, Benelux and North-West Germany; and so on. Even this, however, is simplistic, in the sense that there are basically three kinds of 'products' which have to be considered when looking at such segmentations.

Types of international products

Truly global products

These are either products or services that are inherently global, such as international services, world-standard industrial products, high-technology products, and so on, or they are fashion or national products that have become global, such as Chivas Regal, Coca-Cola, Rolls-Royce, McDonald's, Marlborough cigarettes, and so on. These have become global because their national appeal is replicated in other countries.

National products

These typically exist where the market thrives on supplier responsiveness, client relationships, national preferences, and where global efficiencies are less critical.

Hybrid products

Here, adaptation across countries is possible and this requires a rethinking of simple geographical segmentation bases to ones based on customer groups with similar needs across national boundaries. In advertising, for example, the agency J. Walter Thompson discovered:

- Three broad breakfast types across Europe.
- A fashion lager market across Europe.
- Commonalities in computer software applications across Europe.

There are, thus, significant legal, regulatory, linguistic, communication media and distribution channel differences across Western Europe and even throughout the world. There are, consequently, few truly global products and many traditional habits remain deep-rooted, militating against international segmentation. On the other hand (and this applies particularly to Western Europe), there are a number of growing trends that suggest that the need for international market segmentation will become increasingly important. These include:

- The desire for monetary union, social affairs union, foreign affairs union and defence policy unions.
- Increasing product and technical standardization.
- Deregulation of transportation, telecommunications, pharmaceuticals and others.
- Attitude convergence towards work, individuality, materialism, the environment, and so on.
- Pan-global buying.
- International mergers, acquisitions and joint ventures.
- Increased international travel, education, media exposure, fashion, and so on.

A number of growing trends amplify the need for international market segmentation

International market segmentation, therefore, requires the introduction of market variables that would not normally be used when segmenting a national market. For example, differing legal regimes will be found in different countries and may make a difference to product configuration, safety requirements or importing conditions. In some countries, political circumstances will play a role in creating different consumption or distribution circumstances that might provide a basis for segmentation. The bases for international market segmentation are, therefore, likely to be specific groupings of countries, such as the new 'Euro Regions' outlined earlier, or customer groups across selected countries.

Thereafter, the normal rules of market segmentation apply (see Topic 17 Market Segmentation).

Part 4
Understanding Markets

Marketing Information and Research

Decision-making in organizations requires relevant information if the outcomes are not to be based on those often-used management support tools – 'gut feel' or rationalized personal preference. Within this, marketing information is of vital significance. Indeed, one of the key roles of marketing professionals should be the supply of market and marketing-performance information that will enable the rest of the organization to make decisions about the market-related areas of their responsibilities. As examples, corporate or strategic managers need good market environment and competitor information to be able to set the overall strategic direction of the organization, and operations managers need to understand the critical success factors associated with the delivery of their product or service, since these should form the basis for the design of their operating systems.

These examples illustrate that marketing research is not an activity to be performed in isolation, but one where the results will contribute to many managerial or policy decisions. The implication of this is that the collection, collation and reporting of marketing information needs to be structured in ways appropriate to the decisions it will support. Managers requesting marketing information and research must, therefore, have a clear understanding of exactly what they need to know in order to make the judgements for which they are responsible. This is often one of the biggest problems in drafting a market research brief or in specifying a marketing information system: distinguishing between what it would be 'nice to know' and what is actually needed for management purposes. Tables 14.1 and 14.2 illustrate the areas which commonly form the focus of marketing research.

The activities involved in marketing research can be described in a number of different ways, but together indicate the major issues in conducting marketing research or creating marketing information systems.

Reactive versus passive research

This is sometimes used to distinguish between the different forms or styles of research and is a useful way of classifying the various types of marketing research activities. **Reactive research** implies an interaction between the researcher and the subject(s). It can, therefore, take the form of asking questions as part of a postal survey, an interview, or a group discussion. In each case, the researcher will be prompting the subject(s) to provide their views, state their intentions, or recall their

It is important to distinguish between 'nice to know' and 'need to know'

experiences. Reactive research can also take the form of experiments, such as test-marketing a product, altering an aspect of the marketing mix to establish variations in response, or 'laboratory' studies such as simulated shopping environments.

Passive research concerns the pure observation of subjects, or the collection of data. These could include:

- Consumer panels who simply report their activities on a regular basis so that patterns of behaviour can be established.
- Retail audits, where stock levels and shelf-space allocations are observed on a sample basis to ascertain market share, market penetration, etc.
- Surveys of publicly available reports to identify market trends, market scope or competitor positioning.
- Internally generated data that will provide indications of organizational performance.

Passive research limits the researcher's understanding to his or her own interpretations of observed phenomena or data. Reactive research provides more scope for prompting subjects or for seeking clarification.

Primary versus secondary research

These distinguish between the various sources of data available to the researcher. **Secondary sources** refer to data already available in some form or another and may include the results of previously performed research or other publicly available material such as newspaper reports or government statistics. **Primary research** involves gathering data directly from the market through the collection of opinions, the observation of behaviour, or through tapping into sources within the organization. The advantage of primary research is that it will probably provide information that is unique, whereas secondary sources are likely to be available to everyone else in a market.

Desk versus field research

These are another way of describing the sources that can be used to provide marketing information. **Desk research** usually involves a search of existing data sources, whereas **field research** involves going 'out into the field' or market place to collect, usually primary, data. It is normal to engage in desk research first to establish what information needs to be obtained from field research because it is unavailable elsewhere.

Internal versus external research

This distinction draws attention to the range of information sources which often exist within an organization without having to look outside or commission specific market research projects. **Internal sources** can include sales records, shipping documentation and invoices, as well as reports generated by sales people, service engineers or delivery and installation personnel. Customer correspondence can also be a useful source of data on the way that the market is responding to an organization's offering. Sadly, it is not unusual for organizations to commission, for example, competitor-analysis research when they themselves employ people who previously worked for those competitors and whom their current employers had ignored in their search for information.

When considering marketing research, it is also useful to distinguish between **marketing data**, **information** and **intelligence** when discussing any activity or system. In this context, data can best be thought of as the raw facts, figures or descriptions of the topic being researched. Information is ordered data, or data which has been selected to describe a particular market or performance feature. Intelligence can best be regarded as information from which conclusions have been drawn. As an example, an 80:20, or **Pareto analysis** of an industrial company's customers based on sales invoices (the data) would yield information (a list of their best customers in revenue terms) which could then be interpreted and/or explained to provide intelligence.

Marketing information systems

A comprehensive marketing information system requires attention to four main areas of activity. The first area concerns **performance monitoring over time** and relies heavily on information drawn from internal sources. Such information can include profitability analyses, which can cover customer, segment and product profitability. Also important are sales volumes across different sectors, product mixes and the effectiveness of discount structures. Other points of interest might be trends pertaining to delivery performance, complaints and product returns. Advances in software and the introduction of **Enterprise Resource Planning** systems (ERPs) that concentrate on the efficiency of a firm's internal production, distribution and financial processing provide a good opportunity for the regular generation of timely reports on performance effectiveness. (**Note**: ERPs are management information systems that integrate and automate many of the business practices associated with the operations of production and distribution aspects of a business.)

The second area, **market monitoring**, refers to the regular collection of externally generated materials about developments in the marketing environment. This activity could be performed by an organization's library, if they have one, an outside agency, or by individuals in marketing or marketing associated roles. Whatever the mechanism used, it should be able to deliver steady flows of newspaper, journal and other published matter that will alert managers to changes in their areas of interest. It should also act as a repository from which information required

A wealth of internal information sources is often overlooked

on an occasional basis can be drawn. Market monitoring could also involve the generation of information from employees who operate in the field, from regular surveys, or from panel reports generated at specific intervals. Topics for market monitoring might embrace:

- Competitor activity.
- Publications from standards bodies.
- Legislative activities.
- Technological advances.
- Pressure group campaigns.
- Fashion trends.

And so on.

The third aspect of an integrated marketing information system is a **market investigation facility** for specific questions or *ad hoc* projects. This would involve expert researchers administering questionnaires (postal or telephone), conducting interviews, or engaging in desk research of some form or another. The popular conception of market research usually focuses on this type of activity, but requires careful management if it is to be useful. Critical is the process of problem definition, from which a research plan is developed. The plan will focus on two main elements: the population to be researched and the methodology to be employed. Such projects, however, are very expensive and need to be used carefully for the best effect.

The fourth feature of a system would be a **decision support** mechanism so that marketing personnel can manipulate information and intelligence using the analytical tools of marketing. These may be various statistical techniques such as: correlation; cluster or conjoint analysis; or may be based on analytical models of different kinds. Such models could include:

- 'What if' facilities.
- Portfolio modelling.
- Complete planning systems.

Just as the increased use of computers for administrative systems has enabled much more data to become available for analysis, so the leaps made in information technology towards expert systems and virtual reality will provide ever-increasing sophistication in this type of activity.

Marketing information is now recognized as a source of competitive power and increasing amounts of effort are being spent on the development of marketing information systems. Systems, however, cannot substitute for personal judgement and the creativity required to develop innovative marketing strategies. Such attributes are needed to identify the 'golden nuggets' often hidden by systematic approaches, and to generate the unique positioning or segmentation programmes essential for competitive advantage. In addition, it must be remembered that data, information or intelligence is only ever as good as the specifications from which it was produced, and much information is either too general, or the result of poorly conducted research, to be relied upon. Finally, it must also be remembered that any market research or marketing information systems invariably throw up more questions than they answer. There is no such phenomenon as perfect information.

Market research often creates more questions than it answers

Topic 20 Preparing a Marketing Research Brief

Regardless of who carries out the work involved in a market research project, it is important that a clear brief is produced against which the subsequent work will be undertaken and judged. The research brief, which should be presented in both written and verbal form, is a key document and the starting point. In its preparation it is important that the following questions are to the fore:

- What do we want to know?
- What will we do with the information when we get it?

In this way clearly defined objectives can be set and adhered to.

Contents of a brief

First, the commissioning organization should think very carefully about what, and how much, it wishes to reveal in the brief. Ideally, the brief should be open, precise and factual, but there may be particular points, such as the exact budget, which are best omitted. A good briefing document, preferably accompanied by product literature, may span 1–5 pages. Its elaboration/discussion at a briefing meeting should clarify understanding, confirm contents and remove any written ambiguities. At the end of the meeting, if a quotation is to be submitted, the consultant/agency should try to find ways of demonstrating both competence and a firm commitment to the project.

A good research brief should contain the following:

- Background information on the market, the company, its products/services, market standing, and so on.
- The research objectives, which may include both primary and secondary objectives and, if possible, the precise questions for which answers are required.
- The desired time-scales, such as the completion date, required together with any interim report times or key decision dates.
- Preferred report and presentation format.
- Main point of contact and information to be made available in support of the research.
- Degree of confidentiality required when conducting the research.

It is not suggested that the briefing document be seen as a 'straitjacket' but as a series of well-thought-out guidelines. As such, the expertise of the agency/consultancy should be sought in the briefing meeting, both with regard to information and requirements of the brief, as well as in discussion of the subsequent best methods for achievement of the brief's objectives. The extent to which issues such as budget are discussed with the research agency will depend on the nature of the relationship with them.

Given the expected expertise of the agency/consultancy, it is fair to provide a comprehensive briefing and to ask for a written proposal offering best solutions. This should include the recommended methodologies, the expected time-frames and the costs involved.

Some commissioning organizations set a proposal deadline or tender submission date. At the briefing stage, it may be best to indicate the competitive quoting levels involved without necessarily defining or naming these precisely. Normally, the costs involved in the briefing meeting and preparation of the research proposal are seen by consultants/agencies as part of their prospecting and business development costs.

The research proposal

The proposal, which is also often both a written document and personal presentation, is a 'best response' to the marketing research brief. As such, it represents their ability to communicate, and this should be a selection factor given that the organization subsequently commissioned to carry out the research is providing an indication or preview of its listening, communication and presentation skills. The proposal is therefore an opportunity to provide additional clues as to the likely quality of the final product. This assessment opportunity for the client should not be overlooked!

The research proposal also needs to provide a specification of what the research organization will do, how it will carry out the work and what it will cost. It is important that it conveys its understanding of what is expected and its competence to provide the work most efficiently. A good research proposal should, therefore, include:

- Background information, to convey a clear understanding of the project and the issues involved.
- Objectives, which should be clearly listed and very precisely defined against the specification of the problem.
- Work programme and methodology, covering both the way that the objectives will be achieved and the way that the work programme would be completed including sample size, research stages and questionnaire methods.

The proposal is an opportunity to provide clues to the likely quality of the final product

- Fees/payment terms and time-scales, which should be clearly stated and classified showing expenses, tax, and so on, set against the work schedule.
- Company details and research personnel involved, including research company competence and brief biographies of personnel, plus, if relevant, any business terms.
- Summary of research project benefits and the agency's confidence in its competence to 'deliver' what is required.

The sponsoring organization's response

Acceptance of the proposal should be in writing. It should authorize the work and confirm the points of agreement and costs involved. This should provide a binding agreement as to what is to be done and at what cost, so as to eliminate any subsequent disagreement between the sponsoring organization and the agency/consultancy.

21 Auditing a Market

Basically, a marketing audit is the means by which a company can understand how it relates to the environment in which it operates. It is also the means by which a company can identify its own strengths and weaknesses as they relate to external opportunities and threats. It is thus a way of helping management select a position in that environment based on known factors.

Expressed in its simplest form, the purpose of a marketing plan is to answer three central questions:

- Where is the company now?
- Where does the company want to go?
- How should the company organize its resources to get there?

The audit provides the information from which the first of these questions is answered. An audit, then, is a systematic, critical and unbiased appraisal of an organization's market environment and of its operations. A marketing audit is also part of the larger management audit and is often undertaken as part of a wider business planning process.

Often, the need for an audit does not manifest itself until things start to go wrong, such as declining sales, falling margins, lost market share, underutilized production capacity, and so on. At this point the marketing audit becomes a last-ditch, end-of-the-road attempt to define a company's marketing problem. An equally problematic approach is commissioning an audit from an independent body on an *ad hoc* basis. However, since marketing is such a complex function, it seems illogical not to carry out a thorough situation analysis at least once a year at the beginning of the planning cycle.

There is much evidence to show that many highly successful companies as well as using normal information and control procedures plus marketing research throughout the year, also start their planning cycle each year with a formal review, through an audit-type process, of everything that has had an important influence on marketing activities that year. Certainly, in many leading consumer goods companies, the annual self-audit approach is a tried and tested discipline integrated into their management process, which, like other managerial processes, becomes easier to perform the more regularly the audits are conducted.

A marketing audit answers the question: 'Where is the company now?'

The audit, then, is a structured approach to the collection and analysis of information and data on the complexities of a business and its environment, and is an essential prerequisite to business problem-solving.

Marketing audit variables

Any company carrying out a marketing audit will be faced with two kinds of variables. First, there are variables over which the company has no direct control. These usually take the form of environmental, market and competitive variables. Second, there are variables over which the company has complete control, often referred to as operational variables. These provide the basis for the two critical elements of any audit:

- External variables.
- Internal variables.

An audit starts with an examination of information on the general economy and then moves on to the outlook for the health and growth of the markets served by the company. The purpose of the internal audit is to assess the organization's resources as they relate to the environment and *vis-à-vis* the resources of competitors. Table 21.1 contains a checklist of areas that should be investigated as part of both the internal and external marketing audit.

Each of the headings shown in Table 21.1 should be examined with a view to isolating those factors that are considered critical to the company's performance. Initially, the auditor's task is to screen the enormous amount of information and data for validity and relevance. Some of the data and information obtained for an audit will have to be reorganized into a more easily usable form, and judgement will have to be applied to decide what further data and information are necessary for a proper definition of the problem. Behind the summary headings, however, more detailed questions should be asked. Thus there are basically two phases that comprise the auditing process:

- Identification, measurement, collection and analysis of all the relevant facts and opinions which impinge on a company's operations.
- The application of judgement to the areas of uncertainty remaining after this analysis.

Occasionally it may be justified to hire outside consultants to carry out a marketing audit to check that a company is getting the most out of its resources. However, it seems an unnecessary expense to have this done every year. The answer, therefore, is to have an audit carried out annually by the company's own line managers on their own areas of responsibility.

Table 21.1 Marketing audit checklist

EXTERNAL AUDIT	
Business and economic environment	Economic Political/Fiscal/Legal Social/Cultural Technological Inter-company
The market	Total market size, growth and trends (value/volume) Market characteristics Developments and trends in marketing mix variables as follows: ■ products ■ prices ■ physical distribution ■ channels ■ customers/consumers ■ communication ■ industry practices
Competition	Major competitors Size Market shares/coverage Market standing/reputation Production capabilities Distribution policies Marketing methods Extent of diversification Personnel issues International links Profitability Key strengths and weaknesses
INTERNAL AUDIT	
Marketing operational variables	Sales (by geographical location, industrial type, customer, and product) Market shares Profit margins/costs Marketing information/research Marketing mix variables as follows: ■ product management ■ price ■ distribution ■ promotion ■ operations and resources

The marketing audit provides the basis for many decisions

Objections to this usually centre on the problems of time and objectivity. In practice, these problems are overcome, first, by institutionalizing procedures in as much detail as possible so that all managers have to conform to a disciplined approach, and, second, by thorough training in the use of the procedures themselves. However, even this will not achieve the purpose of an audit unless a rigorous discipline is applied from the highest down to the lowest levels of management involved in the audit. Such a discipline is usually successful in helping managers to avoid the sort of tunnel vision that often results from a lack of critical appraisal.

Alternative structures for a marketing audit include PEST analysis (Political, Economic, Sociological and Technical) and variations on this mnemonic such as STEP, but since these do not cover competitor or internal analyses, they are only a part of the fuller audit referred to here.

A useful framework for presenting the findings of an audit is an adaptation of Michael Porter's Five Forces Analysis under the headings:

- Market influence of supplies.
- Market influence of buyers.
- Potential for new entrants.
- Threats from alternative technologies.
- Intensity of competition in the market.

(**Note**: For further details on Porter's Five Forces Analysis, see Topic 23 Competitor Analysis.)

Once completed, the information gained from a marketing audit forms the basis for many decision-making activities in the organization. For marketing, a summary is required which highlights the key market situations and trends that will impact on the organization's marketing strategy and programmes. The best summary is in the form of a SWOT analysis which displays the organization's key Strengths, Weaknesses, Opportunities and Threats. Regularization of the marketing audit will allow for annually updated SWOTs from which developments in an organization's strategic and tactical approaches to marketing can be made. (**Note**: For further details on SWOT analysis, see Topic 22 Constructing a SWOT.)

22 Constructing a SWOT

A SWOT analysis, covering an organization's strengths, weaknesses, opportunities and threats, is often included as part of an organization's policy and decision-making process. A well-constructed SWOT can provide powerful insights into the situation facing an organization and can demonstrate, in a clear fashion, the direction an organization needs to take. Poorly constructed SWOTs will, at best, provide only a bland interpretation of an organization's position. At worst, they can be misleading and will lead to wrong conclusions and misguided policy. It is, therefore, important for managers to be well-versed in the issues involved in developing a good SWOT, since it is their interpretation of the market and the organization's position within it that will form the basis of a SWOT, wherever the data is derived from.

A SWOT analysis must be derived from a marketing audit. In conducting an audit, it is important to remember that the results will be used to identify points that will appear in the SWOT. In this way, an audit can be given focus, and when the time comes to create the SWOT, the chances of relevant information being absent will be reduced. Poor SWOTs tend to be based on opinion or are constructed without reference to market and marketing information.

It is also important to understand that a SWOT is constructed for a specific market, segment or customer. While it is possible to perform a SWOT for an organization which relates to the whole range of its activities, it is unlikely that the strengths and weaknesses identified will be relevant to all the markets in which it operates. Thus, a hotel might rate its high-class restaurant facilities, which provides meals freshly cooked to order, as a strength for the 'special occasion eating-out market', but would be wrong in thinking this feature was also a strength for the 'business conference market' which requires fast throughput at meal times in order to cover their agendas.

Strengths and weaknesses

Strengths and weaknesses refer to the conclusions of the internal marketing audit in relation to customer requirements. They also refer to the organization's performance against those requirements relative to its competitors. Thus, a strength is only a strength if it is something that is of value to customers and is also something

A well-constructed SWOT can provide powerful insights

which an organization does better than its competitors. For instance, having the ability to deliver against the placement of an order within 48 hours is not a strength if customers require 24 hours' delivery and its major competitors are all able to fulfil this requirement. The converse situation would, of course, be a strength. Also, if a 24 hours' delivery service is the norm and all competitors fulfil this requirement, it is what is known as a 'qualifying' strength and should be omitted from the SWOT.

It is also important to distinguish between a marketing *strength* and a marketing *asset*. An asset is something which an organization possesses which could, potentially, become a strength. A useful means of developing strengths from assets is to apply the question 'which means that . . .?' until a competitive advantage is found. Thus, high-level engineering skills are an asset from which a strength – the ability to supply against a tight specification – can be derived. In a similar fashion, weaknesses will be derived from the absence of an asset of some form, or an asset which underperforms when compared with customer requirements and competitors' abilities.

A useful means of differentiating between strengths, weaknesses and assets is to identify **order-winning** as opposed to **order-qualifying** criteria. Qualifying criteria will be those features or benefits of goods or services that have to be present for a supplier to be a contender for a sale. Thus a holiday company might need to offer packages in Greece to qualify for consideration by a potential customer. Order-winning criteria will be related to those characteristics that it offers as unique or which outperform competitor offerings. Strengths can only refer to order-winning features and benefits, whereas weaknesses can encompass both order-qualifying and order-winning factors.

A similar methodology is to use the concept of **critical success factors** (CSFs). These relate to those factors that a supplier in a market must meet if they are to compete successfully. There are usually relatively few factors that can be deemed 'critical'. Factors such as product performance, breadth of offering, speed of service, low prices, reputation, and so on, are often the most important here. A layout such as that shown in Figure 22.1 can be useful when comparing overall competitive positions using CSFs. Having identified the main CSF for a market segment, each factor should be weighted out of 100, according to its importance to customers. Total weightings should add up to 100. It is then possible to score each major competitor out of 10 on their performance against each CSF. Multiplying each score by its weight will provide a quantitative assessment of the relative strengths of each competitor within a segment. Figure 22.2 illustrates a typical calculation based on this method.

Opportunities and threats

Opportunities and threats refer to external issues and are identified as a result of the external marketing audit. Thus, improving quality or creating a brand name

Critical success factors / Competitors	Weighting factor	Your organisation	Competitor A	Competitor B	Competitor C
CSF 1					
CSF 2					
CSF 3					
CSF 4					
Total weighted score	100				

Figure 22.1 Establishing competitive positions using critical success factors

Critical success factor	Weighting %	Strengths/weaknesses analysis
The few elements of the marketing mix in which any competitor has to perform well to succeed	The relative importance of each CSF scored out of 100	Performance against each CSF is scored out of 10 and multiplied by the weighting

			Competition			
			You	Comp A	Comp B	Comp C
1 Product	20%	1	9 = 1.8	6 = 1.2	5 = 1.0	4 = 0.8
2 Price	10%	2	8 = 0.8	5 = 0.5	6 = 0.6	10 = 1.0
3 Service	50%	3	5 = 2.5	9 = 4.5	7 = 3.5	6 = 3.0
4 Image	20%	4	8 = 1.6	8 = 1.6	5 = 1.0	3 = 0.6
Totals	100%		6.7	7.8	6.1	5.4

Figure 22.2 Strengths and weaknesses analysis

Strengths and weaknesses focus on critical success factors

are *not* opportunities and low stock turnover or poor industrial relations are *not* threats, since they all relate to internal issues for an organization.

Apart from the problem of definition, it is also often difficult to identify *relevant* opportunities and threats. In theory, an organization is faced with limitless opportunities and myriads of threats. These can range from the opportunities created by new markets, new products and poor performance by competitors, to the threats of war, earthquakes and competitor activities. What makes an opportunity or a threat relevant is its *significance* for the organization and its likelihood of occurring. The opportunities and threats matrices depicted in Figures 22.3 and 22.4

Figure 22.3   Opportunities matrix

Figure 22.4   Threats matrix

provide a useful means of prioritizing opportunities and threats for the purposes of inclusion in a SWOT analysis.

A further means of identifying opportunities is to concentrate on those which result from one of two different situations. The first concerns changes that are occurring in the market place. These changes can take the form of legislative developments, a competitor leaving a market, infrastructural changes, market growth, and so on, and can yield some very attractive opportunities. Although such developments may also yield threats, it is important to consider them in light of the organization's marketing asset base. As an example, the current increase in online shopping is a threat to major retailers who rely on expensive high street stores, but will be an opportunity for an organization with well-developed house-hold delivery facilities. Similarly, the present trend towards healthier eating was a threat to McDonald's whose core asset was pre-produced processed foods. It has been very costly for McDonald's to re-engineer its supply chain and menus to regain market position.

Other opportunities derive from situations where an existing need is poorly served by current suppliers. If a supplier services the CSFs for its customers to a high degree of satisfaction, there is unlikely to be an opportunity of any value to competitors. If, on the other hand, a supplier performs poorly against one CSF when compared with customer needs, then an opportunity will exist, so long as the organization has the potential to service that need more effectively than the existing supplier. As a simple example, if a reader is entirely satisfied with their newspaper, there is little opportunity for other newspapers to entice them away. However, if a reader's main interest is soft pornography and celebrity gossip, a lack of good pictures and stories in their traditional paper provides a real opportunity for other journals.

A good SWOT, then, provides a clear presentation of an organization's platform and position within a particular market. The issues it contains will have been refined for relevance and meaning. Each issue will have been the subject of a 'so what?' or 'which means that'. . .?' analysis, so that the true implications of each of the features included are reached. Following the presentation of a good SWOT, it should be easy to understand where an organization's priorities should lie.

A good SWOT should provide a clear indication of future direction

23 Competitor Analysis

An important aspect of a market that needs to be understood and characterized for the development of marketing policies is the substance and nature of the competition within it. In recent years, the work of Michael Porter has become synonymous with the process of such competitive analysis. His 'Five Forces' analytical framework provided a systematic method for exploring the competitive context of a market. Good analysis of these forces will help organizations identify where power lies in the market, who can influence market trends, how the market is likely to develop, where to concentrate when seeking new market opportunities and the basic platforms from which it is possible to compete.

Components of Porter's Five Forces framework

The threat of new entrants

In analysing markets, one of the factors to be appraised is the existence, or absence, of 'barriers to entry'. In other words, how easy is it for new entrants to enter the market? Typically, barriers might be provided by high market share or economies of scale, so that, without a minimum market share, unit costs will be uncompetitive. Similarly, heavy startup costs, whether through the need for capital investment or high levels of marketing expenditure, can also provide a barrier. Conversely, markets may be easy for new competitors to enter where product differentiation is low, where technology changes can overcome cost barriers or where there is the potential for high levels of market fragmentation.

Substitute products or services

One factor that can considerably alter the strategic balance in a market place is the development of products that meet underlying customer needs more cost-effectively than existing products. As an example, the development of oil-based film had a major impact upon the demand for wood-based film. Similarly, the advent of fax machines virtually killed off the demand for telex, whilst fax machines are themselves in significant decline as email takes over.

The bargaining power of buyers

The competitive climate of a market will clearly be influenced by the extent to which customers wield power through purchasing strength. Thus, a market that is dominated by a limited number of buyers, or a situation where a buyer takes a large proportion of the seller's output, will substantially limit the seller's opportunities for individual action or development. The UK and US grocery market illustrates this situation well, with a handful of major retail chains being able to exert considerable influence over manufacturing suppliers' marketing policies, and thus their profitability. A further source of competitive threat from buyers will exist when opportunities arise for backward integration, up the value chain, by buyers.

The bargaining power of suppliers

Many of the threats that potentially exist from buyers can also be posed by suppliers to an industry. If the supply of critical materials is controlled by a few suppliers, or if an individual company's purchases from a supplier constitute only a small part of that supplier's output, then freedom of manoeuvre may be limited. Again, if opportunities exist for forward integration by suppliers, this constitutes a further source of potential competitive pressure.

The degree of market competition

Obviously, the more numerous or equally balanced the competitors, the more intense will be the rivalry within the market. If this is combined with a slow industry growth rate, and if fixed costs relative to variable costs are high, then the prognosis is for a high level of aggressive competition, probably accompanied by severe price-cutting. A further influencing factor will be the extent to which competing products are seen as substitutes by the market place, especially if there are few switching penalties for buyers. Of key importance in this will be the relative cost structures of the major players in the market. These will be determined not just by market share, but by capacity utilization and production technology.

What has become increasingly obvious during the severe shakeouts that occurred in the late 1990s, and which are continuing to occur, is that the most meticulous analysis of an organization's competitors is no longer an option. It is an absolute necessity in order to survive.

Meticulous analysis of the competition is an absolute necessity

Performing a competitor analysis

A good starting point is a summary of the findings of a market audit in respect of major competitors. An organization should understand the sales of each of their competitors within the particular product/market segment under consideration – their share now, and their expected share three years from now. The greater a competitor's influence over others, the greater its ability to implement its own independent strategies and the more successful it will be. It is suggested that organizations should also identify each of their main competitors according to one of the classifications in the guide to competitive position given in Table 23.1,

Table 23.1 Guide to market competitive position classifications

---

■ *Leadership*
Has a major influence on the performance or behaviour of others.

■ *Strong*
Has a wide choice of strategies. Can adopt an independent strategy without endangering their short-term position. Has low vulnerability to competitors' actions.

■ *Favourable*
Exploits specific competitive strengths, often in a product-market niche. Has more than average opportunity to improve their position; several strategies are available.

■ *Tenable*
Performance justifies continuation in business.

■ *Weak*
Currently unsatisfactory performance; a significant competitive weakness. Inherently a short-term condition; must improve or withdraw.

---

based on their influence in the market and their ability to pursue alternative strategies within their markets.

The format shown in Figure 23.1 provides a useful framework for comparing competitors. In this, organizations need first to list their principal products or services; each major competitor's business intention and current strategies (see guidelines in Table 23.2); and their major strengths and weaknesses.

Products/ markets	Main competitor	Business direction, current objectives and strategies	Strengths	Weaknesses	Competitive position

Figure 23.1 Competitor analysis framework

At a more detailed level, it is also important to develop a profile of each major competitor in terms of their contribution to the market in which an organization is interested, plus their basic capabilities. Most organizations will position themselves in terms of one or two of these capabilities. Thus Maytag positions itself as innovative and dependable while Dexion (international storage equipment manufacturer) competes in the 'small user' market on the basis of local retailers

Table 23.2 Alternative business directions

- *Enter*
  Allocate resources to a new business area. Consideration should include building from prevailing company or division strength, exploiting related opportunities and defending against perceived threats. May involve creating a new division
- *Improve*
  Apply strategies that will significantly improve the competitive position of the business. Often requires thoughtful product/market segmentation
- *Maintain*
  Maintain one's competitive position. Aggressive strategies may be required, although a defensive posture may also be assumed. Product/market position is maintained, often in a niche
- *Harvest*
  Intentionally relinquish competitive position, emphasize short-term profit and cashflow but not necessarily at the risk of losing the business in the short term. Often entails consolidating or reducing various aspects of the business to create higher performance for that which remains
- *Exit*
  Abandon a business because of its weak competitive position. The cost of staying in is prohibitive and the risk associated with improving its position is too high

with local knowledge and fast ex-stock supply. Table 23.3 illustrates some of the key ways in which competitors might position themselves in an effort to influence customers' purchase decisions.

Table 23.3 Individual competitor analysis

- Segment shares and trends
- Product line performance and quality
- Promotion strategies
- Pricing strategies
- Channel strategies
- Customer service strategies
- Management skills and philosophies
- Technological capabilities
- Financial strength

To collect, analyse and disseminate this information, some kind of organized, systematic intelligence system is necessary. It is essential to specify in advance the precise information that is needed by the organization about its competitors.

Understanding competitor positioning is critical

Part 5
Product Management

24 Branding

When making a purchase, a customer is influenced by a whole range of factors associated with the complete product offer. One of these may be the product's brand name. In spite of its intangibility, a well-developed brand can be a powerful influence on both customers and competitors alike, and will be a key contributor to the way a product, company, or whatever, is positioned in the market place. It consequently becomes important to understand the scope of branding, the difference between major brands, lesser brands and commodities, the specific components of a brand name and the differences between successful and unsuccessful brands.

The scope of branding

When considering brands, it should be stressed that the term 'brand' is used to encompass not only consumer products such as Flora, Persil or Nescafé, but a host of offerings, including places (such as Paris), transport (such as the *Orient Express* or *Concord*), companies (such as Microsoft and BMW), industrial products (such as Caterpillar), service products, and even individual people. In addition, a distinction should be drawn between a 'brand' and a 'commodity'.

Typically, commodity markets are characterized by a lack of perceived differentiation by customers between competing offerings. Whilst there may be quality differences, the suggestion is that within a given specification this carton of milk, for example, is just the same as any other carton of milk. In situations such as these, one finds that purchase decisions tend to be taken on the basis of price or availability, and not on the basis of the brand or the manufacturer's name. As an example, petrol clearly falls into the commodity category. As a result, petrol companies try to promote 'image'. In the long run, however, they inevitably end up relying on promotions such as loyalty cards, extra services (coffee, groceries etc.) and special offers to attract the vast majority of the public who see little real value in the brand.

There are examples, however, of taking a commodity and making it a brand. A good example is provided by Perrier water: the contents are naturally occurring spring water which, whilst possessing certain distinctive characteristics, at the

Almost anything can become a brand

end of the day is still spring water. Yet through packaging and, more particularly, promotion, an international brand has been created with high brand loyalty. Consequently, it sells for a price well in excess of the costs of the ingredients. A similar approach is nowadays evident for Evian and San Pellegrino.

The difference between a brand and a commodity can be summed up by the phrase 'added values'. A brand is more than just the sum of its component parts. It embodies for the purchaser or user additional attributes which, whilst they might be considered by some to be 'intangible', are still very real. To illustrate the power of these added values, it is only necessary to consider the preference given by consumers to successful brands by dint of the brand name, rather than because of any functional superiority that can be discerned in objective comparisons.

Successful and unsuccessful brands

Successful brand building aids profitability by helping to create stable, long-term, demand and by adding values that entice customers to buy. They also provide a firm base for expansion into product improvements, variants, added services, new countries, and so on, and can help to protect organizations against the growing power of intermediaries. A strong brand name may also help organizations transform themselves from faceless bureaucracies into firms that are attractive both as employers and as businesses with which to associate.

It is important, then, not to make the mistake of confusing successful and unsuccessful brands. The world is full of products and services that have brand names, but which are not successful brands. Successful brands tend to:

- Have a unique identity which is widely recognized by members of the target market.
- Provide sustainable competitive advantage by being more attractive than most other identities or positions in the market.
- Add significantly to the asset value of an organization as demonstrated when the organization is sold or acquired.
- Require continuous investment to avoid the diminution experienced by some previously powerful brands, such as Hoover, Singer, Biro, and so on.

The components of a brand

The first component of a brand is its **brand positioning**. This is concerned with what the brand actually *does* and with what it competes. In other words, brand positioning starts with the physical, or functional, aspects of the product. For instance, Schweppes is positioned in the UK as a mixer for brandies and whiskies, rather than as a soft drink competing with Coca-Cola, Pepsi-Cola and 7Up. Similarly, Tide is presented as a tough, general-purpose detergent, rather than as a powder for woollens. Marks & Spencer goes to great lengths to support its image as a high-quality multiple rather than a low-price chainstore, and SAS is carefully positioned as the business person's airline. Positioning is usually performed against identifiable motivators in any market, only one or two of which are of real importance when developing a brand. These dimensions are best seen as bipolar scales along which brands can be positioned. Examples of these are provided in Table 24.1.

Table 24.1 Bipolar scales for brand positioning

Expensive	Inexpensive
Strong	Mild
Big	Small
Hot	Cold
Fast	Slow
Male	Female

The second component of a brand is its **personality**. This is a useful descriptor for the total impression that consumers have of brands and indicates that in many ways brands are like people in that they have their own physical, emotional and attitudinal characteristics. Thus, they are a complex blend of different characteristics which together create a brand identity. In this way, two brands can be very similar in terms of their functions, yet have very different personalities. As an example, the Ford Fiesta, the VW Polo and the Renault Clio all perform about the same along the functional dimensions of size, speed and price. Yet each one has a totally different personality, which is the result of a blend of three sorts of appeal: sensual, rational, and emotional.

- *Sensual appeal*: refers to the way the product or service looks, sounds or feels. It is easy to imagine how this appeal can differ in the case of, say, cigarettes or cars.
- *Rational appeal*: concerns the way the product or service performs (what they contain, their relative costs, and so on).
- *Emotional appeal*: is perhaps the most important aspect of a brand, and has a lot to do with the psychological rewards it offers, the moods it conjures up, the associations it evokes, and so on; it is easy to see the overt appeal of certain products as being, for instance, particularly masculine, feminine, chic, workmanlike, or 'flashy'.

Brand personality is also the result of a whole gamut of influences, such as: the places where it is sold; the price that is charged; other brands from the same manufacturer; how it is used; the kind of people who buy and use it; after-sales service; the name of the brand; advertising; point-of-sale material; PR; sponsorship; and many others.

A brand converts a commodity into something which can command a higher price

However, for any brand to be successful, all these elements have to be consistent, since they will all affect the brand's personality and it is this personality, above all else, that represents the brand's totality and which makes one brand more desirable than another. At its simplest, it is a brand's personality that converts a commodity into something unique and enables a higher price to be charged for it.

Overall, then, a good brand is an identifiable product, service, company, person, or place, augmented in such a way that buyers or users perceive a personality which incorporates relevant and unique added values which closely match their needs. A brand's success results from being able to sustain these added values against competitors over time.

25 The Product Lifecycle

This topic complements Topic 26 Diffusion of Innovation, which provides an explanation for the shape of the product lifecycle curve.

The product lifecycle is a conceptual tool which provides a means of describing the sales patterns of products over their time in a market. If absolute sales are plotted on a period by period basis (usually annually), the ideal-type lifecycle approximates to an S-curve (see Figure 25.1). In reality, product life-cycles adopt a number of different shapes and are never smooth. However, a good understanding of the concept, its variations, and the determinants of its shape, are a powerful aid to the development of marketing strategies.

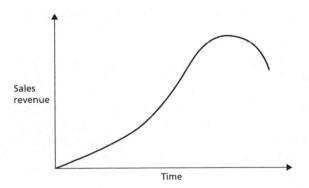

Figure 25.1   Standard product lifecycle curve

Lifecycles and product categories

Understanding product lifecycles requires an appreciation of the different categories of product for which they could be used: product class; form; or brand. These different categories exist because a market is based on a need that will usually be satisfied by alternative technologies over time. Each successive technology will provide a new product class and enhanced performance. The need to store information, for instance, has been satisfied by many product classes, including: stone tablets; papyrus; string; ledgers; microfilm; cards; tapes; discs; and, more recently, CDs, memory cards and i-Pods. Specific needs may, in the end, disappear, such as the need for protection against smallpox, or are greatly reduced, such as the need for telegrams. At this point, a market lifecycle comes to an end. More generic needs are likely to remain current for some time, as is the case for personal security, home entertainment, personal and mass communications, and people's social and physiological needs.

More focused examples of product classes include: televisions; bicycles; internal combustion engines; and personal computers. Each of these classes will have its own lifecycle. Within each class, there are likely to be a number of product forms, or families, which will also experience a lifecycle. Thus, the product-class 'personal computer' has included several product forms such as: desktops; portables; laptops; notebooks; and now hand-held computers.

In a similar way, each product form will include a number of brands or models which may be on the market for a very short time (say, 6–18 months), or which may last for longer (say, 3–9 years). If a brand can become a 'brand name' with a significant customer franchise, or a 'super brand' such as Mercedes, Coca-Cola or Rolex, then it will probably be used to cover a number of successive models, forms and even classes over a number of decades. This has been the case for product brands such as Tide and Persil, and company brands such as Nokia and IBM.

For marketing analysis, the most useful lifecycle is usually that of the product form. Product class lifecycles are often too macro to be of use, except for very long-range planning such as the 50-year strategies common amongst the larger Japanese corporations. This remains true even for the powerful brands which encompass a number of successive generations of a product. Sales of a particular form, such as colour televisions or neon lights, will track the activities of all suppliers to the market and will, therefore, enable judgements to be made in the context of a market as a whole. It is, nonetheless, extremely useful to compare a product or brand's performance against the projected lifecycle of the product form in order to ensure that nothing untoward is happening to it.

Stages in the product lifecycle

Product lifecycles will usually experience a number of successive stages (see Figure 25.2). The **introductory stage** will cover the launch of a new product form into the market to the point at which sales begin to accelerate rapidly. During this stage, sales will be relatively slow while customers get used to the new ideas it incorporates. If the form is to be a successful innovation, the product will move into its **growth phase**, during which sales volumes will increase rapidly from one time period to the next. At some point, sales growth will slow as the number of potential new purchasers reduces, at which time the lifecycle will be in its **maturity stage**.

Once sales growth has levelled off, the lifecycle has reached its **saturation phase** where sales are either replacements or latecomers to the market. Since these will probably be replacing the innovators who were the first to try a new product, and who have probably moved on to replacement product forms, they will add little to the growth of the market. The final stage therefore is **decline**, either as more people migrate to a new product form or the need disappears.

Lifecycles will move into the decline phase for one of two main reasons. The first, as indicated, will be that a replacement technology, usually delivering enhanced performance, will have been developed. In this way, colour televisions replaced black-and-white versions and facsimile transmission is slowly but surely being replaced by e-mail. The second will be a change in another aspect of the marketing environment such as fashion, legislation or standards, the development of a new industry structure or a social trend of some form.

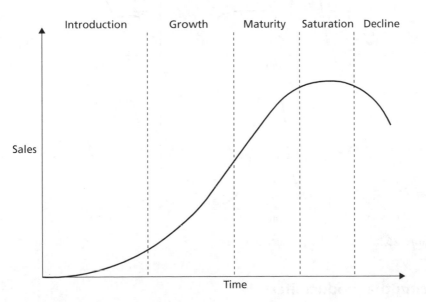

The most useful lifecycle is that of the product form

Figure 25.2   Phases in the product lifecycle

Deviant product lifecycles

Deviations from the shape associated with a 'standard' product lifecycle (see Figure 25.3) will be caused by the nature of a product and its patterns of consumption. Some products will experience growth followed by a sharp slump before levelling out into maturity (Figure 25.3a). This is typical of the sales patterns for small kitchen appliances and will occur because saturation is achieved before replacement purchases come into play. Scalloped lifecycles (Figure 25.3b), where sales continually level off and then grow again, will be associated with products which are constantly finding new markets and new applications. Bar coding and nylon are good examples of this. Rapid growth followed by rapid decline, with sales levelling out at a low level (Figure 25.3c), describes the lifecycle of a fad such as memorabilia associated with a particular event (world cup, royal wedding etc.), the hardly-remembered Clackers or the infamous pet rocks. A double-humped lifecycle (Figure 25.3d) will be typical of products which come in and out of style, such as mountain bikes or fashions, or will be products in markets which respond well to communications so that usage will follow media or industry patterns of promotional activity.

Figure 25.3 Alternative product lifecycles

Using the product lifecycle

Whilst it is never possible to identify accurately which point a product has reached on its lifecycle, or exactly what shape the lifecycle will follow, the concept does enable organizations to consider the future – how strategies will need to alter, and what their market information needs will be. At the introductory stage, competitors will typically be limited and the focus of a marketing strategy will be educating the market. During growth, organizations are likely to face more numerous competitors and will be seeking to establish a strong position in terms of market share, niches, brands and/or reputation, while at the same time, looking for product-range extension and market development. As a market matures and becomes saturated, marketing strategy will tend to concentrate on price, brand protection and customer service. When decline begins to bite, competition will eventually reduce and the organization will tend to concentrate on the next product form or on reducing costs, while maintaining price (see Table 25.1).

Table 25.1 Typical marketing-mix strategies for different lifecycle stages

Stage in product lifecycle	Product strategy	Price strategy	Place strategy	Promotion strategy
Introductory	Limited range for specialist applications	Skim or penetration	Limited to specialized outlets with service often provided by manufacturer	Educate the market and aggressive selling
Growth	Product range expansion	Competitive pricing for market share	Seek wide market coverage	Actively establish image or brand with competitive selling
Maturity	Improve quality and consolidate range	Stabilize prices	Use service for competitive differentiation	Protect brand and market position
Saturation	Reduce costs and range	Push price to limits	Transfer costs to distributors and automate service	Maintain brand or image at low cost
Decline	Further reduce costs and range	Maintain as high as possible	Reduce costs	Focused low cost communications

Different strategies are needed for different lifecycle stages

The problems associated with using the concept of product lifecycle occur either from its misuse or from its misinterpretation. Misuse would result from confusing the lifecycles of product forms with organizational sales or brands, or by trying to use them as predictive tools. Misinterpretation can arise if an organization interprets a 'glitch' in sales for the onset of decline, and pulls out of a market too early. Economic recession can have this effect, when in reality it is more likely to cause a postponement of purchasing rather than an end to it. If used sensibly, however, it can raise questions of importance such as:

■ How fast will growth be?
■ What will limit growth?
■ What could cause the onset of decline?
■ What trading conditions can be expected over the next few years?

If better decisions are made as a consequence, the lifecycle will be a valuable marketing tool.

26 Diffusion of Innovation

The shape of the standard product lifecycle implies that purchasers for a new class of product become customers at different times, and at different rates, following its introduction. This has been described by Everett Rogers as the **diffusion of innovation** or the **adoption process**. Adoption is concerned with the way that a consumer becomes a regular customer for a new product concept.

Diffusion refers to the way in which the product penetrates its potential market, which, in turn, suggests that there will be different stages of adoption. Variations between the shapes of product lifecycles for different products indicate that the rate of diffusion may also vary from one product to another. Effective marketing requires a good understanding of these processes and the causes of any variations.

New product adoption

The adoption process for a product new to a particular consumer will tend to follow a five-stage pattern. The first stage is **awareness**, whereby a consumer learns of the existence of a product. This may happen by accident, or it may be the result of a deliberate communications campaign on the part of the supplier, or of a deliberate search on the part of the consumer. Awareness becomes **interest** if the product is perceived to offer benefits appropriate to the needs of the consumer. At this point, the consumer will actively search for information about the new product. As information is gathered, consumers will go through a process of **evaluation** as they decide whether or not to try the innovation. The next stage is therefore **trial**, where consumers will extend their evaluation by an experimental consumption. The fifth and final stage is **adoption**, whereby either the trial or the appeal of the concept is good enough, or sufficiently strong, to convince consumers to buy again on a regular basis, although not necessarily from the same supplier.

Not all stages will be involved for all new products; consumers could move straight from awareness to adoption if the offer matched their particular need closely enough. More important, however, is the recognition that new purchasers will not necessarily pass from one stage to the next, and could get stuck at any one of the five stages.

New product diffusion

When plotted over time, the adoption process tends to follow a normal distribution. The midpoint of the distribution will represent the average amount of time (months or years) it took people to adopt a product. Most people will come to a new product within plus or minus one standard deviation of the average time. A minority of people, however, will either be amongst the first to become users of a product, or will be behind the rest of the market in the adoption of the innovation (see Figure 26.1). The various categories of adopters can be described as:

- Innovators.
- Early adopters.
- The early majority.
- The late majority.
- Laggards.

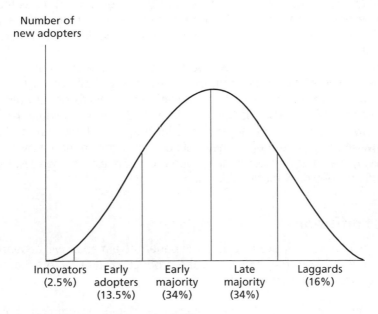

Number of
new adopters

| Innovators (2.5%) | Early adopters (13.5%) | Early majority (34%) | Late majority (34%) | Laggards (16%) |

Figure 26.1 The diffusion of innovation curve

Consumers of new products can be placed into five 'adopter' categories

- **Innovators** are usually characterized as being 2.5 per cent of a market and are the first to become regular users. Innovators are usually venturesome, or find value in being at the forefront of consumption. In industrial markets, innovators will either be technology-orientated and keen on seeking competitive advantage from new products, or will be forced into innovating as a 'distress purchase'. In consumer markets, innovators are usually hard to identify by their demographic, psychographic or media characteristics. It is also the case that an innovator in one product area could easily be a laggard in another; an electronic games hobbyist may be the first to try a new computer game, but the last to adopt a new clothes fashion. Without knowing the individual involved, it is hard to tell who is what.

- **Early adopters**, who comprise 13.5 per cent of a market, will be keen to take up a particular innovation, but will treat it with caution. However, they will often see themselves as being significant community members and therefore at the forefront of opinion in terms of the particular product area. Consequently, they will usually enjoy the attention early consumption brings.
- The **early majority** will cover 34 per cent of the market and will consolidate a new product's success. They will probably see themselves as early adopters, but will tend to be more risk-averse than the early adopters. Their purchase will, therefore, be a statement of their willingness to try something new, but will be tempered by a natural conservatism.
- The **late majority**, again 34 per cent of all adopters, will be even more conservative in their approach to the purchase of this product type, possibly even to the extent of being sceptical about the value of the innovation. Thus, as the innovation becomes more widely used, as its price falls, or as the traditional alternatives become less available, they will move to the new, increasingly acceptable, alternative.
- **Laggards**, the final category, will be the last to come to an innovation and will be the remaining 16 per cent of a market. They will occupy this position for a number of reasons, including: education level; focus of activities; degree of isolation; attitude towards tradition; level of disposable income; lack of any alternative; and so on. For laggards, the innovation will have had to have lost its 'new product' status before they will adopt its consumption. However, there will always be some non-consumers. Even today, there are some West European and US households without a television.

Rate of diffusion

The rate at which a new product class will penetrate a market will depend on the characteristics of both the market and the product. Market factors that will provide hurdles to penetration include:

- The absence of appropriate communications media, distribution channels or physical infrastructure such as regular electricity supply.
- The slow speed of the decision-making process.
- The existence of complicated regulatory or procedural requirements.
- Adverse economic conditions.
- Socio-cultural factors which militate against the product's adoption.

Product factors which can hamper adoption include:

- Little relative performance or cost advantage over the present solutions to the problem which the product is designed to solve.

- Low product compatibility with existing structures in the market, be they physical, social or whatever.
- High complexity, which will make it hard for adopters to evaluate or understand the benefits on offer.
- Few possibilities to try the product before purchase, making it difficult for consumers to judge its value in advance, which is especially true of expensive goods and services.
- Features which are hard to describe, as is often the case for products delivering abstract or intangible benefits, service products, or products that are hard to conceptualize or demonstrate, such as software consultancy or insurance services.

Within this, it should also be noted that word of mouth has often been identified as one of the key features in aiding the diffusion of an innovation throughout its potential market. Unfortunately, this is one of the most difficult aspects of promotion for an organization to influence, even with the opportunities for viral marketing offered by mobile telephones.

These variations help to explain the different shapes of product lifecycles, and the possible hurdles to adoption mean that not all new products will fulfil their market potential. Diffusion and adoption are not inevitable and marketing organizations have to develop strategies which will overcome the blockages they are likely to encounter.

Diffusion and adoption are not inevitable

27 The Ansoff Matrix

The Ansoff Matrix is a 2 × 2 depiction of the options open to organizations if they wish to improve revenue or profitability. The matrix was first described by Igor Ansoff in 'Strategies for Diversification' (*Harvard Business Review*, September–October 1957, p. 114). Although 'old', it remains a very effective framework because it provides a simple framework which encapsulates **all** the strategic directions an organization can adopt in one analytical tool. Unlike some of the other analytical tools used in marketing, the matrix is not diagnostic; rather it is a method for structuring thinking or a means of classifying objectives.

The axes of the matrix focus on the essential relationship an organization has to manage: the provision of products for customers. Whatever an organization's position or industry, the product will be either an existing offering or a product which is new to the organization. Customers, similarly, will be either part of an existing market or members of a market not yet addressed by the organization and, therefore, new to them. An organization is thus faced with four options for commercial action:

- Concentrating on existing products for existing markets.
- Looking for new products for existing markets.
- Seeking new markets for existing products.
- Diversifying into new products for new markets. (See Figure 27.1.)

Figure 27.1 The Ansoff Matrix

Existing products for existing markets

In developing a strategy, close attention should always be paid to existing product/ market relationships. Increased revenue in this option can be gained in a number of ways:

- The easiest method is to attract customers who share the same needs as existing purchasers, but who have not yet become regular users. This is particularly important in growth markets where new customers are appearing all the time. Strategies will concentrate on persuading such people or organizations to test a product and then, if they like it, to use your offering rather than those of direct competitors.
- In mature markets, increased sales will have to come from competitors by persuading customers to use a different supplier or brand. This will usually involve manipulating elements of the marketing mix such as lowering price, broadening a brand's appeal, or initiating sales promotion campaigns. In fact, it is more usual to focus on customer service, since price wars can be damaging to all concerned and product differentiation is often difficult to achieve.
- Improved sales can also come from persuading the market to increase usage of the products. For consumer products, this may be very appropriate, especially during periods of economic growth and increasing levels of disposable income. Thus, the notions of two-car families, two-television households and more frequent clothing purchases have an appeal during times of prosperity. In industrial markets, such a strategy may be more difficult to sell, as purchasers are likely to be seeking better value per purchase, unless they can see competitive value from increased usage or shortened replacement cycles.
- Higher sales revenue can also be achieved through improved productivity, such as: a better mix of products and customers; price increases, or reductions in discounts; charging for deliveries; and so on.
- An alternative to seeking revenue growth is to reduce costs. This, however, may only yield short-term benefits since there is a limit to the scope for cost-reduction. Nonetheless, all good organizations are continuously seeking the benefits of value engineering, process effectiveness and supply-chain efficiencies. All of these can provide useful breathing spaces during which an organization can explore other, longer-term, areas for enhancing revenue.

New products for existing markets

A second strategic option is to introduce new products targeted at existing customers with whom the organization already has a relationship. Within this, the better approach is to build on some aspect of the relationship which already exists. This can take a number of different forms:

- One option is to supply new products which are closely associated with the products which customers already purchase from a supplier. Thus, a computer

The Ansoff Matrix is a method for structuring strategic marketing thinking manufacturer could add computer peripherals, such as printers, plotters and service contracts, or consumables, such as paper, ink and discs, to its range in order to provide a 'one-stop shopping' service.

- A similar approach particularly appropriate for organizational customers would be to identify the way in which they categorize their purchases and endeavour to supply products which meet a customer's purchasing management structures. For instance, a retailer might include shampoo as a personal care item, as a fashion accessory or as a bathroom product. Each classification would provide different opportunities for the shampoo producer to expand the range of associated products they supply.
- An alternative route would be to concentrate on the technology base used to supply existing products and to identify other product needs customers might have which could be produced using current facilities and know-how. A current example is Amazon's expansion from books and CDs into other household goods such as kitchen appliances.
- The other main approach is to build on the way in which existing customers use a supplier. Some relationships might be based on a partnership approach with joint problem-solving, whilst others might use a supplier for convenience or for a particular attribute of their product or service. Each type of relationship will provide different opportunities for the addition of new products to an organization's range.

New markets for existing products

A third option in the matrix is to look for new markets for existing products requiring the identification of users in different markets with similar needs, or new customers who would use a product in a different way. The most obvious example would be to expand from a domestic market into foreign markets (i.e. a geographical market extension). Although such a move would probably require some product adaptation, and maybe some different positioning or selling methods, the experience required to supply the product would be essentially the same. A similar example would be an expansion from, say, the public sector into the private sector, or from financial services to the leisure industry. Again, whilst product modification and adaptation may be required, the core technologies of the product are unlikely to be unaltered.

The same would be true for new markets where the product would be used in a different way. Raw materials, standard components and many service products would be quite easy to adapt, whereas bespoke products, or consumer goods, would be more difficult to transfer. As examples, expanded polystyrene can be used for noise insulation, heat retention in hot water tanks, as a packaging or protection material and as a floor-cushion filler. Similarly, a floor cushion manufacturer could look to expand into cushions for pets, for cars, for beds and for the garden.

New products for new markets

The fourth option, new products for new markets, is the most risky diversification since it utilizes little of an organization's existing expertise or capabilities. It is also the type of expansion which has the highest failure rate. Where organizations have been successful in this domain, it is usually possible to identify some synergy in sales, distribution or product technology. The expansion by BIC, for instance, from pens into disposable razors, utilized both their understanding of the technology of mass production of cheap plastic items and their ability to sell to, and to service, multiple retail organizations. Where no synergies exist, attention to risk management becomes very important.

The Ansoff Matrix can therefore be seen as a framework for describing the range of strategic options open to an organization for expansion. It is also a means of conceptualizing the development of a product over its market life. It provides a useful conceptual approach to diversification. However, rather than moving straight to new products for new markets, organizations should see if it is possible to get there via new products or via new markets first, since these will provide experience that will reduce the risk of managing both new products and new markets simultaneously.

Whether it is preferable to expand into either new products or new markets first is a matter for debate. Some would argue for new products on the grounds that customers are more difficult to manage. Others would prefer new markets, since unfamiliar technologies are fraught with hidden problems. In the end, it is probably the option with the least degree of complexity which will determine the choice.

Overall, the Ansoff Matrix has a certain beauty in its simplicity, because it strips marketing down to its basics, which are to do with getting products to market. Having said this, it does perhaps oversimplify marketing in that there are different kinds of new products and different kinds of new markets. It is important to be clear about what these are, as illustrated in Table 27.1.

Table 27.1 Kinds of new products and markets

Degrees of newness of the product:
- It can stay the same
- It can be extended in some way
- It can be redesigned, modified or improved
- It can be a new product or concept entirely

Different forms of new markets:
- They can be the same
- They can be broader in terms of how they are defined
- They can include new coverage, but on related areas
- They can be totally new

New products into new markets have the highest failure rates

The Ansoff Matrix is good at reminding us that marketing life can become too complicated, but its inference that things are either old or new overlooks those middling shades of grey. One way of clarifying this is to redraw the Ansoff Matrix as depicted in Figure 27.2.

Newness of product

Product / Market	Same product	Extended product	Modified or improved product	New product
Same market				
Broader market coverage				
New coverage but in related areas				
New market				

(left axis label: Newness of market)

Figure 27.2   An extended product/market matrix

28 The Boston Matrix

The Boston Matrix is a vehicle for classifying and characterizing an organization's activities in relation to the markets in which it operates. It can be used to represent strategic business units (SBUs), or product portfolios, which are then located on the matrix for analytical purposes. Such a presentation will enhance the strategic management of an organization and its ability to make judgements about how best to manage each business or product group, and to identify gaps or areas which may prove problematic as markets grow, mature and decline.

The matrix focuses on two key aspects of markets: their growth rates, and a product or SBU's relative market share by value (see Figure 28.1). Market growth rates are ranged on the vertical axis and were originally rated between 0 per cent and 30 per cent, with a growth rate of over 10 per cent being high, and under 10 per cent low. In fact, what is considered a high or low growth rate will vary from industry to industry or market to market, and practitioners need to make their

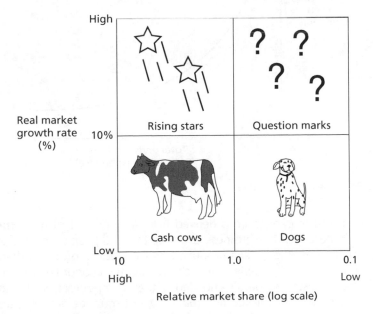

Figure 28.1 The Boston Matrix

own judgements about where the breakpoints between high and low should fall. Market share is depicted on the horizontal axis on a log scale and shows a product or SBU's share *relative* to that of the largest competitor in the market. A relative market share of 1.0 means that its share is equal to that of the largest competitor; 10 will mean that it is ten times larger and 0.1 will mean that it has one-tenth the share of the largest supplier. The log scale is used so that equal distances on the axis represent the same percentage increases or reductions.

The rationale behind the matrix is that growth rates will significantly affect the attractiveness of a market to an organization for investment purposes and relative market share is a good indicator of a business's strength in that market. Growth rates are also of interest because they relate to the stages of a product life-cycle. High growth rates are associated with markets where the customer base is expanding rapidly and in which businesses have to match or exceed the growth rate to maintain their market-share position. Low growth rates indicate that the market is maturing and implies that a business does not have to compete with other suppliers for new customers entering a market, in order to maintain its share of the market.

Figure 28.2 The experience curve

The importance of market share is derived from the concept of the **experience curve** (see Figure 28.2). If a business can maintain the position of market-share leader, it will, by definition, have produced and sold more products than any of its competitors. This will enable it to achieve greater economies of experience and, thus, lower costs and better knowledge than competitors. Such economies and knowledge are not achieved automatically, but must be actively pursued by an organization's management. If gained, such economies should yield cash that can be used for reinvestment in other products/SBUs; protection against price wars; other marketing efforts of competitors; or profit distribution. The knowledge gained from the experience should yield market intelligence, which should, in turn, make competitive activities more effective. High market share also reduces the relative expenditure required for competitive marketing activities and can often provide a business with the power to influence a market in terms of price, technical standards, product development and the way competitive activities are conducted.

The products/SBUs in each quadrant of the matrix are, therefore, faced with different marketing tasks. Those in high-growth markets, but with a low market share (referred to as **Question Marks** or **Problem Children**) need to seek market leadership so that when the market matures, they will be a long way down the experience curve and in a position of strength in the market. This will require investment to challenge the existing leaders and may force a business to prioritize between a number of products/SBUs if they are not to spread their resources too thinly.

A **Star** is a business or product which has attained market leadership in high-growth markets. Here, the priority will be to invest to maintain leadership against challenges from the Question Marks of other organizations. As a market's growth slows, Stars will become **Cash Cows** if they have protected their leadership. Cash Cows still require some investment to keep their leadership position, but not to the same extent as Stars or Question Marks. Thus, they can potentially generate cash that can be used to support Question Marks seeking to become Stars in other markets. If a business has a low relative market share in a mature market, the matrix classifies it as a **Dog**, since it is unlikely to generate cash to the same extent as the market leader. The concept of **Cash Dogs** has been introduced to indicate products/SBUs that have a good market share and which can generate useful cash flows in spite of not being the market leaders.

An unbalanced portfolio can, therefore, have significant cashflow implications for a business either now or for the future. An absence of Stars could mean no Cash Cows in the future. The absence of Cash Cows will imply a need for external funding if it is to be in a cash-generating position in the future. Too many Question Marks may drain a business of cash if it has ambitions for leadership in each of the markets in which they are launched. Dogs consume management time and a business must consider whether they are holding them for good reasons, since they are unlikely to be contributing much to the bottom line on their own, and so on. Figure 28.3 illustrates the cash situation faced by products/SBUs in different parts of the matrix.

The implications of the matrix are that organizations need to invest heavily in those Question Marks and Stars which are potential Cash Cows, and only moderately in Cash Cows and Dogs. Thus, each category of product will have different cashflow connotations and will require attention to different marketing priorities. In this

An unbalanced portfolio can have significant cashflow implications

Relative market share

	High		Low	
High	Cash use	$---$	Cash use	$---$
	Cash generated	$+++$	Cash generated	$+$
Market growth		0		$--$
Low	Cash use	$-$	Cash use	$-$
	Cash generated	$+++$	Cash generated	$+$
		$++$		0

Figure 28.3 The Boston Matrix – cashflow implications

way, a more rational basis for strategy development is possible and the 'health' of an organization can be more easily assessed from a marketing viewpoint.

Like all simplifications, there are a few drawbacks to using the Boston Matrix as a diagnostic and strategic tool:

- The now-popularized names may act as demotivators for managers, especially if they feel that the organization only views them as suitable to manage Dogs.
- Growth and market share are not the only factors that make markets attractive and which give companies strength in markets.
- The data to position products/SBUs accurately on the matrix is not always available.
- A clear and common definition of the market must be agreed so that growth and share positions are not distorted.

As an extreme illustration, it would be quite easy for a business to claim a 100 per cent share of the market if it defined the market as all those customers it supplied! In a similar way, maintaining a Cash Cow assumes that other organizations recognize the position and do not invest heavily in their Dogs and attack the Cash Cows of other organizations, thereby requiring them to spend money to defend their position. Overall, though, the tool can be extremely useful as a means of depicting an organization's situation or market position and as a basis for internal managerial debate.

29 The Directional Policy Matrix

The Directional Policy Matrix (DPM) is a framework that can be used to classify and categorize an organization's business activities in terms of its strengths, capabilities or market position, and the way it perceives markets to be attractive. The basic structure of a DPM is illustrated in Figure 29.1. The purpose of the matrix is to diagnose an organization's strategic options in relation to the two composite dimensions of business strengths and market attractiveness. The DPM enables organizations to conduct an analysis of their portfolio of products or areas of operation.

Figure 29.1   The Directional Policy Matrix (DPM)

The analysis is performed, first, according to the potential each product area or business has to achieve the organization's objectives and, second, according to the organization's ability to take advantage of the range of opportunities it faces. The matrix requires its users to identify a number of factors that will act as indicators of the attractiveness of a market or opportunity to them and, similarly, a number of factors that will act as indicators of organizational strengths. These factors will obviously vary from one product or business area to another since what will be attractive in one area may not be attractive in another. Similarly, a strength or capability in one area may not be a strength in another.

Compared with other portfolio analysis tools, such as the Boston Matrix, the DPM is a more sophisticated mechanism. Like its forerunner, the Boston Matrix, it

The DPM is valuable in analysing and managing product or business portfolios

can be used to derive quantitative comparisons between areas of activities, but, in addition, is able to take into account a wider range of decisional influences. In fact, the DPM was originally conceived by General Electric and developed by McKinsey (management consultants), and later Shell, as a means of overcoming some of the limitations the Boston Matrix was perceived to have. It is usually drawn as a 3 × 3 box matrix, rather than using the more standard 2 × 2 format, in order to encompass the range of strategic options it covers. In the end, the number of lines drawn is irrelevant. What is more important is defining the substance of the matrix and its axes, and adopting an orderly methodology for its application.

Strategic business unit

Since the purpose of performing a DPM analysis is to provide a basis for determining policy and allocating resources for the alternative products or business within an organization, it is important to consider the organizational level at which the analysis should be conducted. This is normally the 'strategic business unit' (SBU) level, but can also be used to plot any portfolio of activity where choices between alternative products or markets have to be made. The most frequently used definition of a SBU is that it will:

- Have common segments and competitors for most of its products.
- Operate in external markets.
- Be identifiable as a discrete and separate unit.
- Be managed by people who will have control over most of the areas critical to success.

It is usually felt that there should be at least three, and up to ten, areas for analysis if the DPM is to be of value.

Market attractiveness

The vertical axis of a DPM represents the degree to which a market is attractive to an organization. The key determinant of market attractiveness is its potential to yield growth in sales and profits. Although what constitutes a market for the purposes of DPM analysis will vary, a useful definition is: 'an identifiable group of customers with requirements in common that are, or may become, significant in requiring a separate strategy.'

Thus, there is a large element of management judgement required at an early stage in the construction of a DPM, which will be critical to the quality of the analysis. To avoid unnecessary bias, it is vital that market definition and the identification of market attractiveness criteria be done in as objective a way as possible. It is also the case that both these judgements need to be made in isolation from the organization's position in its markets. This is difficult to achieve since most of the managers involved in such an exercise will have views about the organization's position, which will potentially influence their judgements. To make the exercise worthwhile, however, as much objectivity as possible should be sought.

For some examples of what might constitute market attractiveness criteria, see Table 29.1. The most important are usually the first four.

Table 29.1 Criteria which might make a market attractive*

- Growth rate
- Accessible-market size
- Competitive intensity
- Profit margins
- Differences between competitive offerings
- Existence of technical standards
- Compatible infrastructure
- Ease of obtaining payment
- Sensitivity to interest rates
- General volatility
- Degree of regulation
- Barriers to entry
- Rate of technological change
- Likelihood of political stability
- Potential for supply 'partnerships'
- Availability of market intelligence

*List non-exclusive

Business strength or position

The horizontal axis of a DPM is a measure of an organization's strengths, or potential strengths, in the market place. The criteria used to judge a product's strengths must be related to customer requirements if they are to have any meaning. The criteria will vary between markets and will need to be assessed against the performance of competitors. The purpose of identifying these criteria is to evaluate the degree to which the organization can take advantage of a market opportunity. Similar to market attractiveness, business strengths or position need to be judged in as objective a way as possible to avoid all products or business areas falling within the same sector of the matrix. Ideally, such judgements should be validated by independent market research.

A list of factors which might be considered when assessing business strengths is shown in Table 29.2.

Ideally, judgements about business strength or position should be validated by independent market research

Table 29.2 Factors which might be considered, or which may yield, business strengths*

- Relative quality
- Production capacity
- Production flexibility
- Product adaptability
- Unit cost of production
- Price position
- R&D capabilities
- Brands owned
- Company image
- Market share
- Range of commercial contacts
- Influence with regulatory bodies
- Delivery performance
- Service facilities
- Channel access or distribution network
- Size/quality of sales force

*List non-exclusive

It is usual, however, to translate these into capabilities that deliver what the market or segment requires. For guidelines on how to do this, see Topic 22 on SWOT analyses.

Constructing a DPM portfolio

Having identified the criteria that will make a market attractive and which will yield business strengths, objective judgements about attractiveness can be made by weighting each factor and then scoring each factor in terms of relative performance or attractiveness. By multiplying each factor's weight by its rating, a numerical value can be obtained. When the values for each factor are totalled, the product or activity can be positioned on the matrix.

The use of a 2 × 2 form of the matrix yields four strategic categories, as shown in Figure 29.2. Each category will have a strategy choice associated with it which managers will have to translate into specific objectives and marketing programmes for that area. Illustrations of what these might be for each quadrant are shown in Figure 29.3. In addition, the steps required for the creation of a DPM are summarized in Table 29.3.

To avoid all products ending up on the left-hand side of a 2 × 2 form of the matrix, scores for performance can be expressed as a ratio where the value is set against a similar value for the best-performing organization in the market. If a log scale is used for this axis, ranging from, say, 3 to 1 to 0.3, this tendency can be overcome.

Notes:

Invest for growth – businesses that are relatively high in business strengths and market attractiveness.

Manage for substained earnings – businesses with medium strengths in markets of medium to low attractiveness. Maintain strong position in moderately attractive markets, but do not invest to increase market share.

Manage for cash – businesses with a relatively weak position in a relatively unattractive market. Harvest for current profitability or divest.

Opportunistic – businesses with low business strength, but high market attractiveness.

Figure 29.2   Four strategic categories

Table 29.3   The ten steps involved in producing a DPM

Step 1	Define the products/services for markets that are to be used during the analysis.
Step 2	Define the criteria for market attractiveness.
Step 3	Score the relevant product/services for market.
Step 4	Define the organization's relative strengths for each product/service for market.
Step 5	Analyse and draw conclusions from the relative position of each product/service for market.
Step 6	Draw conclusions from the analysis with a view to generating objectives and strategies.
Step 7	(Optional) Position the circles on the box assuming no change to current policies. That is to say, a *forecast* should be made of the future position of the circles.
Step 8	Redraw the portfolio to position the circles where the organization wants them to be. That is to say, the *objectives* they wish to achieve for each product/service for market.
Step 9	Detail the strategies to be implemented to achieve the objectives.
Step 10	Calculate the appropriate financial consequences of changes by product.

Main thrust	Invest for growth	Manage for sustained earnings	Manage for cash	Opportunistic development
Market share	Maintain or increase dominance	Maintain or slightly milk for earnings	Forgo share for profit	Invest selectively in share
Products	Differentiation – line expansion	Prune less successful Differentiate for key segments	Aggressively prune	Differentiation – line expansion
Price	Lead – aggressive pricing for share	Stabilize prices/raise	Raise	Aggressive – price for share
Promotion	Aggressive marketing	Limit	Minimize	Aggressive marketing
Distribution	Broaden distribution	Hold wide distribution pattern	Gradually withdraw distribution	Limited coverage
Cost control	Tight control – go for scale economies	Emphasize cost-reduction viz. variable costs	Aggressively reduce both fixed and variable	Tight – but not at expense of entrepreneurship
Production	Expand, invest (organic acquisition, joint venture)	Maximize capacity and utilization	Free up capacity	Invest
R&D	Expand – invest	Focus on specific projects	None	Invest
Personnel	Upgrade management in key functional areas	Maintain, reward efficiency, tighten organization	Cut back organization	Invest
Investment	Fund growth	Limit fixed investment	Minimize and divest opportunistically	Fund growth
Working capital	Reduce in process – extend credit	Tighten credit – reduce accounts receivable Increase inventory turn	Aggressively reduce	Invest

Figure 29.3 Programme guidelines suggested for different positioning on the DPM

30 Developing New Products

A significant proportion of most organizations' revenue is derived from products introduced in the recent past. Such products can take many different forms and can be derived from a number of different external and internal sources. Their development or acquisition, however, is costly and there is a great danger of failure. This danger can be reduced if marketing principles underpin every stage of the acquisition, development and launch of new products.

Types of new products

New products which are not just the acquisition of another organization's established products will have different degrees of 'newness' associated with them. A common way of classifying new products is:

- *Revolutionary new products*: products the like of which have never been seen before and which create entirely new markets.
- *Improved products*: existing products that have been enhanced to provide better performance or greater perceived value – often referred to as the 'next generation'.
- *Modified products*: where current models are replaced by new ones which combine features of a number of different models.
- *Adapted products*: products that have been changed to address needs in other markets or market segments, but whose key functionality remains the same.
- *New brands*: successful new products often stimulate the launch of similar competitive products by other organizations under different brand names or with alternative positions.

An alternative classification based on 'newness' to markets and the businesses launching them is shown in Figure 30.1. The percentages shown for each category demonstrate that only a small proportion (10 per cent) of all new product launches are totally new concepts or in any way revolutionary. This suggests that new product management must cover a wide range of different situations.

Sources of new product ideas

Organizations which are open to new ideas and which actively pursue new product opportunities are usually systematic in their search. They recognize that there

Customers are often the most profitable source of new ideas

Figure 30.1 New product classification

are a number of different sources that can generate good ideas and that sometimes a proactive approach needs to be adopted. Appropriate sources, however, will vary from industry to industry and may require different types of approach, although all ideas must be closely linked with customer needs and wants if they are to be successful commercially.

For many organizations, **customers** are, in fact, the most profitable source of new ideas. This is certainly true in industrial markets where customers often produce the highest percentage of new ideas, particularly if they are **lead users** (i.e. organizations which make the most use of a new product). Lead users are also, therefore, likely to see the limitations of a product first and can recommend improvements ahead of later purchasers. Establishing close development partnerships with such organizations can provide a valuable source of new product ideas, modifications or extensions of existing product lines.

In more highly populated markets, organizations can use different forms of **customer research** as sources of ideas, such as:

- Customer shadowing.
- Surveys.
- Focus group discussions.
- Competitions amongst users.
- Analyses of letters of complaint.

As an example, when Toyota decided it wished to enter the US automobile market it decided to use the VW Beetle as its **benchmark** product. Thus, it closely questioned existing users about the problems they experienced with the Beetle. The result was a car positioned as a 'fun' product for drivers who were prepared to buy foreign cars, with none of the drawbacks of a Beetle, but all the advantages.

Other **external** sources of new product ideas include:

- Competitors.
- Patent offices.
- Intermediaries.
- Universities.
- Commercial laboratories.
- Consultants.
- Market research firms.

The Japanese have often deconstructed **competitor products** (a process known as reverse engineering) as a source of new ideas and are net importers of licences for various technologies, which they often improve for their own commercial purposes. In some countries, as a means of facilitating this process, publications exist which are devoted to advertisers seeking ideas or inventors searching for a business willing to exploit their discoveries. **Internal** sources can be equally valuable and can include: research laboratories; sales representatives; and other employees.

Sometimes, the **chief executive**, as the founder or key technical force within the business, is the main source of innovation. Whatever the source, the organization must be willing to explore new ideas. In many enterprises, their organizational culture can act as a damper and stifle initiatives which could be the future life-blood of the business (see Figure 30.2).

Organizational culture can sometimes stifle new product initiatives

Figure 30.2   Cultural blockages to new product initiatives

Stages in product development

Once an idea for a new product has been conceived, the process of development and placing it on the market needs to be carefully managed to reduce the risk and costs of failure. The initial stage is a preliminary market and technical assessment of the concept to judge whether its creation and sale seem feasible. This should be performed fairly quickly and be at minimal cost. The next step is a detailed technical product analysis and the creation of prototypes, in parallel with some more detailed market research, to test the assumptions made during the initial feasibility or concept test.

Once an organization is satisfied that a new idea has sufficient potential, the technical side of the business should move towards a pilot production stage while marketing begins to establish the springboard from which the product will be launched. This may involve preparing the media, identifying appropriate channels of distribution, understanding the target-market buyer-behaviour, and establishing a market position. Pilot production and a test marketing exercise are often employed as the next stage to confirm or deny the potential before full investment is made in production facilities and the market as a whole.

The cost of developing a new product for commercialization will increase dramatically as an organization moves towards full commercialization. The task of marketing is to reduce the risk by pursuing market knowledge that will enable a project to be dropped before expenditure becomes too high. For mass-market consumer products, the cumulative expenditure at the point of full launch can be well into the £ millions. Of this, 50 per cent can be accounted for by the national **roll-out** of the product. The importance of rigorous procedures to prevent the inappropriate launch of a new product by moving from curve A to curve B is therefore vital (see Figure 30.3).

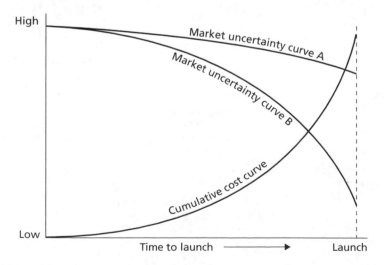

Figure 30.3   Risk and new product development

It has also been estimated that for every successful new product, between 50 and 70 new ideas have to be considered and that only one in four products that are test-marketed prove successful once launched nationally. When products are successful, they tend to be ones that:

- Deliver a significant differentiated benefit.
- Have a good technological fit with the supplying organization.
- Stem from businesses which have 'done their marketing well'.

These features are more likely to be achieved where new product teams are set up which consist of representatives from the major functional disciplines in the organization: operations; engineering; finance; human resources; marketing, and so on. In addition, where development is managed as a parallel process between engineering, production and marketing, as opposed to a linear development process, success is even more likely. Whatever the process, however, without good marketing input, new products become a game of Russian roulette rather than a disciplined management contribution to the organization.

Without good marketing, new products become a game of Russian roulette

Part 6

Key Elements of Positioning

31 Pricing Strategies

A customer's response to an offering from a supplier is affected by all aspects of the marketing mix which constitutes that offer. Amongst these variables, price is always an important feature since it is one of the key determinants of a product's value. Price is thus one of the evaluative criteria used by potential customers, as are the costs incurred in both making the purchase and owning or utilizing the product. Price and associated costs are, therefore, an important adjunct to positioning.

At the same time, price is a very difficult aspect of the marketing mix to manage. This is because it is subject to many pressures which are independent of marketing objectives. These can be both internal (from financial, operations, sales and other senior managers) and external (from customers, competitors and government agencies). To maintain the integrity of prices, a sound pricing strategy is required. A strategy for pricing is also required to support an organization's overall marketing strategy and to protect profitability. The strategy adopted will be determined by the circumstances an individual organization faces, and requires managers to possess a good understanding of the alternative strategies available.

Market skimming

A market-skimming strategy is one where a supplying organization positions itself at the top of the market against its competitors. If there are no competitors, then skimming suggests a price at which only a small number of the potential customers for a product will be prepared to buy. The implication of a skimming strategy is that an organization will be targeting a niche in the market for which the benefits of a product have a high value. A further implication is that product volumes and market share will never be high, but that margins should be good.

Following a skimming strategy is appropriate for products or offerings that are unique or which attract high quality ratings. Uniqueness may be derived from:

- Proprietary access to materials.
- Facilities or the technology a product incorporates.
- The way in which the product is produced.
- Its particular formulation or construction.

Creating a pricing strategy first requires an understanding of the strategic alternatives available

Uniqueness can be protected by patents or by keeping processes and recipes a secret. Quality will be associated with the care with which a product or service is produced, the materials it incorporates or the customer service offered alongside the product. Quality can also be associated with: precision; reliability; longevity; finish; presentation; robustness; and many other features, depending on the product's application.

Maintaining a pricing strategy of skimming over the life of a product obviously requires support from other positioning variables such as image, brand value, relationship management and the way in which a price is presented. It also requires efforts to distance a product away from competitors and a strategy for maintaining differentiation over the product lifecycle. Where significant economies of scale and/or experience are potentially available, skimming and sustaining high price levels becomes difficult unless a really powerful brand has been created, there is a wide patent platform, or proprietary access to the supply of non-substitutable materials or facilities exists.

Sliding or reducing skim

As the name implies, this strategy involves an initially high price which is dropped either as new entrants make a market more competitive or as a market matures. Whilst it does not imply continuing as the most expensive in a market, it does mean that the organization will seek to be towards the upper reaches of the continuum of prices that prevail in a market. In this way, an enterprise can seek to address larger sections of a market with the object of becoming one of the market leader suppliers, if not *the* market leader.

A sliding or reducing skim strategy is also appropriate when it is difficult to sustain a technological advantage or where costs are sensitive to economies of scale and/or experience. Both these factors will make a product attractive to competitors and require price adjustments as the market evolves. In this case, the organization will be following the market and trying to recover product development and investment costs in as short a period as possible. At the same time, it will be seeking to position itself as a dominant player through branding or service quality while using price as a support for its ambitions.

Market penetration

A strategy of market penetration is the opposite of a skimming approach. Here a low price is used to obtain volume sales and to attain market share. The price, however, must not be so low that it becomes indicative of poor quality or unacceptable performance. Sometimes, this can be used as an entry strategy into an already established market, or it might be used to create a market or to speed up its development by making a product accessible to a wide audience early in its lifecycle. In some cases, organizations have been known to price ahead of expected cost gains from economies of experience in order to achieve this.

Such a strategy requires an organization to maintain its price advantage in the face of changes in the general market price structure. It also requires that the benefit to price ratio between supplying organizations is sufficiently different to be significant in the eyes of the consumer, that is, that whatever products act as benchmarks for customers appear to them to be significantly more expensive. The developing Malaysian and Chinese automobile manufacturers provide good examples of organizations adopting this type of approach.

Floor pricing

This strategy implies keeping prices right at the lower end of the price spectrum and will be used to appeal to those who are very price-conscious. High sensitivity to price will be a result of the customer seeing little differential value between the various offerings in the market or having restricted disposable incomes. The perceived benefits of the offer must still match the price adopted. Such a strategy requires close attention to costs at all times and is typical of the bargain basement, no frills, type of operation. Enterprises which can survive on low margins, whether because of high turnover, lower profit requirements, or insignificant overheads, are best able to pursue this type of strategy.

Competitor pricing

An alternative to adopting a proactive pricing strategy is to position an organization a specific distance from a market leader's price. This distance may be large or small, and may be above or below the market leader chosen, depending on the way in which the business wishes to be perceived. Any price changes initiated by the leader will then be followed by the competitor organization, either immediately or at the next available opportunity. In the case of forecourt or retail prices, this may be the following day. Where prices are not openly stated or are part of a competitive tendering process, this can take much longer.

Such an approach is rarely operated in isolation and may be used as part of a penetration or skimming strategy. If the distance adopted is large, then it is likely that a product is being used as a loss leader to attract customers who would then purchase other products at prices closer to the norm. If the distance is significant, but remains constant over time, the position may be held to attract a particular segment of the market by offering a specific value proposition. Whatever the case, the overall benefits offered are likely to be similar to those offered by the leader, who will be providing a 'price umbrella' under which others in the market can 'shelter'.

A market penetration strategy uses low price to obtain volume sales and market share

Cost-based pricing

Under all the strategies discussed above, there is an implication that costs should be managed in the light of the strategy adopted rather than the other way round. In some cases, however, cost will be a significant determinant of price. As an example, where products use expensive capital equipment to be produced, skimming or floor pricing may not be possible options. In other areas, such as some types of government procurement, or where suppliers have been developed as partnerships, prices may be determined and discussed on the basis of costs.

It is also the case that, in the end, income must exceed total costs. These and other reasons, as illustrated in Table 31.1, make costs a very appealing base from which to set prices. Setting prices according to costs, however, is fraught with dangers (see Table 31.2), and can lead to sub-optimization or the absence of any clear market position.

Table 31.1 Appeal of a cost approach to pricing

- Managers usually feel more certain about costs than about what customers will pay.
- Prices are easier to justify in terms of cost rather than benefits.
- A cost-based approach to pricing is administratively easier than judging market-based issues.
- Prices based on cost appear socially more acceptable and are less open to accusations of exploitation.
- A cost-plus approach should ensure than an organization remains profitable.

Table 31.2 Problems of a cost approach to pricing

- Costs are not always easy to identify.
- It ignores the way customers use price.
- It ignores the relative value of an offering compared with competitors.
- Costs will often vary with volume.
- Market objectives are not usually related to costs.
- Costings between products are highly dependent on the way costs are allocated.

The strategy adopted should also, clearly, be appropriate to an organization's marketing objectives, be they in terms of market share, defending markets, establishing a position, managing relationships, stabilizing a market, expanding a market, or whatever. Within strategies, there is also the opportunity to decide whether an organization will operate fixed prices with no discounts, or whether they will adopt a more flexible approach. As a general rule, however, no matter what strategy is adopted, in a buoyant market with rising or excess demand, a business should always seek to raise prices, since it will find it hard, or even impossible, when times are not so good.

32 Setting a Price

Specific pricing decisions should always be made in the context of the pricing strategy an organization has opted to follow. These can vary from a skimming or penetration approach to being the cheapest in the market, or simply following the lead of a major player. Costs are also used as a basis for pricing, although care must be taken not to ignore market conditions. In the end, however, income must always exceed total costs.

As well as strategy, there are a number of situational factors that will also influence the exact price chosen. Thus, when a pricing decision is required, an organization's pricing strategy will provide the main approach to be adopted, but situational variables will determine the actual price paid.

Occasions requiring price decision

The most obvious occasion demanding a pricing decision is when a business sets a price for the **first time**. This can occur when a business launches a product which is new to them *and* the market, or is just new to them; or when they move an existing product into a new market. In some of these situations, a price structure will already exist, and the organization's strategy will determine approximately where it will be positioned relative to competitor products on the price continuum (see Figure 32.1).

Figure 32.1 The price continuum

Pricing decisions should always be made in the context of pricing strategy

In situations where a product is completely new to a market, pricing becomes more difficult, although still driven by the organization's strategy. Here it is sometimes possible to benchmark against similar but non-competing products. Alternatively, it may be possible to establish how target customers evaluate a potential purchase (payback, return on investment, upfront price, lifecycle cost, etc.) or how they perceive value (reliability, availability, brand, security, gaining competitive advantage, associated attitudes, social prestige, etc.). In the absence of these, it may be justifiable to use costs as an indicator for price, in which case it should be acknowledged that improvements to the quality of the organization's marketing are probably required!

Costs, however, *are* a significant issue, when they change. When **costs increase**, it is wise to attempt to maintain margins if the increase is likely to be permanent. This may simply require marginal changes to price lists. In more sensitive markets, it may be necessary to find ways of adding value to justify a price rise. Where costs are likely to be volatile, as is often the case for commodity raw materials or where prices are sensitive to exchange rates, it can be wise to use hedging arrangements, although these can be expensive. Whatever the cause, there is still a decision as to how margins can be maintained without alienating customers. If, on the other hand, **costs drop**, there is an awkward choice to be made between appearing to be exploitative, using the extra profits for investment and using the price flexibility which has become available for competitive advantage.

A price decision will also have to be made when **competitors initiate a price change**. If the initiator is a 'benchmark' competitor, then the response will be fairly straightforward. This will be particularly true for price followers who have adopted a set position in relation to certain key market players. If the initiator has traditionally occupied the role of a follower, then an assessment needs to be made as to their power to make the price change stick and the reasoning behind the move. Should it be felt, for example, that the competitor is trying to grab market-share or penetrate new markets, a defensive response is required.

For organizations operating at either end of the price continuum, a similar judgement has to be made (i.e. do they need to respond or can the move be ignored?). Crucial to this will be an understanding of the segment in which the competitor is operating, the likely response of customers and the relationship between the competitor and the responding organization in the minds of the customer.

The most difficult situation is when a **customer asks for a price reduction**. This may occur during regular negotiations or as a request for a discount from normal prices. Here, it is useful to establish reference points against which to negotiate, such as well-known competitors' prices and the benefits of the product under discussion. It is also useful to establish what motivated the request, since this could help to formulate a response other than a cut in price. This may be more difficult if the relationship with the customer is distant or 'transaction-based'.

If such a situation leads to price negotiations, it is important for the supplier to look for trade-offs which could be made in exchange for price cuts, but which would save the supplier money or gain them advantage. These could include prompt payment, higher volumes, less frequent deliveries, joint promotions, taking a broader mix of products, and so on. This, however, does require a good understanding of operational costs on the part of the supplier to avoid reduced profitability.

Price presentation

When quoting a price to a customer, it must also be remembered that a price is not just an isolated figure, but can be presented in a number of different ways that will make it more or less acceptable. Some prices can be made to look more acceptable if they are 'unbundled' and broken down into component parts. This can include separated delivery charges, packaging requirements, service costs, warranties, upgrades, and so on. The more complex the product, the more scope there is for this type of approach. Some customers, however, may be more interested in the total cost for budgeting or comparison purposes.

Prices can also be made acceptable by providing comparisons with products which are outside a particular customer's price band. If a customer felt, for instance, that the absolute top acceptable price for a suit of clothing was £350 and a supplier was trying to sell one at £375, the supplier might help his case by referring to £750 high-brand suits which the customer would never purchase, but which would make £375 seem a fair price.

In some businesses, it is often worth deliberately presenting a range of models which fall into basic, standard and deluxe categories, in order to enhance the value of the standard model. This offers the potential to migrate deluxe features into the standard model to enhance value over time. Where a product has a tendency to move towards commodity status as customers become more familiar with it, or as a market matures, this can be a useful tactic.

Psychological elements can also be used to enhance the acceptability of a price. This can involve the use of 'attractive numbers' (although what is attractive will vary between different cultural environments) or pricing in relation to certain 'break points' in the market. The existence of such points helps explain the use of £X.99 prices and the significance of keeping below certain price thresholds in a market. Again, such thresholds will vary from market to market.

Price can be presented to customers in different ways to enhance acceptability

Transaction price management

Studies of prices which have compared invoice pricing with the prices customers actually pay have noted that there are often a number of 'off-invoice' concessions which have the effect of reducing the profitability of a customer. These can include:

- Prompt payment discounts.
- Promotional allowances.
- Retrospective volume discounts.
- Free delivery for orders over certain values.
- Sales promotion campaigns.
- Unofficial extended credit.

Since most customer profit calculations are based on invoices, organizations can easily overestimate the profitability of individual customers. The difference between invoice price and the price effectively paid has been shown to be as much as 29 per cent in some cases.

Advantage can be gained by monitoring such income 'leakages' and targeting those customers who incur fewer 'off-invoice' price discounts. It is sometimes possible to move particular elements of 'off-invoice' reductions on to the invoice to demonstrate to customers the real value of their purchase for comparison purposes. In addition, different customers will be sensitive to different elements of 'off-invoice' costs. As an example, one distributor or retailer may be more attracted to promotional discounts than credit allowances. In this case, it may be possible to engineer prices to achieve better results for the supplier by focusing on appropriate elements for specific tactical ends.

For all organizations, what is important is the price the customer ends up paying. However, setting a price, obtaining sales in the right volumes, and collecting the income is not a simple matter. What is important is consistency, which should be driven by adherence to a pricing strategy and which sets the context for a pricing decision. Situations, however, will vary from one customer to another, from one market to another and from one time period to another. Such situational variables will determine which tactics are appropriate and how an organization should respond to the specific circumstances it faces.

Topic
33 Sales Promotion

The term *advertising* (often referred to as 'above-the-line expenditure') can be defined as all non-personal communication in measured media by an identifiable sponsor. This includes television, cinema, radio, print, and outdoor media. Sales promotion, for which the term 'below-the-line expenditure' is often used, is not so easily defined. For example, Americans use the term to describe all forms of communication, including advertising and personal selling. In Europe, some use the term to describe any non-face-to-face activity concerned with the promotion of sales; some use it to describe any non-media expenditure; whilst others use it specifically to mean in-store merchandising. Managers concerned with sales promotions must, therefore, be clear about the nature and scope of such activities and how they can best contribute to the organization's marketing goals.

Nature and scope of sales promotion activities

In practice, sales promotion is a specific activity which can be described as the making of a featured offer to defined customers within a specific time limit. In other words, to qualify as a sales promotion, someone must be offered something which is featured, rather than just being an everyday aspect of trade. Furthermore, the offer must include benefits not inherent in the product or service, as opposed to the intangible benefits offered in advertising, such as adding value through appeals to imagery. As such, it is an important tool to support positioning within the various markets an organization wishes to address.

Seen this way, every other element of the marketing mix, including advertising, personal selling, point-of-sale material, pricing, after-sales service, and so on, can be used as part of a structured sales promotion campaign. Thus sales promotion is essentially a problem-solving activity designed to enhance market position and/or to get customers to behave more in line with the economic interests of the company. Typical objectives for sales promotion include:

- Establishing or reinforcing market positioning.
- Aligning demand and operational capacity.
- Clearing slow-moving stock.
- Counteracting competitive activity.
- Encouraging repeat purchase.

Sales promotion is the making of a featured offer to defined customers within a specific time period

- Securing marginal buyers.
- Getting bills paid on time.
- Inducing trial purchase.

From this, it will be seen that sales promotion is not just concerned with volume increases but can have both strategic and tactical outcomes. Thus, promotions can be used to assist production and distribution scheduling by persuading customers to bring forward their peak-buying from one period to another, or simply as a means of clearing outdated stock. In this way, sales promotion can seek to influence many different audiences in a number of different ways:

Salespeople	to sell	
Customers	to buy	
Customers	to sell	{ more, earlier, faster, etc. }
Users	to buy	
Users	to use	

The many and varied types of sales promotions are listed in Table 33.1. Each of these different types is appropriate for different circumstances and each has advantages and disadvantages. A typical example would be a free item for a multiple purchase which would:

- Allow extra costs and volumes to be easily measured.
- Be fast and flexible.
- Be attractive to profit-conscious customers.
- Last as long as required.
- Be easy to set up, administer and sell.

On the other hand:

- Positioning may be adversely affected.
- It has no cumulative value to the customer.
- It is unimaginative.
- It can often be seen as a prelude to a permanent price reduction.

Amongst the alternatives available, points schemes in their various forms became increasingly popular in the 1990s. Their advantages to the sponsoring organization include: their wide appeal; the absence of any need to hold stocks of gifts; the difficulty faced by customers who try to cross-value gifts; and their ease of administration. On the other hand, they offer no advantages in bulk-buying, are difficult to budget, and lack the immediacy of dealer-loaders. Great care is necessary, therefore, in selecting a scheme appropriate to the objective sought.

In recent years, sales promotion activity has increased to such an extent that it can now exceed expenditure as above-the-line advertising. In spite of this, sales

Table 33.1 Types of sales promotions

Target market	Price promotions		Product promotions		Services promotions	
	Direct	Indirect	Direct	Indirect	Direct	Indirect
Consumer	Price reduction	Coupons Vouchers Money equivalent Competitions	Free goods Premium offers (e.g. 13 for 12) Free gifts Trade-in offers	Stamps Coupons Vouchers Money equivalent Competitions	Guarantees Group participation events Special exhibitions and displays	Cooperative advertising Stamps Coupons Vouchers for services Events admission Competitions
Trade	Dealer loaders Loyalty schemes Incentives Full-range buying	Extended credit Delayed invoicing Sale or return Coupons Vouchers Money equivalent	Free gifts Trial offers Trade-in offers	Coupons Vouchers Money equivalent Competitions	Guarantees Group participation events Free services Risk reduction schemes Training Special exhibitions and displays Reciprocal trading schemes	Stamps Coupons Vouchers for services Competitions
Sales force	Bonus Commission	Coupons Vouchers Points system Money equivalent Competitions	Free gifts	Coupons Vouchers Points system Money equivalent Competitions	Free services Group participation events	Coupons Vouchers Points systems for services Events admission Competitions

promotion will only ever support other positioning activities such as advertising, packaging, pricing and public relations.

Sales promotion strategy and tactics

Unfortunately, the tactical nature of many sales-promotion activities means that they often amount to little more than a series of spasmodic gimmicks lacking in any coherence. This is very different from approaches to positioning, which usually conform to some overall strategy. This is particularly true of advertising, which has always been based on a philosophy of building long-term brand franchises in a consistent manner. In contrast, the basic rationale of sales promotion is usually to help the company pursue a tactical initiative. In fact, there is no reason why there should not be a strategy for sales promotion, so that each promotion consolidates the desired product positioning as well as achieving short-term tactical needs. In this way, tactical objectives can be linked in with some overall positioning plan so that resources can be used more effectively.

One difficulty in using sales promotions strategically is in locating sales promotion expenditure, let alone evaluating it. Some companies include the expenditure with advertising, others as part of salesforce cost; some as a general marketing expense, others as a manufacturing expense (as in the case of extra product, special labels, or promotional packaging), whilst the loss of revenue from special price reductions is often not recorded at all.

Such failures can be extremely damaging, especially since sales promotion can be such an important part of marketing strategy. Indeed, with increasing global competition, troubled economic conditions, and growing pressures from distribution channels, the focused nature of sales promotion is turning into a more attractive, widespread and acceptable marketing tool. This highlights the need for organizations to set good objectives, to evaluate results after the event, and to have some organizational guidelines for their sales promotion campaigns. For example, a £1 case allowance on a product with a contribution rate of £3 per case has to increase sales by 50 per cent just to maintain the same level of contribution. Failure at least to realise this, or to set alternative objectives for the promotion, can easily result in loss of control and a consequent reduction in profits.

Managing an organization's sales promotion expenditure effectively thus requires objectives to be established for each individual sales promotion in the same way that objectives are developed for advertising, pricing, or distribution activities. The objectives for each promotion should be clearly stated in terms such as product appropriate display positioning, image enhancement or competitor positioning at the level of strategy; or trial, repeat purchase, increased distribution, a shift in buying peaks, and so on, at the tactical level. Thereafter, the following process should apply:

- Select the appropriate technique.
- Pre-test.
- Mount the promotion.
- Evaluate in depth.

The in-depth evaluation requires attitudes or product perceptions, both before and after a promotional campaign, to be analysed and spending to be categorized by type of activity (e.g. special packaging, special point-of-sale material, loss of revenue through price reductions, and so on). It is important, however, that the activities planned are compatible with, and complement, other activities within an organization's positioning and promotional activities.

Sales promotion activity is easily undermined by lack of strategy

34 Advertising

Advertising is one of the four major communications and promotions activities in which organizations can engage. Of the four, advertising is probably the most glamorous, although the others (sales promotions, public relations, and personal selling) are nonetheless potent promotional tools. A definition that differentiates advertising from other methods of communication is:

> *Any paid form of non-personal presentation in a measured media by an identifiable sponsor.*

Advertising is also, probably, the most powerful aid to positioning, certainly from within the promotional mix.

Even though there are many relatively cheap forms of advertising, such as small advertisements in local newspapers, any 'serious' advertising campaign is usually an expensive undertaking. This is particularly true for major consumer goods and service companies for whom branding is a key contributor to competitive advantage, although advertising is also important for industrial suppliers, government agencies and other non-profit organizations.

For commercial organizations that see advertising as an important aspect of their promotional activities, expenditures of 5 per cent up to 30 per cent of sales are not unusual. The potential cost and contribution of advertising requires marketing managers to make careful media choices, to understand what advertising can realistically achieve, and to know how to make advertising effective.

Advertising media

The medium traditionally associated with advertising is television. It is the communications channel to which more people are exposed than any other, although, in absolute terms, more money is generally spent on newspaper advertising. More recently, television has been overtaken by the Internet as the media of choice. However, television still arouses more excitement in marketing executives because of its lifestyle, creative and entertainment associations. Other media include:

- Mobile communications devices.
- Magazines.

- Radio.
- Outdoor displays.
- Direct mail (paper and electronic).
- Novelties (airships, hot-air balloons, T-shirts).
- Catalogues.
- Directories.
- Circulars.

Marketing communications managers consequently face a wide range of media choices when putting together an advertising campaign. Their decision should depend upon whom they wish to reach, the product they are promoting, the type of message being sent and the cost-effectiveness of the alternatives. An organization's target audience might, for example, be difficult to identify, may not spend much time reading newspapers or magazines, and may respond better to light-hearted messages. In this case, television or radio might be required to reach them. A special interest group such as joggers or accountants, who take their interest seriously, might be better reached via targeted magazines.

The media chosen should also be able to support the positioning desired for a product, and this again will vary between media. A complicated positioning will require magazines or mailings if it is to be communicated effectively, whilst simple positioning statements such as Nike's 'just do it' can be successfully advertised over television and radio or in daily newspapers and on hoardings.

Whichever medium is chosen, the important financial consideration is the cost per thousand exposures, preferably to the organization's target market, and the impact the advertisement will have. Often, a combination of media is required to overcome the limitations each might have, such as: clutter; fleetingness of exposure; wasted exposures; and the positioning impact which might be implied by the choice of media. Some organizations, for instance, might not want their exclusively positioned Spa to be associated with mass media television advertisements or 'junk mail'.

Types of advertising objectives

There are three main types of advertising campaigns which an organization can adopt depending on the market situation it faces. The first of these is **informative advertising**, which is particularly important when trying to introduce new product forms or classes. The purpose of informative advertising is, normally, to build primary demand by educating a market or by encouraging the formation of attitudes. Such objectives may also be helpful for mature products to reduce false impressions held by consumers; suggest new applications for a product; make consumers aware of upgrades, improvements, new outlets, or special events; and so on. Whatever the case, the information selected for communication, plus the way in which it is communicated, will fundamentally support a product or organization's positioning.

A combination of advertising media is often required to overcome the limitations of each

Positioning is more usually supported by **persuasive advertising**. This is commonly observed in competitive markets where a technology or product form is already established and accepted. The objective will be to create selective demand by building preferences or promoting particular attributes or benefits to differentiate an organization. As part of this, advertisers can compare their offering with those of their competitors, although competitor denigrations and criticism can reflect badly on an advertiser. In addition to positioning and brand preference, persuasive advertising may be used to encourage immediate or early purchase, promote product enquiries or sales appointments, and stimulate a trial purchase or attendance at a demonstration. Of these, the majority of advertising used by, say, holiday time-share firms is of this final kind. Consumer goods suppliers tend to focus on encouraging a purchase whilst industrial organizations usually concentrate on enquiry generation.

The third form of advertising is based on **reminding** consumers of a brand's values or **reinforcing** positioning and other messages already implanted in people's minds. This is often evident in mature markets or where reassurance is an important aspect of post-purchase evaluation for the customer. Established brand names tend to be protected by their owners with this type of advertising. The brochures which come with expensive items are equally concerned with convincing purchasers that they have made the right choice as with persuading people to buy. Where products are subject to seasonal influences, reminder advertising is also important to prevent any loss of position between seasons.

Making advertising effective

Like any other form of communication, to be effective advertising must get people's attention, keep their interest, have a clear message and avoid distortion. In addition, advertisers must start with a good understanding of the effect they wish to achieve.

Although the obvious objective after positioning is the generation of sales, it is hard to link advertising directly with purchases. The main exception to this is direct response advertising, where it is easier to identify sales resulting from advertising campaigns. Objectives are, therefore, better couched in terms of positioning-related issues such as awareness, brand recall, comparisons, knowledge and attitudes.

Once the context of a campaign is established, effective advertising requires the development of a clear message which the advertisers wish to convey. This should be converted into a creative proposition which does not compromise the essentials of effective communications. Much time and effort is usually spent on this aspect to ensure the communicability of the message. Here style, time, language and presentation are important to match consumers' situations. In this, choice of media is also significant, since it will affect the possibility for distortion and the chances that the message will reach the right target group. Good advertising agencies are important contributors to decision-making in these areas. Organizational managers, however, need to be careful not to get too carried away by the artistic and creative sides of advertising at the expense of the original objectives.

Advertising, of course, should never be performed in isolation and requires market research to help define and evaluate its activities. Such research should be conducted both before and after any campaign to identify the directions it should take and the effect it has had. Too often, organizations concentrate on the creation and delivery of a campaign, and whether it obtained sufficient exposure, at the expense of trying to understand what needs to be achieved. Overall, though, there is no substitute for a well-developed advertising plan which follows a logical process of decision-making. The contents and structure of such a plan are illustrated in Table 34.1.

Table 34.1 Suggested pro-forma for an advertising plan

■ **General objectives**
  What are the overall objectives we wish to achieve?
  Should they focus on conveying information, developing attitudes, giving reasons for buying or what?
  What other promotional activities might be needed to support these objectives?
  Are these objectives consistent with activities in other areas of the marketing mix?
  Is it possible to achieve the objectives set through advertising alone? (If not they are not an appropriate objective for advertising.)

■ **Target audience**
  Who are they? How do we describe/identify them?
  What do they already know/feel about us/our competition?
  Where are they? What are their reading/viewing (etc.) habits?

■ **Response required**
  What response do we require from the target audience?
  What do we want them to feel/believe/know about our product?
  Is there anything we wish to avoid conveying?
  Are these responses incorporated in the *specific* objectives set for our advertising activities?

■ **Creative platform**
  How are the key messages translated into a communicable presentation?
  Is the creative platform clearly linked with our specific objectives?
  Does the presentation link clearly with the responses required?
  What evidence is there that the presentation is acceptable and appropriate to our audiences?

(Continued)

Effective advertising conveys a clear message via a creative proposition

Table 34.1   (*Continued*)

■ **Media platform**

What medium or combination of media are to be utilized for the campaign?

Why is this choice appropriate?

What criteria have been used to determine cost-effectiveness?

Do the media chosen match the 'quality' of our product?

■ **Timings**

When are our communications to be displayed/conveyed to our audience?

What is the pattern of activities to be?

Have we considered all the alternative patterns?

What is the reasoning behind the scheduling adopted?

How do the timings adopted coordinate with:

– promotions of the other products we sell?

– competitor promotional and other marketing activities?

– seasonal trends?

– special events in the market?

■ **Budget**

How much will the planned campaigns cost?

When is the money going to be required?

How is expenditure going to be monitored and controlled?

What is the cost justification for spending this amount?

■ **Measuring expected result**

How do we intend to measure the results?

Have we established any benchmarks required to establish change?

Are all objectives sufficiently quantified to be measurable?

What are our criteria for success/failure?

35 Public Relations

As the name suggests, 'public relations' is concerned with an organization's relationships with the various groups, or 'publics', that affect its ability to achieve its goals and objectives. The aspects of these relationships, which act as a focus for public relations, are the image and information a market holds about an organization, in other words, its **position** in the market. At a simple level, this is achieved through publicity in various print and broadcast media. However, the broader views being encouraged by moves towards **relationship marketing** require public relations activities to be more specific in their targeting and objectives. Public relations, therefore, is an important support for both positioning and relationship marketing.

Interest in public relations is also being stimulated by the reducing power and cost-effectiveness of mass-media advertising. As the volume of communications aimed at the public increases and media channels proliferate, public relations offers an alternative means of reaching the audiences which an organization would like to influence. A message received, for instance, via an editorial can be up to five times more influential than one received via an advertisement. Public relations, however, is unlikely to replace advertising or other means of communication and promotion. A more likely development is that it will increase its significance as an integral part of a communications or promotions mix.

Public relations communications tools

Public relations activities cover a number of different areas.

News generation

One of the most widely used is the generation of news. News is best structured around a story which can incorporate information about an organization or its products. Stories can be created around discoveries, achievements, personalities or changes. Often, surveys or projects are commissioned to provide 'objective' reports about topics of relevance to both the sponsoring organization's products and its position. Thus, toothpaste manufacturers might support dental health research or a financial services organization might investigate people's attitudes towards saving. News can also be used to make consumers aware of the existence of a

Public relations messages can be far more influential than advertising

product or service in order to stimulate enquiries from interested parties. It must also be remembered, however, that placing news where it will be accepted for publication is as important a skill as spotting and reporting newsworthy activities.

Events

Organizations can also gain people's attention through staging or sponsoring events. These can range from simple news conferences and seminars to exhibitions, competitive activities, anniversary dinners and stunts. All are likely to gain media coverage and draw attention to the sponsoring organization's name. They can also aid the achievement of credibility or establish images with which an organization would like to be associated. Events are also good opportunities to develop relationships with suppliers, opinion leaders and associates, as well as customers.

Publications

An organization's publications are another method of communication in which public relations will have an active interest. Sales support material is an obvious example, which can include brochures, manuals and presentations, usable by all personnel who have contact with the outside world. Annual reports, other public interest communiqués and special publications such as cookery books and children's stories also provide vehicles for influencing both customers and those who can affect customers' perceptions. Internal audiences and significant stakeholders are often addressed by organizational newsletters and magazines.

Support for good causes

Organizational support for good causes is another means of promoting an image and associating an organization with a certain set of values. This can include charity donations in return for product coupons, the sponsorship of public service activities such as festivals, and individual executives' support for local community interests such as educational establishments, hospitals or crime prevention. All these provide many opportunities for publicity elsewhere.

Expert opinion

Individuals within an organization can also act as sources of expert opinion for journalists, public enquiries or other forms of research and investigation. Public relations managers may seek to promote the expertise in their organization through the dissemination of contact lists and by grooming individuals' interviewing and presentational skills.

Visual identity

Organizations also often seek to establish a visual identity through either conformity of design or logos. While design can make it easier for customers to recognize an organization's products when they come across one, logos and other identification marks can be more important for internal markets as a means of signifying change or commonality of purpose.

Scope of public relations

Public relations can provide a powerful support for an organization's positioning objectives. As examples, **events** can be used to reinforce brand values, or **publications** can help to draw the public's attention to features such as the stability or innovative nature of an organization. Less directly, but still importantly, public relations can be used to establish credibility for either an organization or its technologies, on the back of which a position can be established. Similarly, public relations may be used to build awareness of new products, new processes or other changes which will enhance an organization's ability to serve its customers. Public relations can thus prepare the way for more direct positioning activities such as sales force campaigns; advertising; pricing mechanisms; and packaging.

Developing **relationships** with both customers and other markets can also benefit from public relations activities. At one level, good relationships involve sharing information, and public relations tools such as sales-support materials, specialist publications and research results are useful vehicles here. At another level, relationships should involve demonstrations of commitment and, again, public relations can provide support. This can be through inviting individuals from targeted markets, be they customer markets, influencer markets, referral markets or third party intermediaries, to events. Alternatively this could be achieved by acknowledging their activities with awards, mentions in press releases or by referrals of media enquiries to them. These can be further supported by sales force and sales promotions activities.

An additional role for public relations is in dealing with special problems or disasters and **limiting the damage** such events can have on an organization. In this respect, the tobacco industry maintains a vigilant public relations campaign to limit the effects of adverse health publicity and government restrictions on advertising. An alternative example is provided by Perrier when it became known that some of their product had become contaminated with poisonous chemicals. To limit the potential damage to their brand names, they immediately embarked on a widespread public relations campaign to show that this was an isolated event and that the public were in no danger. Coca-Cola, however, were not so lucky when they launched Dosani (bottled purified water) in the UK in 2004. First, they just survived the revelation that it was simply tap water, filtered with some additives with some good defensive PR ('it goes through a sophisticated high-tech filter system'). However, the death knell came a few weeks later when it was revealed that a batch of minerals had contaminated the water with a potentially carcinogenic bromate, which no amount of PR could overcome.

Public relations are a powerful support to positioning

Public relations, then, can be a significant aspect of an organization's promotional mix and can be very influential in shaping attitudes and opinions. Relatively speaking, it is also a cheap means of gaining publicity and access to media channels. As an example, the value to Fuji of advertising on a modern airship was not the direct effect on the people it flew over, but the television coverage it gained from the novelty of the presentation. On a lesser scale, public relations are also very useful for smaller organizations with limited promotional budgets, although the exact results of public relations spending are always hard to quantify.

Topic
36 Sponsorship

Sponsorship has been a popular means of supporting a product or organization's position in its chosen markets since the 1980s. The impetus to seek a wider variety of communication channels to promote a name or product derived mostly from the growing cost of media advertising. In addition, sponsoring the right kind of person or activity often gave global coverage that would have been difficult to achieve elsewhere, and sponsorship also offered tobacco companies exposure that was increasingly difficult to achieve as they were banned from TV advertising.

Sponsorship can be defined as any commercial agreement by which a sponsor, for the mutual benefit of the sponsor and sponsored party, contractually provides financing or other support in order to establish an association between the sponsor's image, brands or products and a sponsorship property in return for rights to promote this association and/or for the granting of certain agreed direct or indirect benefits.

Types of sponsorship

In general, sponsorship falls into four distinct property types, as shown in Figure 36.1: sport (83%), social (5%), arts and culture (7%) and media (5%).

Figure 36.1 Sponsorship types

Sponsorship can get media exposure that is hard to achieve by other means

Examples of sponsorship activities include:

- The Arts – Unilever and the Tate Modern.
- Social and community – Tesco's 'Race for Life'.
- Educational – BT and information technology in schools.
- Entertainment – T in the Park.
- Broadcast – Nokia and *X-Factor* (ITV1).
- Sports – Emirates and Arsenal FC.
- Personality – Accenture and Tiger Woods.

Sponsorship can be on a local, regional, national, international, and global level, ranging from as little as under £100 to over £1 billion and more. Thus, in 2002, Mastercard spent £20–30 million as official sponsor of the football World Cup, and several million pounds are required to sponsor a high-profile football team for a year.

Growth of sponsorship

As the 21st century unfolds, sponsorship continues to be one of the fastest developing areas of marketing practice in the world today. The global sponsorship market is currently worth over £17 billion, and in the UK is set to grow to over £2 billion, largely because of the sponsorship activities around the London 2012 Olympic Games.

For many organizations, sponsorship has established itself as an essential part of the marketing mix as a result of its perceived ability to make a difference, not only to brand awareness but also, more significantly, to a sponsor's 'bottom line'.

Objectives of sponsorship

To use sponsorship well, organizations have to be clear about the outcomes they desire. Simply requiring a better 'bottom line' is inappropriate since there are few occasions where increased business or acceptance of a price increase can be directly traced to sponsorship. More realistic and potentially more measurable objectives include:

- Competitive advantage from association or exclusivity.
- Alteration or reinforcement of public perception of the sponsor.
- Associating a business with particular market segments.
- Involving the company's employees in the community.
- Generating positive media coverage.
- Building goodwill among decision makers.

Figure 36.2   Sponsorship management cycle

Sponsorship processes

Like all positioning support activities, sponsorship needs to be carefully planned and managed, as illustrated in Figure 36.2.

Phase 1: Existing activity review

The existing activity review should include all positioning support activities and how sponsorship can both complement and enhance them. It is important that any sponsorship programme is consistent with the creative aspects used in other communications and that timings of activities can be coordinated. If, for example, sponsorship is for a high-profile event, other communication activities need to support the build-up to the event, and then consolidate the position as the event fades from the public's mind.

Getting the right balance of activities is particularly important if sponsorship is to be used to support brand positioning where consistency of brand values is paramount. Sponsoring a poor performing Formula One racing team, for instance, may not enhance the brand value as much as desired. Similarly, to ensure return on investment, sponsoring a televised event must take into consideration the expected audience profiles and viewing figures to be worthwhile.

Phase 2: Policy and strategy development

A sponsorship strategy needs to be focused on the positioning objectives being pursued. The core decision is what or who should be sponsored, followed by plans for leveraging the association to the maximum cost-effective extent. In the early 2000s, Vodaphone's sponsorship portfolio included Manchester United, the Australian Rugby Union team and Ferrari. The intended association was excellence

Sponsorship must enhance the sponsor's market positioning

on a global scale and much effort was put into gaining as many spin-off benefits as possible.

Any sponsorship policy and strategy should include:

- Measurable objectives (as far as possible).
- Audience segmentation (including employees).
- Brand essence or image being supported.
- Fit with desired positioning.
- Time-scales and timings.
- Geographical requirements.
- Integration with other communications channels (spin-off opportunities).
- Desired impact on behaviour of audiences.
- Contingency plans if things change.

The key issue is to ensure a good business case for any sponsorship to avoid serving personal preferences rather than positioning objectives.

Phase 3: Negotiation

The objective of the negotiation phase is usually:

- An extension of a sponsorship programme.
- An extension subject to certain amendments.
- A new sponsorship agreement.
- Termination of the old relationship.

Sponsorship negotiations vary depending on the respective bargaining strengths of the parties involved, as well as the nature of the property involved. Whatever the case, however, it is important to ensure satisfactory legal arrangements, that the costs of sponsorship match the value of the intended returns, and that there is sufficient exclusivity.

Phase 4: Activation of the sponsorship programme

Negotiation of the right to associate with a sponsored property is, however, only the first step in a sponsorship programme. Coca-Cola in the US, for instance, spends upwards of four times the sponsorship rights fee in its activation of its FIFA football World Cup and Olympic Games properties. Activation activities based on Nike's sponsorship of US top basketball player Michael Jordon might include:

- Advertising (Michael Jordon wears Nike).
- New media promotions (Nike/Michael Jordon websites).
- Hospitality (Come and join us at a Michael Jordon basketball match).
- Licensing (Special Michael Jordon Nike shoes).

- Public relations (Michael Jordon visits Nike factory in Indonesia).
- Promotions (Free entry into a 'Dinner with Michael Jordon' competition with every Nike product purchase).

Phase 5: Return on investment (ROI)

Establishing an overall ROI for a sponsorship programme can be tricky since it will be hard to link sales directly with sponsorship expenditure given the more powerful impact of other marketing activities. However, if measurable objectives have been set as part of the strategy and activation processes, it is possible to ensure the expected returns in other areas are achieved. These could include:

- Expected media exposure and audience figures.
- Increases in awareness, image, affinity etc.
- Levels of association.
- Attendance at sponsored events.

Phase 6: Review

Following measurements of the ROI of a programme, all experiences need to be evaluated and any lessons to be learnt established. These might include seeking answers to questions such as: 'Did we sponsor too many events?' and 'How did competitors respond to our sponsorships?' Sponsors may decide to withdraw sponsorship of, say, a football team if too many of its players get embroiled in violent conduct. Similarly, a retailer might withdraw from sponsorship of equipment for schools if its competitors find a better way of offering the sponsorship. In the UK in the early 2000s, supermarket giants Tesco and Sainsbury competed by offering vouchers with purchases that could be exchanged for computers and sports equipment respectively by schools. Which will lose momentum first remains to be seen.

Establishing the ROI for a sponsorship programme can be tricky

Part 7
Marketing Relationships

37 Relationship Marketing

The concept of relationship marketing has evolved as a consequence of some of the limitations of traditional approaches to marketing. The most important relationships for marketing purposes are those between the supplying organization and its customers. The focus of these relationships is the activities involved in delivering the marketing mix. Although the four Ps are probably the most universally accepted method for structuring the marketing mix, the idea of a four Ps mix, and customers being the only markets requiring attention, has been questioned. This has led to the propositions contained within the relationship marketing approach.

An expanded marketing mix

The four Ps of product, price, promotion and place constitute the 'offer' which an organization presents to the market place. If the offer is sufficiently well-matched to customers' needs, it should lead to sales. In addition, if it is sufficiently well-managed, these sales should be profitable to the organization. The potential downside to this is that an organization's attention becomes too focused on a 'profitable sale', leading to a *transaction* approach to marketing (see Table 37.1). The danger is that interactions based on transactions can ignore other aspects of supplier/buyer relationships that can provide something of greater substance for longer-term marketing success. The manifestation of this is the development of customer loyalty and commitment which will survive the attempts of competitors to lure away customers.

Table 37.1 Tendencies inherent in a transaction approach to marketing

- Priority is achieving a sale
- Focus on margins rather than profitability
- Meeting short-term sales targets overrides other priorities
- Product is 'pushed' at customer
- Limited commitment to customer
- Acceptance of unrealistic terms of sale
- Responsibility passed to customer at earliest opportunity

The need for such relationships as a means of retaining customers has, in reality, long been recognized. Fast-moving consumer goods organizations have become

A transaction approach to marketing can be dangerously limiting

very sophisticated in developing brands which act as surrogates for personal relationships, and business-to-business selling has traditionally utilized both corporate image and sales teams to keep customers loyal. In general, however, growth and the winning of new customers have tended to attract the greater amount of managerial attention. The increasingly volatile competitive environment, however, has required this approach to change. From a marketing perspective, attitudes towards managing existing relationships have, therefore, had to adopt a higher profile.

The key attitude shifts involved are:

■ Recognition of the value of retaining customers *as well as* attracting new ones.
■ Acceptance that there are elements within the components of the marketing mix that, perhaps, have special significance in terms of managing relationships.
■ Acknowledgement of the influence that people and institutions outside of the customers can have in developing and maintaining relationships.

An examination of the offer presented to the market place in terms of its impact on customer relationships reveals certain elements that are probably worthy of being separated and treated as distinct elements of the marketing mix (see Figure 37.1). The first of these, **customer service**, is normally included as part of the 'P' of place and consists of the activities that support the placement of orders, the delivery of goods or services, either directly or via third party channels, and any post-purchase assistance required. Such support is obviously an important aspect

Figure 37.1 Expanded marketing mix

of an organization's relationships with customers and will help determine customers' experience of a purchase and product utilization. Indeed, in many service businesses, mature markets or markets where the products are technically complex, customer service is seen as a significant vehicle for competitive differentiation.

These factors help to argue the case for isolating customer service as a separate element of an organization's marketing plans.

The recognition that an organization's employees will have a significant impact on the way that customers and other interested parties perceive that organization means that **people** can also be regarded as an extra element of the marketing mix. Whenever a person is identified as a member of a particular establishment, he or she will perform an ambassadorial role, whether they like it or not. Similarly, people will be responsible for the majority of the variations in an organization's performance as experienced by the world outside. Since they will impact on all the other elements of the marketing mix, and since it is difficult to establish sustainable relationships with inanimate objects or intangible features, people become an important competitive aspect of the offer.

An additional element concerns the procedures, mechanisms and routines by which goods or services are created and delivered to the customer, that is, the **processes** which structure an organization's activities. The importance of these is that as a supplier unravels the various elements of its significant relationships the quality of these elements will be determined by the integrity of the processes involved. Where such processes impact on external audiences, be they customers or other parties, they will influence the viability of a relationship and the way in which it develops.

Employees often perform an ambassadorial role

The six markets model

Relationship marketing also recognizes that customer markets do not exist in isolation, but are members of a network of organizations and audiences for which marketing plans may need to develop. These have been termed:

- **Influencer** markets.
- **Referral** markets.
- **Supplier** markets.
- **Recruitment** markets.
- **Internal** markets.

This provides a *six markets* model, as shown in Figure 37.2. Customers, of course, remain the prime focus. The success of an organization in its customer markets, however, can be affected to quite a high degree by these 'other' markets and an organization's strength within them.

Figure 37.2   The relationship marketing six markets model

Influencer markets are important because customers are affected as much by independent third parties as they are by the direct activities of supplier organizations. These may be simple media channels, regulatory bodies that set standards, industry experts with influential opinions, or trade associations that shape practice. Influencer markets can therefore include: banks; government bodies; pressure groups; as well as media activities, all of which influence the perceptions of a supplier.

People who will refer potential customers to a supplier, such as existing customers or professional advisers, are also an important market. They are particularly significant for the generation of new business, but also for the reinforcement of existing relationships. They can include consultants, other professionals, intermediaries, suppliers, and so on.

Suppliers can also be a critical, separate, market for an organization, not just because they are a source of referral, but because their performance can help or hinder a business to fulfil its promises. Thus, many businesses are interested in better relations with their suppliers, particularly following the example set by the Japanese. In some quarters, this is described as 'reverse marketing'.

As well as capital and other physical resources, organizations need to recruit skilled people. The scarcity of skilled people is a consequence of the changing demographics in many developed nations, plus the increased specialization required for people to be able to work with many of the advanced technologies which are so important to organizational efficiency and effectiveness.

As skills become more specialized and less available, and as people themselves become a more significant element of the marketing mix, internal marketing must also be addressed both to retain scarce skills and optimize employees' interactions with external markets.

Traditional marketing is usually outwardly focused and has for too long ignored the people within the organization who have to turn a market promise into a reality. In this way, the concept of relationship marketing brings up to date the efforts of many organizations who have tried to take a broader view of the markets of which they are part and to develop a more sophisticated approach to profitable marketing.

Relationship marketing recognizes the value of internal as well as external marketing

Customer Retention Strategies

Much marketing attention is directed at developing strategies to expand sales through market share dominance; market penetration; finding new markets; and product range expansion. The main reason for concentrating on these is that size, revenue growth and dominance have been shown to be positively correlated with long-term survival and profitability. Recent work, however, has questioned the universality of these approaches, arguing that the cost of winning new customers is high and that, for many organizations, it will be more cost-effective to concentrate on retaining existing customers than attracting new ones.

For some industries, the increased profitability which can be gained from improved rates of customer retention is quite startling. Improvements of a few percentage points in customer retention yield large percentage increases in profits. The basis of this is the mathematical relationship between retention rates and the average life of a customer. Thus, a 90 per cent retention rate implies that 10 per cent of a business's customers are lost each year. In 10 years, the equivalent of all of its customers will have to have been recruited just to maintain the size of its customer base. The average life of a customer can thus be seen to be 10 years. If retention rates are increased to 95 per cent, the average life of a customer doubles to 20 years, since only 5 per cent will be lost each year. Where recruiting new customers costs significantly more than selling to existing customers (five times more in many cases), customer retention may prove a more profitable strategic objective.

Apart from the costs of recruitment, retained customers can also benefit supplier organizations in a number of other ways, although this assumes that such customers become loyal out of choice rather than through some device which 'locks them in'. Such benefits will be obtained because:

- Regular customers will tend to spend less time comparing prices with those of competitors and can become less price-sensitive, providing the opportunity for premium pricing.
- Voluntarily retained customers are more likely to be a source of positive referrals, which can provide a cost-effective source of new customers.
- Administrative procedures and other activities which affect the cost of a sale will be more routinized and, for the supplier as well as the customer, less expensive.

- There is a tendency for loyal customers to make a larger proportion of their purchases with a single supplier and thus boost turnover.

Before focusing on customer retention as a strategic objective, however, it is important for any particular business to understand the relevance of customer retention activities for their customer base. In some markets, customers value the ability to move between suppliers for similar purchases and would resent efforts on the part of suppliers to develop longer-term relationships. In others, many customers are unprofitable, or merely contribute to overheads, rather than adding to the 'bottom line', as is the case for many bank current accounts which are effectively dormant from one year to the next. In addition, the nature of some products means that the majority of sales are only ever going to be 'one-offs', or, at least, very infrequent purchases, as is the case for double-glazing, some large projects and time-share holiday accommodation. Under these circumstances, strategies designed to improve customer retention are likely to reduce customer satisfaction levels and have little impact on profitability.

Where it appears that customer retention is an appropriate strategy, the next step is to identify the type of customers the business wishes to retain. This will provide the focus for both customer recruitment and retention endeavours. In general, the 'right type' of customers will have a particular need in common, so that the costs of servicing these customers can benefit from economies of scale and the organization's positioning will not become too diffused. This essentially requires a benefit segmentation exercise, with the identification of associated needs and benefits enabling subsegments to be developed. Many such subsegments can be adequately managed via the advances being made in database marketing.

Other types of customer who will be a suitable focus for retention strategies include ones who like stable relationships, are reasonable in their demands of suppliers and who have the potential for long-term purchase or usage.

Customers not attracted to stable relationships, often referred to as 'promiscuous customers', will tend to be those who are very price-sensitive, who value change and variety, or who respond well to sales promotion initiatives. Predictions of 'promiscuity', however, do not tend to be very robust and characteristics such as income, sex and socio-economic class, cannot be easily used for this purpose and, indeed, will vary from one industry sector to another. What is true, however, is that loyalty is sometimes a 'default situation' caused by the inability of a customer to purchase elsewhere through legal restrictions, company policy, poverty, or awareness limitations, and who may well turn out to be 'promiscuous' under other circumstances.

The term 'reasonable customers' refers to those who do not cause a supplier to incur costs significantly beyond those associated with the provision of the product. Unreasonable customers would include those for whom the cost of sale was high,

The profitability gained from improved customer retention can be quite startling

who made excessive use of warranty or after-sales services, or who were late payers. Those with the potential to be 'long-term customers' would include customers who recognize that they have a long-term need, who can be easy to locate or keep in touch with and who are likely to experience or maintain an appropriate level of disposable income.

These characteristics highlight the importance of personal recommendations, which have been found to generate more of the better-quality customers than other sources of new customers. They also emphasize the need to target consumers with stable lifestyles or organizations which do not suffer wild fluctuations in their activities, who seem to be well-positioned for growth, or who are diversified enough to survive changing market circumstances. In this context, the value of identifying and developing campaigns for referral markets becomes apparent.

In addition to identifying potentially loyal and profitable customers, it is also important to understand the causes of customer defection, since these will underpin the development of any strategies for retention. Essentially, there are only two causes of customers ceasing to purchase: their need ends, or the product-offering fails in some way or another.

Needs can end for a number of reasons, such as children growing up; retirement; death; bankruptcy; legislative changes; in-house provisions; and so on. Together, these will be either a move from one stage in a lifecycle to another, or changed circumstances.

A failure in a product-offering will be due to the product (including service products) failing to deliver the performances required, a failure in customer service or a competitor offering superior benefits in terms of product performance, service or value. Table 38.1 provides examples of industries with traditionally high defection rates. It is, therefore, very important for an organization to monitor defection patterns as clues to the causes both of customer satisfaction and dissatisfaction levels. These can be supplemented by the use of 'root cause analysis' to get to the heart of defections, rather than just accepting stated reasons, which are not always the real ones.

Table 38.1 Industries with traditionally high defection rates, where customer retention improvements can have a significant impact

- Personal, home and motor insurance
- Credit and charge cards
- Hotels
- Airlines
- Grocery retailing
- Travel and real estate agencies
- Courier services
- Management training and consultancy

Once the rationale and focus for customer retention has been identified, attention must then turn to the choice of strategic options. The main aim of such options will be to convert a potential or actual purchaser into a loyal, long-term customer. This is the process of converting the relationship from that of a simple transaction to something approaching a partnership, which is then maintained over time. The options available fall into three different categories: **validating** the customer's **choice** of supplier; **enhancing** the **value** of the exchange; or creating **interdependency**.

Validating choice means finding ways of reassuring a customer that they have chosen wisely and providing them with clear views as to why their decision was, and is, correct. This will reduce the likelihood of their considering alternative offerings and will enhance their ability to explain their choice to others. Verbalizing the reasons for using a supplier is, in itself, a powerful means of reinforcing personal opinions and beliefs, but does require a high degree of clarity. Validation can be achieved via:

- Influencer markets, such as the media, trade associations and intermediaries.
- Customer communications, such as advertising, PR and direct mail.
- Post-purchase service activities, including instruction manuals, product maintenance or emergency assistance.

Perceptions of *enhanced value* will result from building something extra into the overall product offer which will increase the utility the customer derives from its consumption. Value is provided in either tangible or intangible form. Tangible value can be:

- Monetary, such as loyalty discounts, or terminal bonuses.
- Gifts donated on a periodic or cumulative basis, such as air miles schemes.
- Christmas shopping deals.
- Some form of points collection activity.

Intangible value is more likely to be provided through customer service or database marketing, which makes purchase, use, or ownership of the product satisfying and/or ego-boosting.

Interdependency requires both the supplier and the purchaser to recognize that they rely on each other for either product or revenue. This can be achieved on the part of the supplier by:

- Acknowledging, both publicly and privately, the contribution a customer makes to their business.
- Seeking help from customers so that they become more involved in the organization's activities.

Strategic options fall into three categories

- Finding ways of demonstrating commitment to customers by 'bending rules', public pronouncements or extraordinary efforts to meet individual requests.

Focusing on interdependency is probably the issue closest to ideas of partnership, since any partnership should involve the sharing of risk, information and commitment.

As a final point, and as previously noted, it must be remembered that customer retention should not be taken to involve schemes which 'lock customers' into a supplier. While the idea has appeal in terms of reducing competition and enhancing supplier power, the long-term impact on customer perceptions can be dysfunctional. Locking mechanisms include: financial exit penalties; proprietary technology which is incompatible with other products; or just the sheer administrative problems involved in abandoning a supplier. One only has to think of the problems involved in transferring a house-purchase mortgage from one lender to another to understand the frustrations such barriers can cause.

Recent research has also indicated that an alternative way of approaching customer retention is to ensure product offerings match purchasers' values: values are deep-seated responses which categorize things as 'good' or 'bad', 'right' or 'wrong', and so on. When an offer or brand mirrors the values of a target market above and beyond a competitor product, loyalty is much easier to sustain.

39 Personal Selling

Personal selling is normally seen as part of the communications mix. This is because the key role of the sales person is to present and promote the organization's offer and to engage in two-way communications which negotiate the terms of a sale. However, in order to effect these presentations and negotiations satisfactorily, sales people have to develop and maintain good relationships with their customers, particularly if repeat purchases are part of the desired outcome. Personal selling is, therefore, also an important aspect of the relationship market approach to business management.

The majority of sales people operate in the field of industrial or trade marketing. However, personal selling is also a part of some areas of consumer marketing such as personal financial services or home improvements. Whatever the arena, the sales process is very similar and the tasks which the sales person has to undertake are effectively the same. For organizational customers, the main difference is that there is an added degree of complexity. This results from the greater number of people involved in the decision-making process, the more formalized procedures involved and the distinct steps which an organization tends to follow in the purchase decision.

For business-to-business selling, it is also important to distinguish between a new buy, a straight re-buy and a modified re-buy. The higher the degree of 'newness', the more people tend to be involved and the more involved the selling task becomes. If, in addition, the product is complex, the greater the range of roles the sales person has to play. The way such roles are performed is often critical in determining the strength of the relationship between buyer and seller. Under these circumstances, where there may need to be dealings with engineers, technologists and senior management, as well as financial personnel and purchasing officers, a team approach is often a suitable sales response. Thus sales people might have to become technical consultants; systems designers or integrators; cost accountants; administrative experts; or business strategists in order to deal satisfactorily with the whole range of customers' concerns that are likely to influence the purchase decisions.

The earlier a sales person can become involved in the decision-making process, the better he or she will be able to influence the outcome. This is particularly important given that commitment to a supplier usually grows through the successive stages of the buying process. The commitment of existing customers can also be strengthened if straight re-buy situations can be converted into modified re-buys as this is likely to enhance the involvement of the supplier with the customer and, therefore, the strength of the relationship.

The sales process

Prior to any selling encounter, sales people need to understand as much as possible about their **prospects**. Often, a great deal of effort is involved in such research, but can save much time in the long run if it means that sales people see the right people at the right time and can provide relevant information. The sales process, however, starts with **territory planning** and obtaining **interviews**. This is particularly important to ensure that the maximum time is spent selling as opposed to travelling, administration, wasted calls, and so on. In addition, a systematic approach to territory planning is needed to ensure that all customers receive enough regular visits to maintain good relationships.

Although some calls will be made 'on spec', the majority will be by appointment. Appointments between customers and sales people are usually arranged on the telephone. Thorough preparation is needed before the call to enable the sales person to decide who is to be spoken to, the objective for the call and the lever which is to be used to arouse the prospect's interest. It is not always easy to get through to prospects or, once connected, to persuade them to agree to an appointment. This is equally true for consumer sales calls.

Sales people will only succeed if they handle their **sales interviews** effectively. They must establish clear objectives for each call and have a plan of how they intend to achieve these objectives. A useful sequence to follow in any call is the '*ABC*' sequence. The sales person should gain the prospect's Attention (*A*), sell Benefits (*B*), and move to a Close (*C*). The sales offer also has to be pre-planned and the necessary facts, information and supporting sales-kit of literature, samples, data and other aids needed to achieve the interview objectives must be assembled.

Since customers buy products and services for what they will do for them, that is, the **benefits** of having those products or services, the sales person must focus on selling these benefits rather than the features. For the sales person, a simple formula to ensure this customer-orientated approach is adopted is always to use the phrase 'which means that' to link a feature to the benefit it brings. In this, sales people should seek to identify *standard benefits* (those benefits which arise directly from the features of what they offer), *company benefits* (benefits which are offered by the sales person's company) and *differential benefits* (those benefits which differentiate between the sales person's product or service and those of their competitors). A 'benefit analysis form' can be used to ensure a methodical analysis is conducted and proof should be given to substantiate every claim.

A buyer will almost invariably raise **objections** during a sales interview. An objection is a statement or question which puts an obstacle in the path leading towards closure of the sale. Buyers may raise fundamental objections when they cannot see a need for the product or service on offer. They may raise standard objections when they recognize their need but either wish to delay a decision, or need further convincing before concluding a deal.

When faced with a fundamental objection, the sales person has to sell the need for the product in question rather than the benefits entailed. There is a range of techniques for dealing with standard objections but if the buyer continues to raise objections without actually concluding the interview, there may be a hidden objection. It is often possible to discover what this is by asking an incomplete question, such as, 'and your other reason for not deciding is . . .?' Other objections, such as a price objection, can usually be overcome by talking in terms of value rather than cost.

The sale is **closed** when the buyer makes a firm commitment to place an order. The sales person should constantly look for opportunities to close the sale. The buyer will often show interest, make committing statements and ask questions; these are **buying signals** which the sales person should follow up by asking a question which confirms that they have correctly interpreted the buying signals.

Trial closes can be used throughout the sales offer to test the buyer's reactions, uncover objections, determine buyer interest and speed the sale. Trial closes also help the sales person to retain the initiative and accumulate small commitments from the buyer. The sales person may also use direct and indirect questions to obtain buyer commitment. It is sometimes possible to offer alternatives that lead the buyer into stating a preference which, once expressed, can pave the way to an immediate close. Other opportunities to close can be created by the summary technique, giving a quotation or by offering a concession.

The close, however, is not the end of the matter; it is just a step in a continuous process. Sales people must always remember that their objective is not only to close the sale, but also to open up a **lasting relationship** with the customer. In the final analysis, this is what makes a successful sales person.

Running a sales force, however, is an expensive form of communications and relationship building. The decision to use personal selling must, therefore, be carefully considered and will be based on the appropriateness of the advantages a sales force can provide (see Table 39.1). Clearly, in different markets different weightings will be given to the various forms of communication available. In industries with few customers, such as capital goods or specialized process materials, an in-depth understanding of customers is required and personal contact is of paramount importance. In contrast, many fast-moving industrial or consumer goods

Personal selling is a relatively expensive form of relationship building

are sold into fragmented markets for diverse uses. In these areas, other forms of communications are likely to be more cost-effective.

Table 39.1 The advantages of personal selling

- It is a two-way form of communication, giving the prospective purchaser the opportunity to ask questions of the sales person about the product or service.
- The sales message itself can be made more flexible and therefore can be more closely tailored to the needs of individual customers.
- The sales person can use in-depth product knowledge to relate their messages to the perceived needs of the buyers and to deal with objections as they arise.
- As a purchase is concluded, the sales person can move rapidly from persuasion to reinforcement and maintain appropriate relationships.
- Most important of all, the sales representatives can ask for an order and perhaps negotiate on price, delivery or special requirements.

Key Account Management: Understanding the Concept

The concept of key account management (KAM) has evolved as a natural development of greater customer focus and relationship marketing in business-to-business markets. The emphasis is on moving away from one-off, 'exploitative' transactions to longer-term synergistic relationships. The significance of this for business is that the development of a KAM relationship allows buyer/seller companies to come together and create value in the market place over and above that which either could create individually. The evolutionary nature of KAM makes it possible to identify five distinct stages in the relationship between selling and buying companies. Identifying which stage the company is at is helpful in preparing for the challenges ahead and their implications for company organization and staffing.

Developmental stages of KAM

As the nature of the relationship with the customer develops from being an 'anonymous buyer' to something approaching a 'business partner', the level of involvement with them becomes correspondingly more complex. This gives rise to some characteristic positions on the evolutionary path which are labelled Exploratory KAM, Basic KAM, Cooperative KAM, Interdependent KAM and Integrated KAM, as shown in Figure 40.1.

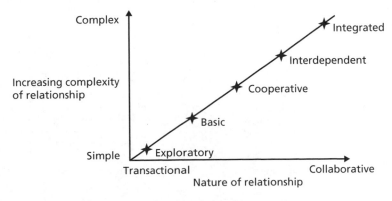

Figure 40.1 Evolutionary nature of KAM relationships

Key Account Management implies more complex relationships

Each stage is distinguished by the nature of the problems faced by the selling company and how it organizes itself in response. As with personal relationships, those between businesses can founder for a number of reasons. The market position and priorities of the buying or selling company may also change over time in a way which negates the strategic necessity for a close working relationship. The evolutionary stages provide an overview of what can happen if all mishaps are avoided, rather than any form of predictive model.

Exploratory KAM

This is a 'scanning and attraction' stage, where both seller and buyer are sending out signals and exchanging messages prior to the decision to get together. Both parties are interested in reducing costs. Commercial issues, such as product quality and organizational capability, are more important than establishing social bonds. Negotiation skills are paramount in the inevitable discussions that take place about price. It is unlikely that either party will disclose truly confidential information at this stage.

Here one of the greatest organizational problems is the ability of a key account manager to persuade the selling company to improve its production processes or to change its internal procedures in a way that makes them genuinely more customer focused.

Basic KAM

Transactions have begun and the supplier's emphasis shifts to identifying opportunities for account penetration. In turn, the buying company will still be market testing other suppliers for price as it seeks value for money. It is essential, therefore, that the selling company concentrates on the core product/service, including all the intangibles, in an attempt to tailor-make a customer-specific package.

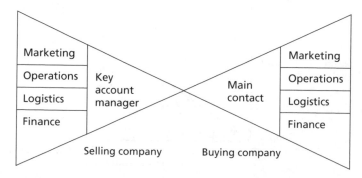

Figure 40.2   The basic KAM stage

Although there may still be a lack of trust, there has been a subtle change organizationally. The key account manager and the main contact in the supplier organization are closer to each other and their organizations are aligned behind them, as shown in Figure 40.2.

Cooperative KAM

By this stage trust will be developing and the selling company may have become a 'preferred' supplier. However, the buying company may still periodically test the market to check alternative sources of supply. With this increasing trust comes a greater willingness to share information about markets, short-term plans and schedules, internal operating systems, and so on. Staff in the selling company are likely to be involved in discussion with their counterparts in the buying company, forging links at all levels from the shop floor to the boardroom. There is often a social context, sometimes in the form of organized events such as golf days.

It is this network of interactions which brings a new strength to the relationship. With it comes the realization that customer service operates at many levels and should be driven by a desire not to let down personal contacts. The relationship is still fragile, however, because of the difficulties in making the transition to higher levels of trust and mutual regard. It is not a highly organized relationship and there are many things that can go badly wrong, particularly if there is high staff turnover. See Figure 40.3.

Figure 40.3 The cooperative KAM stage
Source: Cranfield University School of Management 1996

Interdependent KAM

When this stage is reached, the selling company is seen by the buying company as a strategic external resource. The two should be sharing sensitive information and

Even 'cooperative' key account relationships can be fragile

engaging in joint problem-solving. Each will allow the other to profit from their relationship and there is also a tacit understanding that expertise will be shared.

At this stage, the selling and buying companies are closely aligned and communicating at all levels, as shown in Figure 40.4.

The various functions in each partner communicate directly. The role of the key account manager and the main buyer contact is to 'oversee' the various interfaces and ensure that nothing occurs to discredit the partnership, rather than being the mainstays of the relationship.

The partnership agreement will have long-term profit margins, although there will usually be several categories of performance expectations reviewed and renewed on a regular basis. It will be in the 'spirit of partnership' for the selling company to meet all of these consistently and to the highest possible standards.

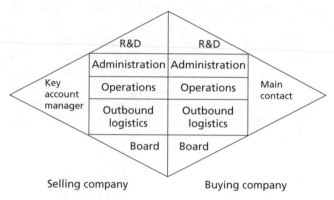

Figure 40.4 The interdependent KAM stage

Integrated KAM

If the seller/buyer relationship can extend beyond partnership so that in effect the two companies operate as an integrated whole, but maintain their separate identities, a more synergistic situation can be created, as shown in Figure 40.5.

The interfaces between the two organizations at all levels will function as focus teams in a way which is largely independent of the key account manager. These teams, made up of personnel from both companies, will generate creative ideas and overcome problems. These may be functional, issue based, project based, or perhaps serve a motivational purpose. Electronic data systems become integrated, information flows are streamlined, business plans are linked and the 'unthinkable' is explored.

About the only issue which remains sacrosanct for the selling company is likely to be its brand. Any requests from the buying company which could undermine this will probably be greeted with great suspicion.

Figure 40.5 The integrated KAM stage

Challenges for the future

Although transforming the tactics of repeat business into a strategic thrust sounds deceptively simple, the implementation of KAM has proved to be more problematic. Many organizations have tried the partnership approach whilst failing to recognize the demands that true partnership brings. There are obvious benefits to be had, but it is important to acknowledge that managing the transition from traditional selling to general accounts to KAM will not be easy.

Indeed, as shown in Table 40.1, there are a number of key questions that need to be addressed if the KAM approach is to provide a relevant model for organizations faced with the changing demands of continuously evolving markets.

Table 40.1 Key questions for the future of KAM

- How are organizations going to find or develop KAM executives with sufficient skills to build buyer/seller relationships?
- Is Integrated KAM the ultimate stage in the evolutionary development of KAM or will another form emerge?
- What is the best way to build key account teams?
- What are the particular problems for key account managers operating in complex supply chains or on a global basis?
- What are the organizational implications of global KAM?
- What kind of decision support systems are required for effective KAM?
- How should the differences between key accounts and non-key accounts be managed?
- At what level may the KAM relationship be seen as a barrier to competition and fair trade?

The brand should be sacrosanct

Key Account Management: Implementing the Concept

In order to implement KAM effectively, organizations need a clear understanding of the areas in which KAM differs from traditional account policies.

Difference between KAM and traditional selling to general accounts

Account management has long been recognized as an important sales function in business-to-business markets. However, general account management systems are notorious for being difficult to extend beyond a sales-based relationship. The tendency is for the performance of the account manager to be measured in terms of numbers of transactions and contract renewals. Negotiations are invariably focused on cost, product availability and quality issues. The aim of sellers is to keep their liabilities to a minimum whilst buyers are focused on value for money and are keen to keep options open. Under a general account management system, account turnover is accepted as a fact of life, new customers are constantly being sought and little differentiation is made between customers except, maybe, in terms of size or location.

Recasting these efforts as a KAM system recognizes that it may be more cost-effective for a supplier to focus resources on retaining existing profitable accounts rather than constantly signing up new customers. Further, it recognizes that not all customers have the potential to be long-term partners and that developing such relationships requires the allocation of disproportionate resources. The emphasis becomes one of tailored service rather than sales, and supply coordination rather than delivery. Accounts are considered whole entities instead of buying points and key account managers become responsible for the quality of the relationship as well as the negotiation of sales.

As an example of the flexibility required, DHL operates a global account policy that enables it to offer a strategic partnership to customers, with a global account team located either in the country that the customer prefers to deal with or based at DHL's headquarters.

Strategic marketing benefits of KAM

The first benefit of successfully developing a KAM system is that less profitable accounts are identified and managed accordingly, thereby consuming fewer resources. Similarly, if key accounts are identified and kept for longer, less effort is required to attract new customers, except for those with the potential to become longer-term customers.

Broadening the relationship so that it goes beyond sales negotiations will increase the amount of two-way communications between the seller and buyer organizations. As communications increase, then so do the chances of doing more business.

If customer satisfaction levels can be raised in this way, a virtuous circle can be created in which it becomes easier to sell to satisfied customers, as shown in Figure 41.1.

Organizations that use KAM systems to evolve accounts successfully into business partners also become more strategically secure. Their customers become less fickle and more willing to accommodate mistakes. Mutual problem-solving will reduce the costs of 'doing business' and resources can be devoted to creating value for customers further along the supply chain.

Figure 41.1   Customer satisfaction virtuous circle

In addition, buying companies will benefit by having their supplies safeguarded in terms of both quality and quantity, and are able to concentrate their resources on operations rather than procurement or supply management.

Skills required of a key account manager

Key account managers must be able to recognize how a relationship with a customer changes and how to respond positively to events in a way that enhances the relationship. This requires an ever-increasing repertoire of skills and knowledge as the scope of KAM widens and becomes more complex, particularly in global markets. Different skills are needed at each stage of the KAM relationship.

■ In the early stages, as the main point of contact for a buying company, key account managers must represent the selling organization in a way that makes it appear competent. In this, they must appear likeable, approachable and trustworthy while at the same time demonstrating sound selling skills and good product knowledge.

Key account managers require a repertoire of skills and knowledge

- As the relationship moves to interfaces at all levels, high-level business skills are required of key account managers, particularly since they have to act as a key facilitator between the different areas of the business. They will also need to develop an understanding of department or functional issues and how these might impact on the key account.
- Key account managers also require general management skills so that they are equipped to deal with any tensions that arise over differing organizational priorities. These can occur as a result of demands on staff who report to other functional managers as well as the key account manager, and the cross-functional nature of advanced KAM.
- Where key account managers have team responsibilities, they must keep all members fully briefed about operational and strategic issues that have a bearing on the KAM relationship. This requires high-level organizational and team skills.
- Key account managers also require strategic business skills to deal with a key account's specific problems or needs, particularly as they become more involved in all aspects of managing an account.

Organizational positioning

Organizationally, KAM must be positioned at the highest level as a result of its potential strategic impact and the authority that the key account manager requires in order to call in resources from across the organization. This positioning should reflect the significance of the role in bringing about and maintaining large tranches of long-term business. In order to be effective, KAM cannot be perceived within the organization as a simple re-titling of the existing sales group.

The authority and status of the key account manager can easily be undermined if the buying organization is allowed to gain the ear of somebody higher in the business. Thus, when dealing with key accounts, more senior managers and directors should be seen to defer to the account manager.

Such authority will help to overcome adversity within the selling organization during the early stages of the KAM relationship as other managers seek to fight proposed changes to the internal procedures needed to support the development of the relationship.

Implementation issues

For the effective implementation of KAM, organizations need to address all of the above areas and develop policies to accommodate them. In particular, it is important that specific measurements are put in place to measure its success. These might include: key account sales relative to general accounts; industry and own customer satisfaction systems; and executive feedback and development procedures.

Ignoring the differences between KAM and traditional selling to general accounts, the skills required, or the strategic organizational positioning of KAM, are likely to create difficulties in implementation. At the same time it is important that the entire organization appreciates the benefits that adopting KAM can bring to the long-term profitability of the business.

KAM's organizational positioning can make implementation difficult

42 Channel Strategy

A major concern for any producing organization is how they can best make their products available to the market place. The options available are many and the wrong choice can have significant consequences for an organization's success. In addition, once made, such choices tend to be long term, in that a distribution system takes time to build and make effective, and, once established, is not easily changed. The development of a strategy for the channels through which products will be placed on the market is, therefore, an important aspect of marketing.

Evaluating the use of intermediaries

The basic channel-strategy decision is whether to sell direct to users or whether to use some form of intermediary. The choice may be straightforward in that the costs incurred by selling direct may be just too high. Thus Volkswagen would have difficulty finding enough capital to fund a retail network for the sale of its cars in Germany, its home market, let alone the rest of Europe or the rest of the world. Similarly, the German consumer electronics company, Braun, would have to sell a large number of competitor manufacturers' products in addition to its own before it could consider owning retail outlets which would be of interest to shoppers and have sufficient turnover to cover the overheads of retail premises.

When the decision is not so clear-cut, the choice will depend on an evaluation of the advantages and disadvantages of using intermediaries. The main advantages include:

- Reduced **distribution costs** since an intermediary will be able to use the same transport and storage facilities for the output of a number of suppliers and spread the costs across a greater number of products.
- Better **access** to remote or fragmented markets, which would be too costly to service directly, or markets about which an intermediary has special knowledge and in which they can operate more efficiently.
- Reduced financial and physical problems associated with **stock holding**. If intermediaries pay for goods on receipt, rather than when sold, and operate warehouse facilities which match the particular requirements of local markets, original suppliers gain working capital benefits without having to invest in supply chain facilities.

- Improved **service response** can be achieved by intermediaries who are closer to customers geographically, or who possess better local knowledge of the needs of customers in their area.
- Enhanced **value** can be provided by intermediaries for customers via a number of different means. These may include one-stop shopping; systems integration; special packaging; or just simply breaking bulk and supplying in smaller quantities.

The disadvantages to a supplier of using intermediaries are smaller in number, but can have significant consequences. Since intermediaries tend to be independent organizations, there is an inevitable **loss of control** on the part of the supplier. Thus, there will be no guarantee that the products will be presented or positioned in the most appropriate way, or that intermediaries will actively sell one supplier's products rather than another. The other problem which can result from the use of intermediaries is a **loss of customer contact** and the information such contacts provide. Apart from the inconvenience involved in passing information to a supplier, intermediaries will often be keen to hold on to information for the power it can add to their side of the relationship.

The functions performed by intermediaries are not usually optional; they are all required in order that the final customer finds the overall offer worthwhile. Strategic decisions about channels are, therefore, concerned with who should perform these functions and where they should be located. The decisions will be based on efficiency in terms of who can best execute a function, plus the other marketing requirements of a supplier. Thus, apart from being more cost-effective, an intermediary should also complement the supplier's product range, pricing aspirations and service policies.

Channel and intermediary alternatives

There is a very wide range of channel intermediaries who will perform sales, distribution and service functions on behalf of a supplier. The exact number and appropriate forms will vary enormously between industries. However, the major types in existence are illustrated in Table 42.1.

Table 42.1 Major forms of intermediaries

■ Retailers in or out of town	■ Catalogue distributors
■ Wholesalers	■ Direct mail retailers
■ Distributors	■ Franchised outlets
■ Dealers	■ Freight forwarders
■ Agents	■ Merchandise clubs
■ Value added re-sellers	■ Party sales organizers
■ Original equipment manufacturers	■ Licensed manufacturers/service operators

The functions performed by intermediaries have to be performed by someone

Any particular intermediary may be a combination of two or more of the types listed in Table 42.1. In reality, for strategic purposes, form is irrelevant. More important are the costs they incur and the advantages they provide. In general, many organizations utilize a combination of intermediaries, and may even operate a direct sales activity as well, to match the different markets in which they desire a presence.

In addition to varying the types of intermediary, an organization will also include the number of intermediaries as part of their strategy. The first strategic option is to seek **intensive distribution** by stocking their products in as many outlets as possible. Thus, milk can be made available through doorstep delivery; supermarkets; convenience retailers; vending machines; garages; caterers; and, in some cases, directly from the farmer, to match consumer need and utilization. The second option is **selective distribution** which involves some, but not all, of the intermediaries who would be willing to supply a product. This can be a cheaper option and allows a producer to concentrate his or her efforts more effectively and thereby maintain greater control. Many financial services and products with a high brand value are marketed in this way. The third option is to offer **exclusive distribution** by limiting the number of intermediaries who handle a product. While this will reduce market coverage, it offers the supplier the possibility of greater control, better access to information, and can encourage intermediaries not to stock competing products or brands. New automobiles, plant and equipment, spare parts, major appliances and high brand apparel are often distributed in this way.

Developing a channel strategy thus requires an organization to make some long-term decisions about how to make its products available to end-user markets. The decisions are long term because each party will require commitment from the other and the creation of any arrangement will involve considerable investment of both time and money. This can include:

- Familiarization.
- Training.
- Establishment of routines.
- Even an investment in special tools, equipment or facilities.

The basis of the decision will be the trade-offs involved between control, cost and market objectives.

A supplier must also decide where to focus marketing efforts: on a **push strategy**, whereby attention is concentrated on the intermediary to 'sell-in' more products, or on a **pull strategy**, whereby the supplier emphasizes the creation of demand so that intermediaries are encouraged to deal in that product. The strategy might also involve the development of different channels over time. For example, a direct sales force can help an organization to prove that a market exists through obtaining early market penetration, but is then replaced by dealers to obtain intensive distribution as a market grows. This may be followed by a move to exclusive distribution to create brand value in a mature market. Whatever the case, the decisions involved are not easy, but can significantly influence success in the market.

Channel strategy involves long-term decisions

43 Channel Management

Having devised a channel strategy, a supplier organization has to develop appropriate relationships with its intermediaries to enable it to take good advantage of the opportunities it wishes to address. The major drawbacks to using intermediaries, rather than supplying direct, are the loss of control which intermediaries imply and the lack of access to direct feedback from user markets. Channel management must, therefore, seek to work with intermediaries so that they complement the suppliers' marketing objectives and minimize the problems of control and access to market information. Organizations can achieve this through attention to channel motivation, treating intermediaries as business partners and managing channel conflict.

Motivating intermediaries

Intermediaries' prime focus of attention is *their* customers, since it is they who provide them with their income. Apart from the usual marketing issues involved in attracting and retaining such customers, the nature of the job performed by intermediaries also highlights issues of stock turnover and margins. Stock turnover will be an important issue as a result of the working-capital implications of holding inventories. Margins are important since production costs are outside an intermediary's control, which means that profitability is very dependent on the bought-in price and margin management. In addition, intermediaries will tend to concentrate their efforts on the products which sell most easily.

Suppliers must work hard if they are to motivate intermediaries under these circumstances. The simple solution is to reduce prices or make the margin available to the intermediary more inviting. Efforts will also be required from suppliers to reduce the risk of stock-outs on the part of the intermediaries, which may result from their reluctance to hold large inventories. At the same time, suppliers must encourage intermediaries to promote *their* products rather than just wait for customers to turn up.

Possibly the most important aspect of motivating intermediaries is to remember that they are, themselves, a market and not just middlemen being paid to provide a service for the supplier. If the latter approach is adopted, the tendency will be for suppliers to seek the **compliance** of their channel members rather than any more substantial form of **cooperation**. This can lead to interactions based on transactions rather than a relationship built on mutual long-term needs. In transaction mode, motivation will tend to be 'deal-orientated' and focus on discounts, advertising allowances, merchandising arrangements, and sales incentives. While these tools are not, in themselves, inappropriate, they need to be used as part of a wider marketing approach if they are to provide longer-term cooperation and stability.

As a market, intermediaries' problems need to be solved in a way which encourages them to become 'advocates' for their suppliers. This requires an understanding of how value can be supplied, rather than looking at the problem as one of efficiency or a simple transfer of cost. Important areas of value to middlemen that go beyond the approaches implied by a deal-orientation include:

- Sales support materials.
- Market research about intermediaries' markets.
- Advance information about product development.
- Fast responses to technical queries.
- The creation of market pull.
- Rapid fault tracing.
- Product training.

Developing partnerships

An organization's relationships with its intermediaries are often better managed if they can be formed into **partnerships**. Under a partnership arrangement, intermediaries are more likely to see themselves as a meaningful part of their supplier's enterprise. The essence of this will be **agreement** between supplier and intermediary about the supplier's general market policies plus positive demonstrations of **commitment**. Agreement and commitment between supplier and middleman will reduce the need to exert control, since channel markets should now, voluntarily, implement supplier policies and increase the flow of information from end-users to suppliers. Having the incentive to collect it they should be more willing to pass it back.

One way of promoting agreement within channel partnerships is through the creation of distributor panels, in the same way that equipment suppliers might set up user groups. Two-way communications between people at different levels of each organization will also be a means of cementing relationships. At a deeper level, this might include cross-board membership, personnel exchanges and participation in the marketing planning process.

Commitment to creating a feeling of partnership can be demonstrated in a number of ways. One significant action is the referral of customer enquiries to the relevant intermediary. Others can be:

- Inclusion in public statements.
- Mentions in company newsletters.

Intermediaries form a market in themselves

- Invitations to trade entertainment events.
- Acknowledgement of achievements.
- Consultancy advice.
- Not opening competing outlets in their territory.

A significant demonstration is to devote a specific part of the supplier's marketing management structures to channel marketing to show that the relationships are important.

This is not to say that channel partnerships cannot be changed. As a product matures through its lifecycle in the market, different arrangements may be required to match different market developments. As a simple example, mass markets need to be addressed in a different way from niche markets, and products which are tending towards commodity status do not require the same level of dealer sophistication to be competitive. Similarly, as the competitive status of a product improves through, for instance, brand value development, different types of intermediary may be required to maintain product positioning. In the early 1990s in the UK, both Nissan and Mazda (Japanese car manufacturers) made significant changes to their franchised dealer network; the former to gain better control, the latter to upgrade the quality of their dealers in order to complement better the perceived quality and status of their newer models.

Channel Conflict

Since channel members are normally independent organizations there is always the potential for conflict, either between channel members themselves or between an intermediary and their supplier. Resolution of such conflict is important so that intermediaries will remain responsive to efforts to motivate them and a partnership relationship can be maintained.

The majority of the conflict between intermediaries and suppliers usually occurs because suppliers have not paid proper attention to, or are inconsistent about, their channel management policies. As an example, equipment manufacturers will naturally want distributors to offer high levels of service, local advertising and competitive prices. They will also want their products promoted, presented and displayed, to the disadvantage of their competitors. If intermediaries were to adopt such policies unconditionally, they would incur significant costs, but not necessarily fulfil their own profit objectives or provide the right type of service for their customers. As indicated above, suppliers need to take channel members' ambitions and problems into account before demanding gold-star service for knock-down prices from them.

Inconsistent channel management can also arise when suppliers make their products available through a number of competing intermediaries. In the more extreme cases, suppliers find themselves competing directly with their intermediaries, which can leave channel members feeling a little betrayed. During the 'shake-outs' in the world personal computer markets in the late 1980s and early 1990s, many manufacturers and volume wholesalers started bypassing their intermediaries in an effort to survive. It must be added that this was only necessary as a result of poor channel relationships and short-sighted channel management in the first place. More recently, many UK insurance companies now sell direct as well as through traditional insurance brokers to keep up with the trends started by Direct Line insurance.

Conflict between channel members, rather than between intermediary and supplier, can occur for a number of reasons. One cause can be the appointment of too many intermediaries in one geographical area so that they end up competing with each other and find it difficult to sustain sufficient volume to make it worthwhile doing business. Another can result from the supplier seeming to favour one channel member against another.

Alternatively, individual channel members may start 'letting the side down' by engaging in overvigorous competitive activities or reductions in quality. Here, suppliers must fulfil a role of **channel captain** and seek to maintain a state of distribution equilibrium.

Conflict is best resolved by anticipating its occurrence and trying to pre-empt the causes. Well-motivated intermediaries who see themselves as partners can significantly reduce the potential for such conflict. A well-developed strategy should seek to balance the needs of suppliers and intermediaries so that it adds value to products beyond the costs they generate and advances the strategies of both.

Channel conflict is best resolved by anticipating its occurrence

44 Customer Service Strategies

Customer service is an increasingly important factor for both competitive advantage and customer retention. Indeed, the service element of many product offerings is sometimes the only aspect that distinguishes one organization's marketing efforts from another. In addition, once a supplier/customer relationship has been established, customer service provides a significant contribution to the augmented product offering that enhances the value of a purchase and cements relationships. To manage this adequately, in some organizations, customer service is treated as a separate aspect of the marketing mix for which individual plans and strategies are created.

Customer service can most easily be thought of as all those activities that support a customer's purchase from the time they decide to buy from a particular organization to the point at which they take full ownership and responsibility for the product. Whilst this is obviously a simplification, the approach covers most of the major elements that need to be considered when devising an organization's customer service strategy.

Elements of customer service

The key elements of customer service include:

- The organization's response to **placing the order**, which provides the initial encounter. The ease by which an order is taken and facilitated can provide a lasting impression, and can win and sustain customers if managed more effectively than by other organizations. Apart from just being accessible, this can also involve advice, assistance in creating a specification and personal attention.
- The **information** provided by a supplier while an order is being processed and delivered will also influence a customer's experience of an organization. Such information could include: order confirmation; delivery notification and delivery variations; plus information that will facilitate installation or utilization. Regular contacts with a supplier will reduce the possibility of customers feeling isolated or forgotten and can increase a customer's feelings of being important to a supplier.
- Final **delivery** of the goods or service, which will also affect a purchaser's experience of a supplier. This does not involve just availability and delivery lead times,

but also the *way* in which the product is delivered. Thus, the ability to deliver at specific times, the degree of delivery time variability, the completeness of an order and fill rates (the percentage of orders shipped complete) will all contribute to customer service levels.

- The support provided **after sales** have been completed, which can substantially enhance or reduce the value of a purchase. In fact, customer service is often taken to mean after-sales service, despite the other elements which customer service covers. Post-sales support ranges from straightforward maintenance and repairs to training activities; helplines; assistance with, and notification of, upgrades; instruction manuals; returns policy; and fault tracing.
- The ease with which **problems are solved**, which can be the true test of an organization's commitment to customer service. This is particularly the case for many service organizations such as insurance, transport and hotels, where the core product is, to a large extent, customer service, but where customers often only learn of an organization's true qualities when something goes wrong. This is also true where tangible products are concerned and can cover action on complaints, crisis repairs and an organization's ability to respond to emergency orders. Also included here will be the way in which an organization deals with problems such as design faults, contamination or other supply problems which may arise from time to time.

Developing a strategy

Forming a customer service strategy first involves the identification of the critical elements of service associated with an organization's activities. Some of these will be 'order-qualifying-type' activities, in that they have to be provided for an organization to be on the shortlist of potential suppliers. For most computer vendors, for instance, the ability to offer 'on-site' or 'next-day' service contracts falls into this category. Others can be characterized as 'order winning', in that they will act to differentiate one supplier from another.

Once identified, an enterprise can then compare its performance in these customer service elements with the expectations of customers and the performance of competitors. This will provide appropriate targets for customer service levels, for which policies and processes can be established. As an example, many organizations now operate a 'three-rings' policy which tries to ensure that any telephone call is answered on, or by, the third ring to avoid the frustration a caller can experience from not knowing whether they have the right number, or from just feeling ignored. Other targets may involve on-time delivery levels, minimum notification times for late deliveries, emergency response times, and so on. Many Internet suppliers now offer an 'order-tracking' facility as part of the purchase experience.

A good method for establishing customer service priorities is to perform **trade-off analysis** with customers. This asks respondents to prioritize different aspects of

Customer service priorities should reflect customer preferences

customer service against each other, such as delivery time variability against order lead times (see Figure 44.1). In this example, it is assumed that all customers would find a short order lead time with no delivery time variability the most preferable combination (scored 1), and the converse the least acceptable (scored 9). Customers are then asked to complete the remaining boxes with the numbers 2 to 8 to represent their order of preference. These rankings will show exactly where customer preferences lie. If this is performed for the half-dozen or so elements which are critical for attracting new customers or retaining existing ones, it is possible to develop quite sophisticated customer service programmes. It is also possible to use such an analysis for segmentation purposes, so that differing requirements can be serviced at the appropriate levels, should distinct patterns of need appear.

	Delivery time variability		
	On time	± One day	± Two days
One week	1		
Two weeks			
Three weeks			9

Order lead times

Figure 44.1 Example of customer service trade-off matrix

The final decision in creating a customer service strategy revolves around the implementation of the service programme. The basic options are contracting out, or doing it yourself.

Here, the decisions will depend on the resources available to an organization, plus the trade-offs between costs, quality and control. As an example, whilst it may be cheaper to subcontract repairs, it may be hard to monitor quality. Similarly, whilst good asset management might dictate using third parties for infrequently used and expensive service operations, a situation of rapid change might make it more desirable to keep the activity in-house to retain control over market or new product developments.

One answer to the problems of managing customer service has been to reduce the need for service by allowing customers to perform certain activities themselves. Thus, the developments in electronic data interchange (EDI) have enabled customers to place orders direct via terminals on their own premises, thereby reducing the need to order during opening hours, etc. Similarly, central diagnosis facilities via EDI can locate equipment faults and perform tests which can save much time and expense for both parties. In addition, 'plug-in maintenance', whereby a whole module or aspect of a product is replaced, sometimes by the customers them-selves, rather than sending out a specialist to locate a faulty part, has reduced the need for service calls.

Overall, then, customer service can be a powerful contributor to the competitive position of an organization and its ability to maintain good customer relation-ships. As product reliability improves, the need for after-sales service decreases. However, a customer service package covers more than just after-sales service and should facilitate much of a customer's experience of dealing with a supplier.

Customer service facilitates a customer's experience of dealing with a supplier

45 Databases for Marketing

Technological advances and reducing costs have made databases a much more versatile and cost-effective tool for the support of marketing activities. Where an organization's customer base numbers a few hundred up to several thousand, databases are relatively easy to construct and keep up to date. For FMCG companies, the task is greater. However, the introduction of loyalty cards, the proliferation of organization-specific credit cards, and the increasing volume of online purchases have all created the potential for much larger databases built on information captured through monitoring spending and activity patterns. Many larger organizations now also use databases to support marketing activities in a number of different ways.

The increased importance of direct marketing, telemarketing, sales performance management (using laptop computers), and delivery performance (using handheld point-of-sale or point-of-delivery computing) are examples that have encouraged the development of good databases, which can then also be used to enhance the quality of an organization's relationship with its customers. Good databases will enable the personalization of communications; performance analysis; faster notification of changing consumption patterns; and comprehensive customer records to be available at the 'touch of a button'. In addition, good databases can allow for micro-segmentation based on such criteria as buying patterns, customer-initiated communications, fine-tuned demographics and other, normally difficult-to-discern, characteristics.

Problems with databases

One drawback to using databases is that managers sometimes fall prey to the many pitfalls, and believe many of the myths associated with them, as illustrated in Table 45.1. The consequence of these problems is that databases often hold data that does not fit the purpose of the tacticians, far less the needs of strategic planners. The attempt to develop databases that serve both strategic and tactical purposes is often referred to as **database marketing**.

One of the most acute problems is that of reconciling internal and external views of markets. The usual problem is that data retrieved from the sales

Table 45.1 Myths and realities about databases

Myth	Reality
The database collects what we need.	We collect what is easily available.
The database measures what matters.	We measure what is least embarrassing.
The database users understand what data they need.	We know what we used last, what the textbooks say and what might be interesting on a rainy day.
The database needs to hold more and more data.	We feel safer with 'loadsadata', even when we haven't a clue how to use it.
The database must integrate the data physically.	We like neat solutions, whatever the cost.
The database will save staff time.	We need more and more staff to analyse data.
The database will harmonize marketing, finance and sales.	We all compete for scarce resources, and this involves fighting.
The database is the one source of our market intelligence.	We haven't thought through the business problems.

The costs of developing data-fusion routines emphasize the need to collect data at source

ledger rarely possesses the details needed to link customer records to market segments. Some of the problems are described in Table 45.2 against the key issues involved in identifying a market segment: what is bought; by whom; and for what reason.

Fusing together data from external sources and internal data is becoming increasingly common as a solution to this external–internal problem. This is often referred to as data fusion. Where large volumes of data are involved, computer programmes, known as **deduplication routines**, are used to automate the matching of the data. However, automation rarely achieves more than 80 per cent accuracy in matching, and manual matching has to be applied to the remaining data.

The cost of matching external and internal market-coding schemes is driving some companies to collect customer profiles at source. This occurs either when they first enquire, or when their sales ledger records are first created. However, the cost of making changes to the sales ledger, and the fact that it is 'owned' by the finance department, are often barriers to success. In the future, marketing will need to work much more closely with finance and IT departments if it is to develop databases successfully.

Table 45.2 Problems of reconciling internal and external market audits

External audit variable	Problem with internal audit
What is bought	Internal systems have rich detail on accounts and stock-keeping units. However, information about products such as colour, style, etc., can often be missing. Information on the outlets or channels through which they were sold is also very often lacking.
Who buys	Internal systems record who paid the invoice and who received delivery of the goods. They rarely record who made the buying decision or who influenced it. Even when buyer details are on the system, it is rarely easy to determine their characteristics such as age, sex and so on.
Why	Internal sources of information on why people purchase is scarce. Enquiries can be qualified, using survey techniques, to provide some clues about why people respond to an advertising campaign. Customer satisfaction surveys may also yield clues. Call reports from field sales and telesales can also provide valuable clues, especially if survey disciplines can be observed by the sales staff.
Reconciling variables	Reconciling external with internal variables involves: ■ matching accounts to customers ■ matching stock-keeping units to products ■ matching external variables to internal records ■ collecting data from sources other than the sales ledger (e.g. from surveys of sales representatives)

Avoiding badly constructed databases

Information, in the minds of most marketing managers, lies in a strange 'no man's land', part way between the 'nitty-gritty' stuff of marketing management and the abstractions of technologists, cyberneticists and 'boffins'. Widely misunderstood, or equated to 'keyboard literacy' or 'technology awareness', the management of marketing information often ends up neglected or delegated to the most junior member of the marketing team. In reality, this should be a responsibility addressed by senior marketing managers (i.e. those who have a good view of the decision areas a database will be required to support).

In addition, it must be remembered that information is not all hard, objective data, and organizations will not necessarily become better-informed by collecting more and more raw data and storing it until they end up knowing 'everything'. The belief tends to be that accounting systems are a source of hard facts, since most accounting transactions have to be audited and therefore must be reasonably accurate. Constructing good marketing databases must take into consideration the fact that most accounting data has little direct relevance for marketing strategy.

Information needed to support a marketing strategy

The information needed depends upon the marketing objectives for which a strategy is developed and the tactical decisions that have to be made on an ongoing basis. If strategic marketing objectives are changed, then different kinds of information are needed to support the new strategy that will have to be developed. Table 45.3 illustrates how different objectives require different supporting information. At this point, the sales or marketing director might feel that, because the situation changes so radically every year, there can be no hope of developing an effective system or procedure for obtaining marketing information.

Table 45.3 Examples of business objectives and segmentation methods

Business objective	Segmentation method	Information source
Market extension		
▪ new locations	Geodemographics	Electoral roll (consumer)
▪ new channels	Prospect profiles	Companies House (business)
▪ new segments	Survey analysis	Prospect lists and surveys
Market development	Customer profiling	Sales ledger and added profile data
	Behavioural scoring	Models from internal data source
Product development	Factor analysis	
	Surveys	
	Qualitative methods	
	Panels/discussion groups	

However, without seriously addressing the problem, marketing managers will end up ill-informed when they come to develop their marketing strategies or make tactical decisions.

For all the problems, there are, in practice, a limited number of basic underlying marketing issues with which all companies have to contend. Furthermore, the solutions usually adopted can be seen as variations on relatively few themes. The basic model of information flows to support a marketing system can, therefore, be visualized as shown in Figure 45.1. The main components of this system are explained in Table 45.4.

The critical issue, then, when building such a system is that it is not self-contained within marketing. It requires interface programmes that will alter the systems used by finance, sales and other internal departments, so that information can be produced which will be of direct relevance to marketing management. In addition, it will need to capture appropriate data-feeds from external sources to provide other supporting information. The secrets of success in developing such systems for marketing are:

▪ Understanding the information needs of marketing and particularly how internal and external views of a market will be reconciled.

Different marketing objectives require different supporting information

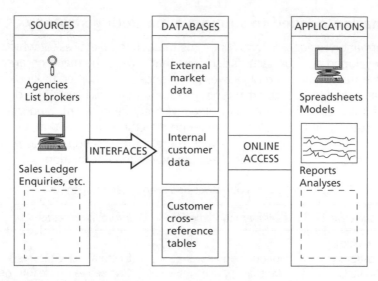

Figure 45.1 Information flows in a marketing system

Table 45.4 The main components of a market database system

External market data: which is purchased from external agencies. These include governmental agencies, market research firms, list brokers and so on.

Internal customer data: which is collected from the sales ledger and other internal sources such as customer service, field sales, telesales, etc. It is coded and segmented in such a way that market-share figures can be created by comparison with external data.

Customer reference table: which is needed to make the system work effectively. It identifies customers (as defined by Marketing) and provides a cross-reference to sales ledger accounts. Whenever a new sales ledger account is created, the cross-reference table is used to determine the customer associated with that account. This avoids the need for costly manual matching or deduplication after the account is created. It is also used by marketing applications as a standard reference table for customers.

Databases: refer to all three of the above data types. They need to be structured using a technique known as *data modelling* which organizes the data into the component types that Marketing wants, and not the structure that Finance or anyone else provides. Usually, the data is held using *relational database* software, since this provides for maximum flexibility and choice of analysis tools.

Interfaces: refer to the computer programs that grab the data from the source systems and restructure it into the components to go onto the marketing database. These programs have to be written by the in-house IT staff, since they obtain and restructure data from the in-house sales ledger, and other in-house systems.

Applications: are the software programs that the planners use to analyse the data and develop their plans. They include data-grabbing tools that grab the items of data from their storage locations; reporting tools that summarize the data according to categories that Marketing defines; spreadsheets that carry out calculations; and 'what-if' analyses on the reported summary data.

- Developing a strong cost-benefit case for the development of information systems, given that other systems, including financial ones, will have to be altered to accommodate the needs of marketing.
- Working continuously with internal IT staff until the system is built whilst recognizing that they are/will be under pressure from other sources, especially finance, and that unless marketing maintains momentum and direction, then other priorities will inevitably win.

Marketing planners need to become far less insular and parochial if they are to obtain the information they require to plan effectively. Cross-functional understanding and cooperation must be secured by the marketing department if it is to develop the systems it needs. In many companies, marketing staff are, at best, tolerated by their colleagues in finance, operations, IT, and on the board. Building the interdepartmental bridges to secure data, information and knowledge is possibly one of the greatest challenges facing marketing today.

(**Note**: Tables 45.1 to 54.3 and Figure 45.1 are reproduced with the kind permission of Dr Robert Shaw of Shaw Consulting, London.)

Cross-functional cooperation is an essential prerequisite for the creation of marketing databases

46 M(obile) Marketing

The concept

Mobile or m-marketing is the process by which organizations satisfy consumer requirements by exchanging messages and content that have value for individual consumers via mobile devices such as phones and PDAs. Currently, mobile marketing covers the transmission of text, graphics, video or sound to (or between) mobile devices via wireless networks using long-range or short-range radio frequencies. Short-range networks include Bluetooth technology which, since 2003, has permitted the transfer of messages from local hotspot-systems direct to a consumer's mobile phone. The growth of messaging for direct marketing purposes has been exponential from its introduction in the early-1990s. Communication possibilities between organizations and consumers have since been enhanced by technologies that also allow consumers to access the Internet and e-mail via mobile devices.

For today's active consumer (particularly the young) the mobile phone is not only a communication device but also a direct source of entertainment (through gaming, photography and music), an organizational device (through diaries and alerts), a source of information and news (direct or via the Internet), a navigational device, and even an important personal accessory and image statement. The almost ubiquitous ownership of such highly personal devices offers the marketer a valuable tool for highly targeted, direct, personal and immediate communication and exchanges – connecting with the consumer at the very heart of their personal space, location and even their consumption context.

The seven brand enhancements

Of great significance is the value mobile marketing can add to the brand-consumer relationship (see Figure 46.1). First, contact with customers is **direct** – allowing the marketer to cut through a saturated media landscape with highly targeted communication for the user. It offers a valuable channel to reach certain consumer segments, particularly highly mobile younger groups that have become difficult to reach through traditional media.

The contact is also highly **personal**. A mobile phone resides at the heart of a consumer's personal and psychological environment. It is a highly treasured – and often customized – accessory and status symbol. Mobile phones often remain with

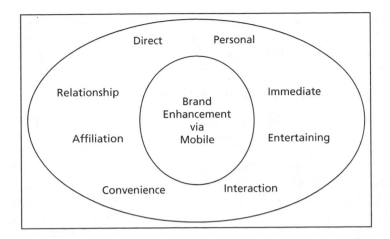

Figure 46.1 M-market brand enhancement

a consumer 24/7 and become intricately integrated into their daily lifestyle and routine. Brands reaching into this environment will be communicating through a highly personal medium.

Mobile communication campaigns also run in 'real time' and offer the marketer **immediacy**, boosting top-of-mind awareness and recall by engaging with consumers at critical and specific moments of potential impulse and purchase. The immediacy characteristic also offers a rapid response to changes in market conditions.

Mobile devices permit the ultimate in **convenience** for consumers. Mobiles break free of the traditional gravitational e-commerce model. Exchanges with consumers are not constrained by time or location, and communication and transactions are possible any time, any where. Mobiles can take a user's location into account and provide users with access to information at the specific instant they are within range of a particular business.

Mobile campaigns can also strengthen brand associations through engaging and **entertaining** multimedia content which can be personalized through context and location. As such, it will facilitate frequent **interaction** and dialogue between consumers and brand owners. This is achieved through the provision of messages, content and games, but also by allowing consumers to access advice and support and raise queries, place orders and give feedback through both voice and low-cost texts. Mobile marketing therefore provides a direct response mechanism (via short codes or single word texts) to track consumer responses to direct marketing campaigns.

Mobile marketers can additionally create communities and brand **affiliations**. Magazine publishers, for example, ask readers to text demographics to a dedicated

Mobile communications campaigns are run in 'real time'

number in order to receive news and information. It can similarly strengthen **relationship** building efforts. Some banks, for instance, will text alerts when accounts reach a dangerously low level.

Leveraging value from mobile marketing

As a communications tool, mobile marketing can be highly cost-effective and a valuable complement to other media in the promotions mix. Text messages are low cost and response rates can be substantially higher than for a direct mail campaign. Creative costs are low and production costs negligible. Furthermore, if the product or service being marketed has sufficient value, consumers may be willing to respond through premium chargeable texts – enabling partially-financed campaigns.

Mobile marketing can also facilitate the initiation of **viral campaigns**. Viral marketing seeks to exploit consumer social networks to spread a particular message exponentially, deploying processes similar to the spread of an epidemic. Effectively it mirrors the effect of word-of-mouth campaigns but uses SMS or MMS messaging to initiate and prompt rapid dissemination of interesting and entertaining images, video or text. Viral 'tell-a-friend' campaigns can be used to generate high awareness levels at relatively low cost, with effective targeting. The technique avoids the irritation of spam mail by encouraging targeted consumers to pass genuine and personal messages to friends, effectively creating positive word-of-mouth recommendation.

To fully leverage the benefits of mobile marketing, strategies need to maximize the level of customer personalization through engaging portal interfaces, personalized messages and highly relevant value-added content. Marketers also need to appreciate the precise role and contribution of mobile marketing within a wider and fully-integrated marketing communications mix. Mobile is more likely to enhance than replace other media and will itself require support from other media. A mobile campaign designed to encourage consumer interaction with a brand by downloading wallpapers, browsing a specific website, searching for a brand's outlets and stimulating a viral surge of interest in the brand, for example, may itself need to be promoted through traditional media in order to prompt the initial consumer interest.

Challenges for mobile marketing

While mobile marketing offers potential enhancements to a brand, there are challenges that could, if not managed effectively, weaken the brand proposition for customers and hinder mobile transactions.

Wireless communications are notoriously less secure than communication over fixed lines, and this potentially opens the door for security and privacy breaches and the transfer of unwanted viruses. Mobile communications strike at the heart of the consumer's personal environment, and consumers could perceive an unsolicited message or a virus as far more intrusive and threatening than if received through a PC. Some countries are clamping down on unwanted commercial advertising through mobile phones and, to avoid consumer backlash, brands will increasingly need to deploy permission-based opt-in marketing programmes.

A key challenge for brands using mobile marketing is to achieve a level of interaction with consumers that adds value to the relationship but which does not threaten privacy. In addition, marketers must avoid alienating customers with multiple or untimely messaging, and particularly uncoordinated messaging from different parts of the organization. In relation to mobile financial transactions, organizations need to bolster consumer confidence by employing highly-secure connections. Businesses and consumers need to feel safe transmitting personal details, profiles and passwords, and marketers must provide for appropriate authentication, privacy, integrity and information to reassure consumers.

The technology itself also remains a challenge. Screen sizes limit the visual impact of marketing messages, and the unpredictability of breaks in wireless connections can be a source of considerable frustration for consumers. Device compatibility is another issue since devices vary widely in their display capabilities; input options, processing power, memory and battery life, and constantly emerging technologies can make it difficult to determine the best technical platform for a new marketing campaign.

Alliances are also a major strategic issue for marketers seeking to access mobile channels. Achieving access and exploiting the potential may well require relationships with hardware manufacturers, network providers, agencies that design the interactive software, content providers and aggregators, advertising agencies for the creative message, and even partner brands. The challenges include both aligning and coordinating the various inputs for the development of effective and timely strategies.

The key questions in deciding whether mobile marketing is an option for a business are listed in Table 46.1.

Table 46.1 Key questions in choosing mobile marketing

- Are our target customers using mobile devices?
- Are our customers likely to transmit sensitive and financial information?
- Are there benefits to be realized from the time-critical and/or location-specific contribution of mobile marketing?
- How will the medium improve customer service or enhance the brand?
- How will the organization assess the effectiveness of mobile marketing?

Permission-based programmes are a key dimension of mobile marketing

Measures of registration numbers and proportions proceeding to download are straightforward, but many mobile marketing techniques – such as viral marketing – are still in their experimental stages and metrics will be needed to fully measure effectiveness and efficiency.

Mobile phones are rapidly becoming the single most important personal medium that consumers possess and the most versatile communication, entertainment and information device. Successful penetration of a consumer's personal space while on the move can offer timely and powerful intervention in the consumer-decision process, but strategies require content that compels, engages and inspires along with secure and convenient interaction functionality.

Successful mobile marketing campaigns

The following are examples of successful mobile marketing campaigns.

Pot Noodle

In 2005 Flytxt was commissioned to run a mobile mechanic on behalf of this Unilever brand to generate data on participating customers. Consumers could win a Pot Noodle horn by texting a code number from a winning pack together with their address. Unilever used the address details to profile consumers in terms of geodemograhics and lifestyles to inform subsequent targeting decisions, media selection and CRM plans. With TV support, at its peak, the Flytxt campaign generated 3000 responses per day.

Orange Wednesdays

Through advertising and sponsorship, Orange has used mobile marketing to associate its brand with the cinema and to provide real added-value to its customers. Orange Wednesdays is a three-year campaign offering customers a '2-4-1' deal on cinema tickets every Wednesday evening, using vouchers delivered direct to handsets. Customers request the offer by texting 'film' to a given number and receive a unique SMS code in return. The codes are validated in real-time by participating cinemas using Orange redemption units. Orange and the cinemas then benefit from detailed usage, cinema and film preference data.

Novartis

Novartis used a Pollen Count Alert text message service to support the launch of its Allereze nasal spray and eye drops for hay fever sufferers. The text messages contain personalized pollen count information at specific times of the day and when pollen counts are high in particular locations. The service was free for the first month but then users are required to register (texting their postcode) and pay a 10p fee per message. An integrated marketing communication campaign supported the service: sampling, trade magazine advertising, bus tickets, pharmacy POS, and database marketing. High brand awareness, response and conversion were achieved.

Bradford Bulls

The immediacy in the timing of broadcasting and consumption is a key benefit of mobile marketing. Bradford Bulls – a UK Rugby League team – created the Bulls Mobile Match service to offer their fans the opportunity of information updates and subscription-based interactive services. Text messages from the club build pre-match anticipation with news on injuries and team selection, and on match days fans are encouraged to interact by texting opinions on players. While interacting, fans are tempted with special offers on tickets and the latest merchandise. The timely information and quality of content provides real value to fans and this value translates to revenue generating opportunities for the club.

Text messaging is proving to be a significant marketing tool

47 Category Management

Category management (CM) is a concept that has developed as a radical alternative to brand management in retail marketing since the mid-1990s. The process of CM can be summarized as: 'The strategic management of a group of products clustered around a specific customer need. This group, or category, is managed as a strategic business unit with clearly defined profitability goals.' The impact of CM is that it shifts attention from individual brands to the management of overall categories as defined by local customer needs.

CM emerged from the development of ideas within the concept of efficient customer response (ECR) that was initiated industry-wide in the US from the mid-1980s onwards. The emphasis of ECR is on sales profitability rather than sales volume and spans the entire business process from the purchase of raw materials to manufacturing, distribution and sale. It is founded on the recent improvements in technology that have allowed suppliers and buyers to reduce waste and stock-holding as well as reduce discounts as a means of generating sales. The focus of the concept is the business processes to be found in retail organizations.

Growth of category management

Brand management focuses on individual brands from the manufacturer's perspective, grouping all functions that affect a brand's profitability under one manager. Retailers however, will often group brands together by product (e.g. soap powder) because that is more convenient for their customers and reflects the way in which customers shop.

The resultant categories are therefore defined by customers, but this can lead to problems of definition. For instance, when a customer wants a cleaner for the bathroom, does he or she categorize it as a bathroom product, a cleaner, or a home safety product? In addition, categories tend to vary regionally and according to customer types, rather than on a broader cross-cultural basis. In response some manufacturers have had to recast their brands for categories, but this in turn raises the question of whether some products should appear in more than one category (for instance, should herbs be categorized with fresh produce, baking goods or both?).

In the final analysis, what is important to retailers is that their shelf space sells more than it would if managed another way. Retailers' expertise lies in providing the space to sell products and services to facilitate that. Sometimes, an external supplier is appointed as category manager, who is then made responsible for optimizing sales from that space. By doing so, retailers are exploiting manufacturer skills in such areas as display, sales promotion and merchandising.

The retailer will normally set minimum standards for the category such as demanding that there must be at least one major brand name and one 'own label' product displayed. After that, the category managers make their own stocking and communications decisions on behalf of their assigned category. For example, if GSK were to identify opportunities for increased toothbrush sales within the oral hygiene category for which they acted as category manager, they could spend their own budget on promoting them.

Contrary to traditional practices, CM obliges manufacturers to consider the profitability of an entire product segment rather than that of just their own brands. The fact that retailers have forced this change is another example of the evolution of retailers from passive distributors to proactive marketers and the shift of power from manufacturer to retailer.

Where category managers are appointed internally, they usually have a similar role, that is, the management of a partnership between a supplier or a number of suppliers with the objective of sales and profit enhancement.

From brand management to category management

The trend towards CM has also required a shift from the traditionally narrow focus of brand management. Looked at from a category perspective, it is possible to see that the consumer choice is not just about selecting from competing brands such as Coca-Cola or Pepsi, but involves an entire drinks portfolio of soft drinks, juices, beverages and alcohol. Heinz began realigning its business along category management principles in 1997 and now has seven global categories: ketchups, condiments and sauces, infant feeding, seafood (tuna), organic and nutritional food, pet food, frozen food, and convenience food (**Source**: H.J. Heinz Company Corporate Profile 2000).

Rather than relying on the power of their brand names, organizations need to ensure that all of their support systems demonstrate to retailers that they are capable of managing categories to advantage. This might mean a review of all of the organization's systems for retail supply such as the logistics of keeping the shelves fully supplied or maintaining efficient electronic data interchange systems for stocks.

Limitations of CM

Viewed purely as a strategy to reduce waste and therefore costs, CM loses its focus on the end customer as the absolute priority. Concentrating on the maximization

Category Management requires suppliers to look beyond their own brands

of shelf space profitability may not improve customer satisfaction levels and that, in the long run, may reduce profits.

One recent report concluded that the availability of a wide selection of goods is a major determinant in customers' decisions about where to shop. CM limits the product choice to those which are most profitable for the retailer and this can have a negative impact on the customers' shopping experience. If customers feel hindered in their purchase decisions by the inability to compare prices of different brands, the CM process will ultimately rebound.

Further difficulties arise from the issue of positioning different product categories. Should paper tissues, for instance, be categorized with bathroom products or health and beauty? And, should the two categories be set next to each other or apart? In addition, different retailers and manufacturers could well work to different category definitions.

These limitations reflect the fact that much of the emphasis of CM has been on the manufacturer/retailer relationship. As far back as 1994, a *Financial Times* survey found that consumers have effectively been demoted as the focus of marketing strategy as retailers have grown in importance, with consumers attracting 30 per cent of marketing expenditure against retailers at 54 per cent.

Challenges for the future

One of the most difficult challenges facing CM is reducing the number of superfluous items on the shelves. This is in opposition to traditional brand marketing which aims to prolong the life of the brand by extending the product range. Possible ways of evolution are demonstrated by Figure 47.1.

Mass customization has been made possible by the increased sophistication in consumer information which has allowed marketers to provide variations on the central product to suit each customer. The growth of retailers' own label products (e.g. Tesco's 'finest' and 'value') reflects this, but further limits the available shelf space for branded supplies. The difficulty for retailers is ensuring that limiting consumers' brand choice is not perceived as limiting their category choice just because they cannot find their favourite products.

The future of CM must necessarily take account of the distribution systems for an increasingly 'global village' market. Many mass retailers are unable to market so many products properly, even when redefined as categories. Providing marketing expertise is therefore one way in which manufacturers can hope to retain some kind of balance in the relationship with such international retailers.

In order to sustain a customer focus, manufacturers need free access to customer information. This can be obtained through large panel companies such as Nielsen

Figure 47.1 Category management evolution

or Taylor Nelson Sofres (TNS), or through the development of a manufacturer's own database, such as Heinz. Manufacturers can also try to establish a reputation for themselves as leaders in ECR.

Future emphasis will probably be on targeting customer satisfaction more effectively, in order to maximize long-term profit. CM can help by focusing on the retail audience and the way in which category sales are driven. This in turn helps retailers build an effective vehicle for appealing to the variety of customers' product decisions and needs. The challenge is to make this happen on a store-by-store basis, at an affordable cost.

Category Management can help deliver customer satisfaction by focusing retailers on customer preferences

48 Multi-channel Integration

The advent of the Internet plus the enormous growth in digitized products and service suggests that a significant business theme of the early part of this century will be innovation in the route to market, that is, the channels used to both communicate with customers *and* deliver products. Companies such as Direct Line, First Direct, easyJet, eBay and Amazon are already competing by exploiting IT-enabled remote channels to add value and/or reduce costs. For other businesses, the challenge is deciding how to respond to the opportunities and threats that these pose.

Packages for sales force automation, direct mail, telemarketing, customer service, e-commerce and marketing analysis have all been available for some time, both individually and in combination, as integrated customer relationship management suites. But these packages, while providing an essential infrastructure, need to be supplemented by managerial processes to address such questions as 'Which channels to use?' and 'How should they work together to deliver customer value?'.

Research from Cranfield School of Management suggests that companies can select from the following broad channel strategy options:

- A single channel that is used for the bulk of customer interactions. Direct Line and First Direct, for example, both started as telephone operations. In the Internet world, this approach is referred to as 'pure play', as exemplified by Amazon, eBay, and so on.
- Channel migration starts with one single channel, but then attempts to migrate customers to another channel on the grounds of increased value or reduced cost. Thus, easyJet initially sold tickets by telephone but now provides financial incentives to its price-sensitive customers to buy online; most of whom now do so.
- A discrete multi-channel strategy uses different channels to perform different tasks in the customer's lifecycle. As an example, Thomas Cook's corporate foreign exchange business uses the Internet to generate leads, a direct sales force to sign up new clients, and a call centre or the Internet to take orders.
- An integrated multi-channel strategy involves offering different channels to the customer without attempting to influence which the customer uses. First Direct, for instance, now offers both telephone and Internet channels as equal alternatives, although the Internet has much lower unit costs and has also proved better for cross-selling. However, since First Direct competes on the basis of

customer service, it accepts the higher costs generated by telephone customers without penalty or the offer of reward to Internet users.

- A channel segmentation strategy offers different channels to different customer groups to meet their varying needs. Each of these routes to market may use the same or different brand names. The insurer Zurich's multiple brands (Allied Dunbar, Zurich, Eagle Star and Threadneedle) use different routes to market (the direct sales force, independent financial advisers and company pension schemes, etc.) in order to serve customer groups with differing needs and attitudes.

- A customer value strategy uses channels selectively according to the financial value of the customers. Many IT firms use account managers for high-value customers but steer smaller customers to lower-cost channels such as the Internet, call centres or value-added resellers.

Which channels will customers choose?

When deciding on the extent to which an integrated channel strategy is required, the starting point must be customers themselves. If organizations do not offer them the channels they prefer, a competitor will. However, the business risk of using new channels requires organizations to attempt to predict customer take-up. Figure 48.1 illustrates a simple technique for doing this based on the 'customer value curve'.

The first step is to establish those factors that determine a customer's choice of supplier. These are shown on the horizontal axis of Figure 48.1, along with weightings out of 100 representing their relative importance in the buying decision. These factors will vary by customer segment. In the segment illustrated, customers are most interested in the cost they incur – the book price plus any other

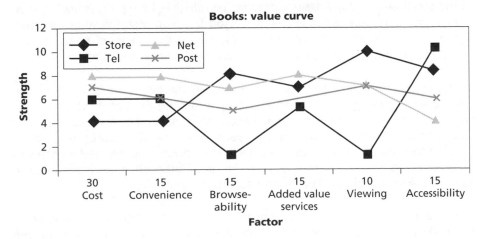

Figure 48.1 Choosing channels – the value curve

The starting point for an integrated channel strategy is customers

charges such as delivery – but are also concerned with a number of other factors such as convenience of purchase and the ability to browse for the book they want. The channel choices might include a traditional book shop, telephone ordering from a magazine advert, an Internet store such as Amazon, or purchase through the post from a book catalogue.

The ability of each current or future channel to deliver against each factor is then either researched or subjectively assessed and allocated a score out of 10. In this example, it can be seen that taking all the factors together, the Internet and physical stores have the best matches.

One factor in assessing a channel's economics is the transaction costs involved. The TPN Register business-to-business exchange set up by General Electric (GE), the first significant e-hub, saves GE 50–90 per cent on processing costs for each order. However, acquisition and retention costs should not be forgotten. The dot-com arm of one retail chain recently discovered that customer acquisition through banner advertising was costing £700 per customer, when the average sale was only £50 – good news for this bricks-and-clicks retailer in its competition with pure-play dotcoms, as it could leverage its physical stores for customer acquisition at a cost of just £13 per customer.

How channels work together

In most markets, purchasers use a number of channels in combination to meet their needs at different stages of their relationship with a supplier. This can be demonstrated using channel-chain analysis as illustrated in Figure 48.2.

Channel-chain analysis involves describing which channels are used at which stages of the purchase and value delivery process. The stages of the process are listed on the left of Figure 48.2, and the channels used to accomplish the stage are listed against each stage. The channel used for one stage will often affect which channel is likely to be used at the next stage as shown by the lines joining each box.

In this example from the business-to-business PC market, three of the common channel-chains being used by various competitors are illustrated. The channel-chain on the left shows the traditional account management approach, as used by most competitors at the start of the 1990s, when the sales process was largely handled face-to-face by account managers. This approach is still used for the sale of larger computers or contracts. For smaller deals, other channel-chains are used as they offer better channel economics for this type of sale.

With the introduction of 'selling from the page', as illustrated in the middle of Figure 48.2, press advertising became the dominant marketing tool, with further information being provided by product brochures and call centre staff. The actual

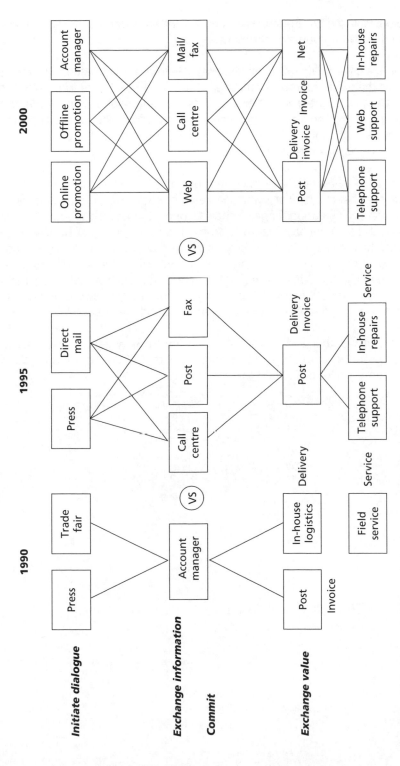

Figure 48.2 Channel-chain analysis: the corporate PC market

order could be placed by a number of means – often a traditional fax or mailed order placed by the accounts department.

More recently, many competitors have added the Internet to the channel mix, as illustrated on the right. But most of these are far from pure-play Internet providers. Account managers might serve major accounts, building relationships and negotiating discount levels. The account managers are freed from the details of product configuration and pricing by the website, while the order itself is as likely to be placed by fax or post as it is on the Web.

Having drawn the channel-chains in current use, the next step is to consider possible future channel-chains. For some markets, interactive TV, e-mail and mobile telephony offer an increasing range of channel opportunities. This requires experimentation with channel-chain diagrams to think through, not just how sales can be made, but how all aspects of a customer's needs will be satisfied. For example, will a mobile phone purchaser buying over the Web be able to return a faulty phone to a nearby store? Will an e-hub be able to handle not just price negotiations, but also information flows on stock levels, complaints, returns and product development – and if not, what additional channels will be needed?

The acid test of whether a channel-chain will flourish is whether it represents a better value proposition to some group of customers. Channel-chain analysis can be used a useful way of evaluating the alternatives.

Integrated Marketing
Topic Communication and
49 Distribution Channels

As distribution channels proliferate with the advent of new media and improved physical distribution infrastructure, the distinction between communications channels and sales and distribution channels is steadily reducing. At the same time, this increase in choice has encouraged further fragmentation within markets with individual customers preferring different sales and communications channels. Integrating these channels within a coherent strategy is not an easy job. The first task is to choose which medium to use for which customer interactions. The choices are illustrated in Figure 49.1.

The choice of medium is generally a complex one often involving different media for different communications and product delivery with the same customer. For example, a Hewlett Packard (HP) customer may find out about the company from colleagues or from press advertising; investigate which product to buy, what the price is and what configuration is required using the HP website, a PC retailer and Web-based discussion groups; print out order details and pass them to the purchasing department to place the order via fax, phone or e-mail; check on the

Figure 49.1 Communications strategy

delivery time via telephone or interactive Web dialogue; take delivery via a parcels service or from a retailer; and obtain customer service using technical help telephone lines or e-mailed communications. Customers are no longer content to have the medium dictated by the supplier.

From this illustration, it can be seen that the choice of communications medium is clearly closely intertwined with the distribution strategy. Distribution channels often have a mix of purposes:

- Conveying a physical product to the customer.
- Communicating and exchanging information with the customer.

A garage selling motor cars, for example, provides information on the model, an opportunity for a test drive, a location where price negotiations can occur, and a step in the physical delivery of the car to the customer, as well as post-purchase service and problem-solving. A clothes shop provides a location where information about a garment can be exchanged by trying it on, feeling it, examining labels and talking to a shop assistant. Such detailed information exchange would be hard to replicate using direct marketing approaches.

Basing promotional strategies on information exchange in this way encourages an organization to forge close linkage with the physical issues of distribution. As illustrated in Figure 49.2 the physical development of a tangible product and many service products provides numerous opportunities for communications with the market and individual customers/consumers. This is a far more sophisticated model of marketing communications and forces a direct link with operations distribution channels.

Figure 49.2 Value chain and associated communications activities

Under this model, sales personnel will be included in communications plans. The key messages that are at the core of a communications plan will need to be supported by field sales staff and actively brought into both formal presentations and informal conversations. Performance targets in terms of message continuity, sales seminars and the reporting of customer information exchanges could all have measurable objectives associated with them.

Regarding communications as an interactive process, rather than a one-way stream of promotional activity, adds new dimensions to sales planning. A traditional sales and communications programme might include a direct mail campaign, an outdoor advertising programme, participation in a number of local fairs, some in-store promotions, and so on. The overall approach can be described as a 'push' strategy whereby customers are identified and/or found, and then persuaded to make a purchase. Under an interaction approach, communications are seen more as a dialogue in which information is exchanged and the propensity to purchase becomes the subject of negotiation. The product may still be pre-manufactured, but the customer experience is significantly different. As product customization becomes increasingly feasible in a larger number of industries, and markets become more fragmented, the potential for sales based on interactive dialogue becomes much greater.

The ability to capitalize on these developments and the potential for integrating communications and distribution channels does, however, depend on senior managers understanding the opportunity and adjusting the organization's processes accordingly, as illustrated in the following example.

An international business-to-business financial services organization was one of the first businesses in its sector to develop a website. Their early experience immediately identified that the site enabled them to reach new customers considerably more cost-effectively than their traditional sales force. When the website was first launched, potential customers were finding the company on the Web, deciding which products were appropriate on the basis of the website, and sending an e-mail to ask to buy. So far, so good.

However, stuck in a traditional sales process mode, the company would allocate the 'lead' to a sales person, who would phone up and make an appointment, perhaps three weeks hence. This gave the customer plenty of opportunity to investigate other suppliers and even have purchased from a competitor who could respond faster. Those that didn't were subjected to a sales pitch complete with glossy materials, which was totally unnecessary, the customer having already decided to buy. Those that were not put off would proceed to be registered as able to buy over the Web, but the company had lost the opportunity to improve its margins by using the sales force more judiciously.

In time, the company realized its mistake, and changed its sales model and reward systems to something close to the interactive model. Unlike those prospects which the company proactively identified and contacted, which might indeed need 'selling' to, many new Web customers were initiating the dialogue themselves, and simply required the company to respond effectively and rapidly. The sales force was increasingly freed up to concentrate on major clients and on relationship building.

The changing perspective of sales processes and broader communication opportunities clearly raises questions for the design of marketing communications, such as: Who initiates the dialogue, and how do we measure the effectiveness of our attempts to do so across multiple channels?; How do we monitor the effectiveness not just of what we say to customers but what they say back?; and How about the role of marketing communications as part of the value that is being delivered and paid for, not just as part of the sales cost?

Part 8
Management, Planning and Control

50 Managing the Sales Team

As the importance of managing relationships with customers has increased, organizations have had to pay particular attention to the productivity of one of their scarcest and most expensive resources: those individuals who have the greatest amount of direct contact with customers, otherwise known as the sales force. The standard measures of sales force productivity have traditionally included call rates; revenue targets; volume targets; and an increased client base. In more enlightened organizations, results-oriented sales managers have come to recognize that other objectives and productivity yardsticks are also required. In addition, this has led to the understanding that organizations also have to address issues of motivation and training to complement this expanded set of requirements.

Sales force objectives

One of the major problems in achieving sales force productivity is that the way sales people have to spend their day leaves comparatively little time available for selling. Much of it is occupied in planning, travelling, sales administration, and so on. In these circumstances, it is crucial that an organization should know as precisely as possible what objectives it wants its sales force to achieve. The sophistication of these objectives has led to the development of both quantitative and qualitative targets for sales activities.

The principal quantitative objectives employed are usually concerned with:

- How much to sell (the value of unit sales volume).
- What to sell (the mix of unit sales volume).
- Where to sell (the markets and the individual customers that will take the company towards its marketing objectives).
- The desired profit contribution (where relevant and where the company is organized to compute this).
- Selling costs (in compensation, expenses and supervision).

The first three types of objectives are derived directly from an organization's marketing objectives, and constitute the principal components of the sales plan. However,

Sales force objectives should be as precise as possible

Table 50.1   Further quantitative objectives for a sales force

- Number of point-of-sale displays organized
- Number of letters written to prospects
- Number of telephone calls to prospects
- Number of reports turned or not turned in
- Number of trade meetings held
- Use of sales aids in presentations
- Number of service calls made
- Number of customer complaints
- Safety record
- Collections made
- Training meetings conducted
- Competitive activity reports submitted
- General market condition reports delivered

there are many other kinds of quantitative objectives which can be set for the sales force; these are summarized in Table 50.1.

Qualitative objectives are more intangible in nature and can be a potential source of problems if sales managers try to assess the performance of the sales force along dimensions which include abstract terms such as 'loyalty', 'enthusiasm' and 'cooperation', since such terms are difficult to measure objectively. Thus, in seeking qualitative measurements of performance, managers often resort to highly subjective interpretations which cause resentment and frustration amongst those being assessed.

However, it is perfectly possible for managers to set and measure qualitative objectives that directly relate to the performance of the sales force. It is possible, for example, to assess the skill with which a person applies his or her product knowledge for a customer, the skill with which the work is planned, or the skill with which objections are overcome by the representative during a sales interview. While still qualitative in nature, these measures relate to standards of performance which are likely to be understood and accepted by the sales force.

Given such standards, it is not too difficult for a competent field sales manager to identify deficiencies; get agreement on them; coach in skills and techniques; build attitudes of professionalism; show how to self-train; determine which training requirements cannot be tackled in the field; and evaluate improvements in performance and the effect of any past training. Table 50.2 shows an example of setting objectives for an individual sales representative.

Table 50.2 Setting objectives for an individual sales representative

Task	Standard	How to set standard	How to measure performance	Performance shortfalls
■ To achieve personal sales target	Sales target per period of time for individual groups and/or products	Analysis of: – territory potential – individual customer's potential Discussions and agreement between sales person and manager	Comparison of individual sales person's product sales against targets	Significant shortfall between target and achievement over a meaningful period
■ To sell the required range and quantity to individual customers	The achievement of specified range and quantity of sales to a particular customer or group of customers within an agreed time period	Analysis of individual customer records of: – potential – present sales Discussion and agreement between manager and sales person	Scrutiny of: – individual customer records – observation of selling in the field	Failure to achieve agreed objectives. Complacency with range of sales made to individual customers
■ To plan journeys and call frequencies to achieve minimum practicable selling cost	To achieve appropriate call frequency on individual customers. Number of live customer calls during a given time period.	Analysis of individual customer's potential. Analysis of order/call ratios. Discussion and agreement between manager and sales person	Scrutiny of: – individual customer records Analysis of order/call ratio Examination of call reports	High ratio of calls to individual customer relative to that customer's yield. Shortfall on agreed total number of calls made over an agreed time period

(Continued)

Table 50.2 (Continued)

Task	Standard	How to set standard	How to measure performance	Performance shortfalls
▪ To acquire new customers	Number of prospect calls during time period. Selling new products to existing customers	Identify total number of potential and actual customers who could produce results. Identify opportunity areas for prospecting	Examination of – call reports – records of new accounts opened – ratio of existing to potential customers	Shortfall in number of prospect calls from agreed standard. Low ratio of existing to potential customers
▪ To make a sales approach of the required quality	To exercise the necessary skills and techniques required to achieve the identified objective of each element of the sales approach	Standards to be agreed in discussion between manager and sales person related to company standards laid down	Regular observations of field selling using a systematic analysis of performance in each stage of the sales approach	Failure to identify: – objective of each stage of sales approach – specific areas of skill, weakness – use of support material

Motivating the sales force

Sales force motivation has received a great deal of attention in recent times, largely as a result of the work undertaken by psychologists in other fields of management. It is, therefore, now widely accepted that it is not enough to give someone a title and an office and expect them to achieve good sales results. Effective leadership is as much 'follower determined' as it is determined by management, and it is important to remember some of the main factors that contribute to effective management of the sales force.

If a sales manager's job is to improve the performance of his or her sales force, and if performance is a function of incentives minus 'disincentives', then the more he or she can increase incentives and reduce disincentives, the better will be performance. Research has also shown that an important element of sales force motivation is a sense of doing a worthwhile job. In other words, the desire for praise and recognition, the avoidance of boredom and monotony, the enhancement of self-image, the freedom from fear and worry and the desire to belong to something believed to be worthwhile, all contribute to enhanced performance.

Other methods and ideas that have been used to improve the productivity of sales forces over recent years have included:

- The development of imaginative and thorough training modules covering areas such as communication techniques, body language, human behaviour and motivation, observation skills, transactional analysis and effective planning.
- The introduction of performance measurement, supported by evaluation procedures.
- The design of creative and productive sales aids.
- The establishment of systems for tapping and cross-fertilizing creative ideas generated by the firm's sales force.
- The development of effective incentive systems.

Remuneration

Remuneration will always be a very important determinant of motivation. This does not necessarily mean paying the most money, although, clearly, unless there are significant financial motivations within a company, it is unlikely that people will stay. When drawing up a remuneration plan, which would normally include a basic salary plus some element for special effort such as bonus or commission, the objectives summarized in the following list should also be considered:

- Attract and keep effective people.
- Remain competitive.
- Reward sales people in accordance with their individual performance.
- Provide a guaranteed income plus an orderly individual growth rate.

Believing a job to be worthwhile contributes to enhanced performance

- Generate individual sales initiative.
- Encourage team work.
- Encourage the performance of essential non-selling tasks.
- Ensure that management can fairly administer and adjust compensation levels as a means of achieving sales objectives.

A central concept of sales force motivation is that the individual sales person will exert more effort if he or she is led to concentrate on:

- *Expectations* of accomplishing the sales objectives.
- *Personal benefits* derived from accomplishing those objectives.

The theory of sales force motivation is known as the *path–goal* approach because it is based on the particular path which the sales representative follows to a particular sales objective – and the particular goals associated with successfully travelling down that path. Representatives estimate the probability of success of travelling down various paths or sales approaches, and estimate the probability that their superiors will recognize their goal accomplishments and will reward them accordingly. Stated less formally, the motivational functions of the sales manager consist of increasing personal pay-offs to sales representatives for work-goal attainment, making the path to these pay-offs easier to travel by clarifying it, reducing roadblocks and pitfalls, and increasing the opportunities for personal satisfaction *en route*.

51 Forecasting Sales

The size and complexity of the marketing task in all kinds of enterprise has substantially increased in recent years. The growing diversity of customer needs in a rapidly changing environment has resulted in shorter product lifecycles. Distribution patterns have changed dramatically in most markets, and have been complicated by the geographical dispersion of operations and the growing internationalization and scale of businesses. In addition, the sociocultural, legal and political environments in which managers have to operate have become more volatile and the volume of data and information available has mushroomed. Added to this is the ever-present difficulty of measuring the behavioural aspects, such as organizational and psychological influences, which impact on marketing decisions.

The result of all this is that it is increasingly difficult to forecast with anything like the accuracy that was possible when markets were more stable. Nevertheless, this is a necessary task and one which has to be done well, since the consequences of being wrong can be very severe indeed. Crucial to this is a good understanding of the differences between **macro** and **micro** forecasting and the ability to utilize both **qualitative** and **quantitative** methods.

The selection of an appropriate forecasting approach or set of techniques is dependent on four main factors:

- The **degree of accuracy** required, which, in turn, will depend on the risk associated with the decisions which will be based on the forecast.
- The **availability of data** and information, which will determine the techniques which can be utilized for making forecasts.
- The **time-horizon required**, which will, again, affect the approach to be adopted.
- The **position of a product in its lifecycle**, which will influence both the time-horizons sought and the types of data and information which will be available.

Macro and micro forecasting

Macro forecasting is essentially concerned with forecasting markets in total. In adopting a macro approach, the emphasis is on observing the broad picture and, from that, deducing the implications for the products and markets in which an

Sales are increasingly difficult to forecast

organization is interested. Some form of macro forecasting has to precede the setting of marketing objectives and strategies. Other forecasts should come after the company has decided which specific market opportunities it wants to take advantage of and how best this can be done.

Micro forecasting is more concerned with detailed unit forecasts and should normally come after the organization has set its major objectives and strategies. These obviously deal with shorter time-horizons such as an organization's sales predictions for the next period. For this type of forecast, extrapolative techniques may be appropriate, although, in general, simple extrapolations are fraught with dangers. It must be recognized here that such projections are based on the assumption that what has happened in the past will be a guide to what will happen in the future. A more appropriate micro approach is to build up, from an individual customer level, an estimate of what the total sales of a product could be in a given period.

Forecasting techniques

Whilst there are many techniques that can be used for forecasting, they usually fall into one of two categories: **quantitative techniques** and **qualitative methods**. Quantitative approaches, as the name implies, refer to a forecast made on a numerical basis of some kind and usually involve some form of statistical analysis. Qualitative estimates are more intuitive in nature and rely on the skills of individuals in interpreting the world around them as they see it, based on their experience, the quality of their imagination and their knowledge of the area under discussion. In the end, the outcome of a qualitative forecast should, of course, also be quantitative in nature. It is the methods of arriving at the projection which differ.

It is also the case that, particularly at a macro level, it would be unusual if either of these methods were used entirely on their own, mainly because of the inherent dangers in each. Thus a combination of approaches is usually far more appropriate. As an example, it is comparatively easy to develop an equation that will extrapolate statistically the world population up to, say, the year 2025. The problem here is that the method would not have taken account of likely changes in past trends. Better would be an approach which listed a whole series of possible events which could affect world population, and then assigned probabilities to the likelihood of those events happening. From this, a more sophisticated and more realistic forecast could be produced.

A similar approach is adopted by many business forecasters who use leading indicators, that is, indices of related or even non-related activities as aids to estimating changes in market conditions at a macro level. Examples include:

■ The *Financial Times* Ordinary Share Index, which is reckoned to provide a lead of about six months.

- New housing starts, which can give a lead of about 10 months.
- The net acquisition of financial assets by companies, which can be used as a lead for about 12 months.

Such indicators will only provide approximate pictures of general business conditions and cannot be guaranteed to offer consistent correlations. On the other hand, forecasters may discern, from their experience and their understanding of business, that there is a close fit between seemingly unrelated activity and the sales performance of a particular product.

In recent years, there has also been a considerable growth in the use of marketing models to provide a macro-type basis for sales estimation. Generally, these models incorporate a number of statistically derived relationships drawn from empirical observations, the purpose of which is to explain the observed market behaviour in terms of marketing trends. However, not everybody is enthusiastic about such models, particularly if they are used for large-scale situations, because of the problems of quantifying what are often qualitative and intangible relationships. In addition, such relationships will often change considerably over time, thereby making the model obsolete. Another factor militating against the use of models is the considerable expense involved in collecting the necessary data.

An example of a qualitative macro-estimation technique is the Delphi forecast (named after the Greek oracle who foretold the future). Here, a group of experts discuss a problem, such as 'How will retailing be structured by the year 2025? ', and give their consensus of the answer to this problem.

As noted, good micro approaches are based on building up, from an individual customer level, an estimate of what total sales of the product could be in a given period. Quantitative micro methods sometimes involve surveys of actual and/or potential customers or seek to extract information from internal sources. Although the procedures involved may be very sophisticated, these studies basically rely on indications from respondents as to their likely purchasing behaviour. An example of a qualitative micro estimate would be an estimate based on the judgement of members of the sales force concerning future sales.

Forecasting and uncertainty

Forecasts deal with uncertainties, which require market forecasters to establish the nature of the 'either/or' associated with the area under study. Thus, the output of a forecast should be expressed in terms of a range of possible outcomes. Beyond this, it should also be recognized that the process by which any market prediction is achieved is essentially probabilistic. Forecasts thus can and should be made to incorporate the probabilities that are implicit in the marketing environment in which the organization operates.

The output of a forecast should be a range of scenarios

As an example, sales forecasters are concerned to establish what proportion of a total market potential will be represented as their sales estimates. This will be based on an assessment of the effect of a specific marketing mix and marketing programme in competition with alternative means of satisfying the same need. The danger here is that it can be possible for such estimates to become self-fulfilling prophecies, in that both the estimate and the marketing mix programmes are dependent on each other. In this sense, a given level of market achievement is predicted by what an organization believes to be potentially achievable. More useful, here, would be alternative scenarios based on different probabilities so that optimum levels of investment can be assessed, and risk factors built into the various activities of the organization.

The task of marketing managers, when adopting a forecasting role, is to take whatever relevant data is available to help to predict the future. They must apply to them whatever quantitative techniques are appropriate, but then use qualitative methods, such as: expert opinions; market research; analogy; and so on, to predict what will be the likely discontinuities in the same time series. It is only through sensible use of the available tools that management will begin to understand what has to be done to match its own capabilities with carefully selected market needs. Without such an understanding, any form of forecasting is likely to be a sterile exercise.

52 Marketing Planning

All organizations operate in a complex environment, in which hundreds of external and internal factors interact to affect their ability to achieve their objectives. Managers need some understanding, or view, about how all these variables interact and they must try to be rational about their decisions, no matter how important intuition, feel and experience are as contributory factors in this process of rationality. Most managers accept that some kind of formalized procedure for planning the organization's marketing helps to sharpen this rationality so as to reduce the complexity of business operations and add a dimension of realism to the organization's hopes for the future.

The essence of marketing planning

The contribution of marketing planning to organizational success, whatever its area of activity, lies in its commitment to detailed analysis of future opportunities to meet customer needs, and a wholly professional approach to selling to well-defined market segments, products or services that deliver the sought-after benefits. Such commitment and activities, however, must not be mistaken for budget forecasts, which have always been a commercial necessity. The process of marketing planning is a more sophisticated approach which is concerned with identifying what, and to whom, sales are going to be made in the longer term to enable revenue budgets and sales forecasts to have any chance of being achieved.

In essence, marketing planning is a managerial process, the output of which is a marketing plan. As such, it is a logical sequence and a series of activities leading to the setting of marketing objectives and the formulation of plans for achieving them. Conceptually, the process is very simple and is achieved by means of a planning system. The system is little more than a structured way of identifying a range of options for the organization, of making them explicit in writing, of formulating marketing objectives which are consistent with the company's overall objectives, and of scheduling and costing the specific activities most likely to bring about the achievement of the objectives. It is the systemization of this process which lies at the heart of the theory of marketing planning.

Marketing planning is a managerial process

Types of marketing plan

There are two principal kinds of marketing plan:

- The strategic marketing plan.
- The tactical marketing plan.

The **strategic marketing plan** is a plan for three or more years. It is the written document which outlines how managers perceive their own position in their markets relative to their competitors (with competitive advantage accurately defined), what objectives they want to achieve, how they intend to achieve them (strategies), what resources are required, and with what results (budget). Three years, however, is the most frequent planning period for strategic marketing plans. Five years is the longest period and this is becoming less common as a result of the speed of technological and environmental change. The exceptions here are the very long-range plans formulated by a number of Japanese companies which may often have planning horizons of between 50 and 200 years!

The **tactical marketing plan** is the detailed scheduling and costing of the specific actions necessary for the achievement of the first year of the strategic marketing plan. The tactical plan is thus usually for one year.

Research into the marketing planning practices of organizations shows that successful ones complete the strategic plan before the tactical plan. Unsuccessful organizations frequently do not bother with a strategic marketing plan at all, relying largely on sales forecasts and the associated budgets. The problem with this approach is that many managers sell the products and services they find easiest to sell, to those customers who offer the least line of resistance. By developing short-term, tactical marketing plans first and then extrapolating them, managers merely succeed in extrapolating their own shortcomings. Preoccupation with preparing a detailed marketing plan first is typical of those companies that confuse sales forecasting and budgeting with strategic marketing planning.

The contents of a strategic marketing plan

The contents of a strategic marketing plan are as follows:

- *Mission statement*   This sets out the *raison d'être* of the organization and covers its role, business definition, distinctive competence, and future indications.
- *Financial summary*   This summarizes the financial implications over the full planning period.
- *Market overview*   This provides a brief picture of the market and includes: market structure; market trends; key market segments; and (sometimes) gap analysis.

- *SWOT analyses* These are the strengths and weaknesses of the organization compared with competitors against key customer success factors plus the organization's opportunities and threats; they are normally completed for each key product, or segment.
- *Issues to be addressed* These are derived from the SWOT analyses and are usually specific to each product or segment.
- *Portfolio summary* This is a pictorial summary of the SWOT analyses that makes it easy to see, at a glance, the relative importance of each; it is often a two-dimensional matrix in which the horizontal axis measures the organization's comparative strengths and the vertical axis measures its relative attractiveness.
- *Assumptions* These are the assumptions which are critical to the planned marketing objectives and strategies.
- *Marketing objectives* These are usually quantitative statements in terms of profit, volume, value and market share, of what the organization wishes to achieve. They are usually stated by product; by segment; and overall.
- *Marketing strategies* These state how the objectives are to be achieved and often involve the four Ps of marketing: product; price; place; and promotion.
- *Resource requirements and budget* This is the full planning period budget, showing in detail, for each year, the revenues and associated costs.

The contents of a tactical marketing plan

The contents of a tactical marketing plan are very similar, except that it often omits the mission statement, the market overview and SWOT analyses, and goes into much more detailed quantification by product and segment of marketing objectives and associated strategies. An additional feature is a much more detailed scheduling and costing of the tactics necessary to the achievement of the first year of the plan.

The marketing planning timetable

Figure 52.1 depicts the relationship between the marketing planning process and the output of that process: the strategic and tactical marketing plans. Figure 52.2 shows the same process in a circular form, as this indicates more realistically the ongoing nature of the marketing planning process and the link between strategic and tactical marketing plans.

Marketing vs business plans

Good marketing plans and business plans have many overlaps since they both try to provide an overview of important managerial processes. However, marketing plans do not cover other areas of a business such as operational activities, financial management, HR developments, which are all areas that will be referenced in a

Good marketing plans and business plans have many overlaps

Typical timetable for creating
unit strategic marketing plans

March

Planning team 'kick-off'
Meetings with Unit
managers to discuss
overall guidelines for the
three-year planning period

What Unit managers present
in their strategic marketing plans

Between March and May

Unit managers carry out
marketing audits

May

1 Unit mission statement
2 Summary of Unit's
  performance last year
3 Summary of financial
  projections for the next
  three years
4 A market overview
5 SWOT analyses (of major
  products/markets)
6 Portfolio summary
7 Major assumptions
8 Marketing objectives
  and strategies for next
  three years
9 Financial projections
  for next three years

Stage 1
meetings

May

Planning team discuss
three-year business plans
with Unit managers and
amend as necessary

**Between September
and October**

Prepare detailed one-year
operational plan with
forecasts and budgets

Stage 2
meetings

November

Present amended three-year
plan and detailed one-year
plans to planning team

December

HQ consolidation of one
and three-year plans

Note: The marketing planning process must not be confused with what appears
in the plan itself, which is described on the right.

Figure 52.1 Strategic and tactical marketing plans

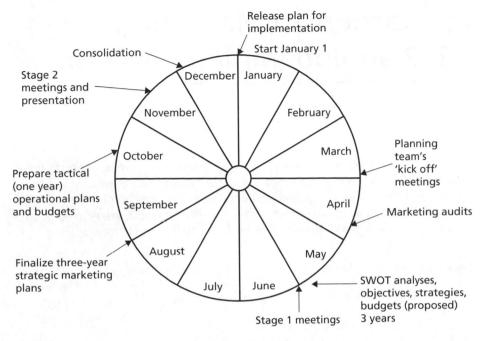

Figure 52.2 Strategic and operational planning cycle

full business plan. A marketing plan should, however, provide clear market-based performance requirements that will act as a starting point for, say, engineering plans, financial plans, logistics planning, and so on, that will impact on the marketing mix. The challenge for senior managers is finding a way of bringing all these together in one larger and comprehensive corporate or business plan.

A marketing plan should provide clear performance requirements

Barriers to Marketing Planning Implementation

Successfully implemented marketing planning systems will have profound benefits for a business. However, recent research has confirmed that 80 per cent of organizations do not have an integrated, coordinated and internally consistent plan for their marketing activities. The most frequently encountered barriers to successful marketing planning are shown in Table 53.1 and elaborated below.

Table 53.1 Barriers to the integration of strategic marketing planning

1. Weak support from the chief executive and top management.
2. Lack of a plan for planning.
3. Lack of line management support.
4. Confusion over planning terms.
5. Numbers in lieu of written objectives and strategies.
6. Too much detail, too far ahead.
7. Once-a-year ritual.
8. Separation of operational planning from strategic planning.
9. Failure to integrate marketing planning into a total corporate planning system.
10. Delegation of planning to a planner.

Weak support from chief executive and top management

Since the chief executive and top management are the key influencers in a company, without their active support and participation any formalized marketing planning system is unlikely to work. Any sign of indifference will very quickly destroy any credibility that emerging plans might have had. This is the most frequently encountered barrier to effective marketing planning.

Lack of a plan for planning

The next most common cause of failure is the belief that, once a system is designed, it can be implemented immediately. One company became very worried when it achieved virtually no improvement in the quality of the plans coming into headquarters over a year after the introduction of a very sophisticated system. Evidence indicates that in fact a period of around three years is required in a major company before a complete marketing planning system can be implemented. Failure or partial failure is often the result of not building the following into the timetable when introducing a planning system:

- The need to communicate why a marketing planning system is necessary.
- The need to recruit top management support and participation.
- The need to test the system out on a limited basis to demonstrate its effectiveness and value.
- The need for training programmes, or workshops, to train the management in its use.
- Lack of date and information in some parts of the world.
- Shortage of resources in some parts of the world.

Lack of line management support

Hostility on the part of line managers to the introduction of new marketing planning systems is a further barrier. The reasons for this are related to the initiators' lack of a plan for planning. New systems inevitably require considerable explanation of the procedures involved and are usually accompanied by *pro formas*, flow charts and the like. Often these devices are most conveniently presented in the form of a manual.

When such a document arrives on the desk of a busy line manager, unheralded by previous explanation or discussion, the immediate reaction often appears to be fear of their possible inability to understand and comply with it, followed by anger, and finally rejection. They begin to picture headquarters as a remote 'ivory tower' totally divorced from the reality of the market place.

Allied to this is the fact that many line managers are ignorant of basic marketing principles, have never been used to breaking up their markets into strategically relevant segments, nor of collecting meaningful information about them. This lack of skill is compounded by the fact that there are many countries in the world which cannot match the wealth of useful information and data available in the USA and Europe. The problem of lack of reliable data and information can only be solved by devoting time and money to its solution, and where available resources are scarce, it is unlikely that the information demands of headquarters can be met.

Confusion over planning terms

Confusion over planning terms is another reason for the failure of marketing planning systems. The initiators of these systems frequently use a form of planning terminology that is perceived by operational managers as meaningless jargon. Those companies with successful planning systems try to use terminology which

Hostility from line managers can be a barrier to implementation

will be familiar to operational management, and where terms such as 'objectives' and 'strategies' are used, these are clearly defined, with examples given of their practical use.

Numbers in lieu of written objectives and strategies

Most managers in operating units are accustomed to completing sales forecasts together with the associated financial implications. They are not accustomed to considering underlying causal factors for past performance or expected results, nor highlighting opportunities, emphasizing key issues, and so on. Their tendency is to extrapolate numbers and to project the current business unchanged into the next fiscal year. When a marketing planning system suddenly requires that they make explicit their understanding of the business, they cannot do it.

Too much detail, too far ahead

Connected with this is the problem of overplanning, usually caused by elaborate systems that demand information and data that headquarters do not need and can never use. Systems that require vast quantities of data are generally demotivating for all concerned.

Once-a-year ritual

One of the commonest weaknesses in the marketing planning systems is the ritualistic nature of the activity. In such cases, operating managers treat the writing of the marketing plan as an unpleasant duty. The *pro formas* are completed, not always very diligently, and the resulting plans are quickly filed away, never to be referred to again. They are seen as something which is required by headquarters rather than as an essential tool of management. In other words, the production of the marketing plan is seen as a once-a-year ritual, a sort of game of management bluff.

Separation of operational planning from strategic planning

Most companies make long-term projections. Unfortunately, in the majority of cases these are totally separate from short-term planning activity. This separation tends to discourage operational managers from thinking strategically. In reality, the detailed operational plan should be the first year of the long-term plan, and operational managers should be encouraged to complete their long-term projections at the same time as their short-term projections. The advantage is that it encourages managers to think about what decisions have to be made in the current planning year, in order to achieve the long-term projections.

Failure to integrate marketing planning into a total corporate planning system

It is difficult to initiate an effective marketing planning system in the absence of a parallel corporate planning system. This is yet another facet of the separation of operational planning from strategic planning. Unless similar processes and time-scales to those being used in the marketing planning system are also being used by other major functions such as distribution, production, finance and personnel, the sort of trade-offs and compromises that have to be made in any company between what is wanted and what is practicable and affordable, will not take place in a rational way.

Another facet of this is the lack of participation of key functions of the company, such as engineering or production. Where these are key determinants of success, as in capital goods companies, a separate marketing planning system is virtually ineffective. Where marketing is a major activity, as in companies with fast-moving goods, it is possible to initiate a separate marketing planning system.

Delegation of planning to a planner

Planners should really act as coordinators of planning, not as an initiator of goals and strategies. Without the ability and the willingness of operational management to cooperate, a planner becomes little more than a kind of headquarters administrative assistant. In many large companies, where there is a person at headquarters with the specific title of marketing planning manager, they have usually been appointed as a result of difficulty controlling businesses that have grown rapidly in size and diversity, and which present a baffling array of new problems to deal with.

Their tasks are essentially those of system design and coordination of inputs, although they are also expected to formulate overall objectives and strategies for the board. In all cases, it is lack of line management skills and inadequate organizational structures that frustrates the company's marketing efforts, rather than inadequacies on the part of the planner. This puts the onus on planners themselves to do a lot of the planning, which is, not surprisingly, largely ineffective.

One consequence of employing a marketing planning manager is that they will need to initiate changes in management behaviour in order to become effective. Usually these are far-reaching in their implications, affecting training, resource allocation, and organizational structures. As the catalyst for such changes, the planner, not surprisingly, comes up against enormous political barriers, the result of which is that they often become frustrated and eventually ineffective. This is especially true in larger companies.

Without cooperation, a central planner becomes an administrative assistant

Overall, to be successful it is important to distinguish between the *process* of marketing planning and the *output*. Indeed, much of the benefit of a planning system will derive from the process of analysis and debate amongst relevant managers and directors rather than from the written document itself. Being aware of the barriers to implementing a successful planning system will go some way to helping organizations overcome them and obtain these benefits.

International Product Planning

Although there are many factors that inhibit successful international marketing, inadequate product planning is one of the more significant contributions to poor international marketing performance. This is because the product is at the heart of the marketing mix that constitutes a supplier's offer, and to which customers and consumers respond. Since trade is about selling products into markets, the product, as the leading edge of the marketing mix, must be as 'right' as possible to avoid becoming another example of products which fail once they move outside their home territory. The two key questions that need to be answered to enhance the chances of success are:

- Which of its product lines should an organization sell in overseas markets?
- Does it need to adapt them for those markets?

Product line choice

In all but the most exceptional cases, overseas markets will already have trade in similar or competing products to those a domestic supplier wishes to introduce. This implies that the overseas market will already support a distribution infrastructure with established trading practices, including exclusivity agreements and networked relationships. In addition, it will imply that there are existing consumer habits and preferences, competitor promotional activities and accepted pricing structures. Choosing a product line for such a market will require the identification of an opportunity derived from a good understanding of these market features. This should include:

- An analysis of potential competitor product performance.
- Market usage patterns and important application requirements.
- The composition of the market in terms of supply chain structures, the major determinants of price, communication channels and the major positioning variables.
- Customer expectations of a product.

The analysis should seek to highlight any trends in the market that will reduce the attractiveness of products currently available and to identify any products from existing suppliers which leave a gap between customer expectations and product performance. Where an organization can identify a product line that has a cost or performance advantage that fits one of the gaps identified, it has an opportunity which it may be possible to exploit.

Before entering the market, however, the business must engage in product trials to ensure that the line has no fundamental weaknesses which will prohibit sales or that will be too costly to adapt. This, in turn, will be a function of market potential, market accessibility and the possible margins available.

Product adaptation

Unfortunately, it is rarely the case that a domestic product can be introduced into an overseas market without any form of adaptation. Research has shown that some of the biggest problems in product internationalization have occurred when organizations have followed the rather naive belief that products are transferable from home to foreign markets without change of some kind. Thus, product application is hardly ever universal and even globally branded products such as Coca-Cola use different formulations for different parts of the world to accommodate taste variations between countries.

Apart from taste and cultural influences such as colour requirements, adaptations may be required by distribution complexities not encountered in home markets. Thus packaging and unitization practices may differ by country and aspects such as product tracking mechanisms will often require modification once consignments enter a foreign land. Additionally, there are often legal or semi-legal requirements which must be satisfied. Thus, if a similar product or service already exists in a target country, there is likely to be a standard for it to which products will need to conform. Organizations must, therefore, have regard for:

- Legal requirements (such as environment/pollution legislation).
- Mandatory standards (such as electrical safety standards).
- Industry standards (such as light alloy wheels in Germany).
- Voluntary standards (such as paper size).

A further complication here is that, whereas standards are always well-defined, they tend to be:

- Different by country.
- Many in number as a result of covering measurement, quality, material, properties, performance and safety, etc.
- Different in legal backing/adherence and rationale.

As well as standards, products may also require adaptation as a consequence of the way in which they are used. Thus, other product characteristics that need to be most carefully researched in all foreign countries include:

- Physical properties, such as size, weight, materials, tolerances and instrumentation.
- Performance characteristics, such as mechanical, electrical and raw materials.
- Others, such as applications, symbols, codes, language, commissioning and service requirements.

As examples, in respect of physical characteristics, paper size is different in photocopiers in different markets and different flour quality affects the design of baking machinery. Similarly, with reference to performance, there are different generator-size requirements in different countries and in the case of application, tyre requirements differ significantly in hot countries, although the product is essentially the same. In addition, instruction and installation manuals will need to be rewritten and maintenance requirements may need to be altered to take account of service facilities in other countries.

Whilst it is tempting to stop at product/market analysis, it is also prudent to consider product adaptation at a much broader or company level. Thus, it might be important for an organization to consider whether it has: the design/technical capability, the raw material processing capability; the labour know-how; the equipment/technical know-how; the correct production processes, such as special assembly versus batch assembly; and so on. A good example is provided by power cables, where a European manufacturer had to switch machines and provide additional tooling in order to produce a product. In turn, this led to pressure on existing work-flows, resulting in a production plan change, with consequent capacity constraints, slower throughputs, lower earnings for employees and, worst of all, increased production costs.

Overall, issues such as these lead to the conclusion that the financial risks involved in entering overseas markets need to be most carefully evaluated. In particular, an organization is interested in the cost of adaptation, the resulting margins, the investment requirement and the likely return on investment (ROI), leading to a preliminary assessment of the volume required in any specific foreign market. In particular, the successful international company should be looking continuously for synergy and cost savings from any essential product adaptation. These are possible from:

- Economies of scale in production.
- Economies in product research and development.
- Economies in marketing as a result of consumer mobility.
- The impact of technology.

To plan satisfactorily for these circumstances, product managers thus have to be rigorous in their approach, as summarized in Table 54.1.

The financial risks involved in entering overseas markets must be carefully evaluated

Table 54.1 Areas requiring attention in international product planning

The product functionality	Standardization
	Adaptation
Packaging and labelling	Protection/security
	Promotional/channel aspects
	Cultural factors
	Package size
	Language
Brands and trade markets	Global or national
	Legal
	Cultural
	Other marketing considerations
Warranty and service	Transferability of domestic terms and conditions
	Safety
	Varying quality control standards internationally
	Varying use conditions
	Service networks

Topic 55 Organizational Structure and Marketing

One of the problems of managing marketing occurs when deciding exactly how marketing should fit within the existing and developing structures of the organization. The first problem concerns whether or not to have a specific marketing department at all. If it is thought that this is the right option, the second decision is judging what scope, or range of activities, it should oversee. Once a department's overall responsibilities have been determined, the third step is to decide how it should be structured and who should do what job. If it is felt that a discrete marketing department is not appropriate, establishing and maintaining strong marketing leadership throughout the organization becomes more than usually important.

The significance of these problems is that organizations can only provide the environment within which people carry out their work; they cannot determine how the work is performed. However, structures, and the control systems associated with them, provide evidence of how senior managers value a particular activity and the role it plays in the organization. In addition, it must be remembered that structure can also place hurdles in the way of people trying to get on with achieving their responsibilities by making communication, coordination and decision-making more difficult. It is, therefore, vital that organizations think carefully about the structures they create and how they are commensurate with the long-term objectives they are trying to achieve.

The typical evolutionary pattern for an organization that has grown over time will lead it from a 'one-man-band' situation, where one person will perform all tasks and where sales essentially involve order-taking with small amounts of prospecting or advertising, to the multifunctioning super-department incorporating a whole range of specialist activities as illustrated in Figure 55.1. As an organization grows and becomes more sophisticated in its approach to marketing, it becomes faced with a number of options for structuring its range of marketing activities.

Typical evolutionary pattern of marketing

One-man band
Basically an order-taker, probably
involved in technical side as well.

Sales team marketing
Sales people sent out to 'drum up
orders'. Self-generated sales support
materials.

Sales force plus marketing sales support
Marketing provides materials and
information which support sales activities.

Sales force plus ancillary marketing
Marketing expands activities and employs
specialists to manage a range of
functions – still essentially sales support.

Separate sales and marketing departments
Marketing takes on product or brand
management responsibilities and starts to
coordinate/influence sales strategies.

Unified sales and marketing departments
A sales and marketing director/VP
appointed to coordinate all activities.

Figure 55.1   Organizational structure and marketing

Central and decentralized activities

For organizations which have expanded so that they operate in several regions, the
first choice is between centralizing and decentralizing their marketing activities.
Centralized operations make coordination much easier and are better at avoiding

duplication. Decentralization allows for more flexibility and better exploitation of local opportunities. In this respect, there are no 'right' or 'wrong' options. The choice will depend on the organization's product diversity, the need for local variations and the management's ability to achieve a good balance between coordination and control. The latter is necessary to avoid fragmentation and to prevent managers feeling that they have no effective freedom of choice. Sadly, in many international organizations, it is not uncommon for local (i.e. decentralized) marketing personnel to find themselves with no influence over product decisions, price or delivery, and who then become frustrated at having to manage a marketing mix over which they have little control.

An ideal arrangement, of course, is to organize around a combination of both in order to gain the benefits of each. This involves putting marketing as close to the customer as possible, whilst also having some kind of centralized marketing function. In this way, the potential for costly and unnecessary duplication is minimized and the possibility of achieving economies of scale and effective knowledge transfer is optimized.

Departmental structures

For organizations with marketing departments, the second area of choice is the methodology for structuring the department's activities. The main decision is whether to organize around functions; products; markets; key accounts; geographical area; or some combination of two or more of these options. A functionally organized department would separate activities such as: new product management; market research; customer service; advertising; market analysis; public relations; sales promotions/special campaigns; and so on.

Alternatively, a department could be organized around a series of product managers who would be responsible for the whole range of activities associated with their products or brands. This would include stimulating activity within the sales force and third party re-sellers, as well as intra-company coordination. Organizing around markets would involve the creation of market managers, whether geographically, by sector, or by segment. Variations on this theme have been referred to as vertical marketing, trade marketing and industry marketing.

In some cases, such as, for example, where there are very few customers, it is sensible to organize around key account management, whilst in others it is appropriate to have marketing specialists with responsibility for all activities within a definable area. In many organizations, a combination of approaches is often in evidence. As examples, some businesses organize around brand managers, but separate the functions of public relations, customer service and planning, whilst others use both product and market managers in a matrix-type relationship.

The dangers inherent in any approach or methodology cover a number of areas. The first is that sometimes products or markets are lost from managers' perspectives.

The main structural decision is what to organize around

For instance, organizing around markets would seem to be sensible for corporations which are interested in developing a marketing-orientated business. However, focusing on markets can lead to the neglect of smaller brands, the dilution or loss of functional skills or product knowledge, and excessive product customization so that economies of scale are reduced. The second danger, therefore, is that focusing on functions, products and/or markets reduces the chances that all the tasks which need to be completed actually get done, and are performed in as professional or as effective a way as possible. The third is that responsibility and accountability become imbalanced, so that the objectives people have to achieve are not commensurate with the areas over which they have control.

One of the key problems in operationalizing marketing in organizations is achieving the correct balance between responsibility and accountability in the management of the marketing mix. Marketing managers are obviously concerned to manipulate the mix to create an offer irresistible to targeted customers. Many of the elements of the marketing mix, however, are quite rightly under the control of non-marketing managers, since they require specialist or technical skills to be managed well. Marketing managers are therefore in the position of being responsible for the profitable sales of the organization's products, but without the authority to control the elements that will promote such sales. In many organizations, the conflict and poor relations that exist between sales and marketing or engineering and marketing typify this problem.

Process redesign

One attempt to overcome some of these difficulties has been to reorganize an organization's activities around its core processes which either obtain value from suppliers or deliver value to customers. Instead of structuring a business around their functional activities such as operations, finance and human resources, etc., some organizations have adopted processes such as new product development, order fulfilment and cost reduction as the basis for managing operating units. Each process is managed by a team which has responsibility for delivering efficiency in that area and for meeting the objectives appropriate for competitive advantage. The teams may still be product or customer focused, depending on the nature of the business. The key difference between conventional structures and a core process, team-based approach, is that the team becomes multifunctional with responsibility for, say, inbound logistics, production, sales and supply, rather than each activity stage being a distinct and separate operation.

Under these circumstances, marketing functions would be provided by each of the teams, with ultimate marketing responsibility resting with the top team for each process. The organization would also include a specialist marketing unit, which would provide information, advice or assistance on specialist topics such as conducting market research or designing a customer service strategy. Marketing would thus be brought closer to the areas it needs to influence, since a good part of all the elements of the marketing mix would be the responsibility of the cross-functional process team. Under this approach, marketing expertise would be injected into the team either through consultancy, training or 'contracting out'.

Other developments

In addition to the 'business process redesign' described above, there are a number of other developments that are likely to affect the position or structure of marketing within organizations.

The first of these is the decline of traditional brand management as retailers become more powerful and, in some cases, substitute brands. Rather than a brand's franchise in the market influencing the choice of supplier, retailers are now much more interested in costs, strategy alignment, and response to regional differences, as a basis for choosing suppliers.

The second development is the advancements being made in micromarketing, which are encouraging marketing managers to look at differences between consumers in more elaborate ways and to use sales promotion activities and database marketing for more accurate targeting.

The third is the reduction in the effectiveness of mass advertising as media channels proliferate and as it becomes harder to reach mass markets. These trends will support moves away from national and international brand management as a basis for organizing marketing, towards market-focused management structures, either as part of a process team, or as a framework based on relationships.

Fourth, the current popularity of category management as a basis for organizing consumer goods marketing is also affecting how suppliers organize their marketing activities. To match their retail customers, suppliers are organizing brand portfolios and appointing category managers, or 'champions', whose focus is on maximizing profit from a category for the retailer rather than developing brand franchises.

In the end, however, it must be remembered that structure is of only secondary importance in establishing marketing as an effective force within an organization. Of greater significance is the attitude of the managers working within the structures and the ways in which they are able to influence other managers towards a market-orientated approach to their own responsibilities. If a market orientation is well embedded and stretches across its range of activities, it is almost possible to argue that structure is irrelevant to marketing effectiveness.

The position and structure of marketing is being challenged

56 Budgeting for Marketing

One of the most vexing questions for any marketing manager, or indeed any marketing organization, is 'How much, and where, should we spend on marketing?' The question is difficult because it requires an understanding of what should be included in a marketing budget, the way in which costs are generated and the relationship between marketing expenditure and the results sought. Each of these areas is problematic and often requires sophisticated financial information and analytical tools for the development of effective programmes and budgets.

Budgeting practices

For many organizations, such information and tools are not readily available. In their absence, the most appealing approach is to use last year's figures as the base and to project forward. This, of course, takes into account inflation, prevailing market conditions and adds on an amount which senior controllers will deduct at the budget review!

Zero-based budgeting

More preferable is an **iterative zero-based** approach that starts with marketing objectives and the programmes designed to achieve these objectives. Once activities have been identified, the incremental cost of these can be calculated and a budget can be established. If these are deemed to be too expensive, alternative activities or structures can be investigated. If these prove equally unacceptable, then a review of strategy is required, and so on. In this way, every item of expenditure can be traced back to specific objectives, and indeed to the overall corporate objectives of the organization.

Variable cost budgeting

A less wide-ranging approach is to base the budget on **variable costs**, particularly for short-term budgeting, since certain costs, such as human resources and physical facilities, can only be significantly altered in the longer term. Periodically, however, this would require a zero-based approach to be used to review all products, markets and related activities. This would enable organizations to abandon obsolete and unnecessary features and to make appropriate structural alterations.

Many of the moves away from brand management towards category, or business process, management are a result of such reviews.

Lifecycle budgeting

Budgeting for marketing can also incorporate **lifecycle costing**. This involves assessments of the total costs involved in managing products over their life in the market. Such an approach requires marketing managers to plan ahead in terms of product upgrades, changing promotional activities, service and distribution support, and the way price is likely to alter over the life of a product. Long-term assessments of return on investment, payback and cash management can therefore be made, which will help both short-term budgeting control and organizational financial planning.

Operating and opportunity budgeting

A further approach to structuring a budget utilizes the notions of **operating budget** versus **opportunity** or **exceptions budgets**. Operating budgets cover those activities that are a continuation of existing programmes. The key issues here are in terms of efficiency and the maintenance of expected performance levels. This highlights the fact that marketing managers should be seeking constant cost-reduction and better ways of managing the marketing mix and obtaining marketing information, whilst at the same time countering adverse developments. An opportunities budget should be developed for unexpected circumstances which can yield financial and marketing benefits for the organization. One of the critical roles of marketing managers is to spot such opportunities and to feed them into the general management of their enterprise.

Marketing costs for budgeting

Since marketing management requires the development of an offer, which consists of the various elements of the marketing mix, a marketing budget should, in theory, include all costs associated with operationalizing this mix. In practice, marketing managers do not, of course, have control over all these elements. In addition, the activities over which they do have control will vary from one organization to another.

For an organization that buys in products which are then sold via a direct sales force, some form of catalogue or a direct mail activity, the marketing budget may be comprehensive and include selling costs; order processing; stockholding; merchandising; packaging; and credit. For a manufacturing concern with complex logistics, which sells via distributors or retailers and utilizes significant financial activities such as credit card or electronic data interchange (EDI) facilities, marketing may be more focused on the generation of demand and market forecasting.

Marketing budgets depend on what marketing managers control

For budgeting purposes, the important factor here is to distinguish between **controllable** and **uncontrollable** costs. This is a particularly difficult problem when sales and marketing are organized as two separate activities. Whilst marketing managers may be held accountable for sales and profits, they may have no responsibility for selling, merchandising and discounts. Thus, the contents of marketing budgets need to be set in the context of specific organizational structures, the way in which senior management see the priorities of their business and the role of marketing within it.

Costing marketing activities

Even where marketing responsibilities are clearly identifiable, budgeting problems can still arise as a result of difficulties in allocating costs between different marketing activities. As an example, the ultimate profit centre for a business is each individual customer. For industrial companies with only a handful of customers, costs and profits may be easy to identify on a customer basis. Where larger numbers of customers exist, the allocation of expenditures such as advertising, sales and customer service between customers becomes confused. This is especially so since some customers can be easy to sell to whilst others may require much greater efforts. Similarly, some customers may place great demands on their suppliers, whilst others may be more self-sufficient. In addition, some customers may take a very profitable mix of products whilst others may only purchase those with low margin. Thus, establishing the profitability of a customer may be a very confusing process.

The problem for marketing managers lies in determining the most profitable courses of action and in targeting the organization's activities in the best way possible. This requires good information about both customer profitability and product profitability, and as indicated, it may be hard to attribute costs in a way which will yield the appropriate information. In addition, the expected results of different types of campaign such as sales promotions, additional sales people, product upgrades and price adjustments may also be difficult to judge.

Some assistance can be gained from historical data which can be used to assess trends or to establish relationships between expenditure and results. Unfortunately, simple input/output relationships rarely exist in marketing, except at a very low level, since purchases are the result of a complex series of events which are unlikely to repeat themselves from one time-period to another. In the end, marketing managers must utilize both the information which does exist and their professional judgement, based on experience and sound marketing principles, to set their budgets.

Overall, then, budgeting for marketing is an imprecise science which will depend on an organization's structure, its approach to marketing and the sophistication of its information systems for its quality. The process can be enhanced by focusing on the areas which are important to a business and ensuring that expenditure is related to specific marketing objectives. Distinguishing between order-filling activities and order-getting activities can help identify marketing responsibilities and is a basis for analysing the effectiveness of marketing activities. Ultimately, however, the interweaving of a market orientation into all areas of operations, so that appropriate judgements can be made, will be most beneficial in directing and controlling marketing expenditure.

Expenditure must be related to specific marketing objectives

Legal Issues in Marketing Communications

Marketers and general managers alike will probably know and understand the differences between, say, an Ansoff and a Boston Matrix. It is less likely, however, that they will know the difference between contract and tort. Or for that matter the difference between civil and criminal law. More dangerously, they may be completely unaware that a claim in a news release could be subject to review by the Committee of Advertising Practice (CAP).

Unfortunately, ignorance of the law as it applies to modern marketing communication is no longer acceptable in today's highly litigious industry, which has only recently (2006) seen two giants of the mobile world slug it out over the rights to use the colour orange, and the founder of Apple computers being pursued by the remaining members of the 'Fab Four' (The Beatles) over alleged trademark infringement.

Rules and regulations have a purpose in business and marketing best practice should comply automatically with the laws of the country in which an organization operates. Thus, a business based in London should conform to British and European Union (EU) laws; although it can't always be assumed that it does given that

Table 57.1 Sources of legal information

- Advertising Standards Authority (www.asa.org.uk)
- Brand Republic (www.brandrepublic.com)
- British Copyright Council (www.britishcopyright.org)
- Committee of Advertising Practice (www.cap.org.uk)
- European Commission Office (http://europa.eu.int/index_en.htm)
- Ethics Resource Centre (www.ethics.org)
- Equal Opportunities Commission (www.eoc.org.uk)
- Fax Preference Service (www.fpsonline.org.uk)
- Freedom of Information (www.dca.gov.uk)
- Human Rights (www.humanrights.gov.uk)
- Information Commissioner (www.ico.gov.uk)
- Mailing Preference Service (www.mpsonline.org.uk)
- Office for Communication (www.ofcom.org.uk)
- Office of Fair Trading (www.oft.gov.uk)
- Pinsent Masons (www.out-law.com)

laws change so frequently. Most law and regulation is based on common sense, so any person who finds themselves engaged in activities likely to discredit, rather than enhance, strengthen or protect your organization's *reputation*, is highly likely to be doing something that is unlawful as well.

However, navigating the legal thicket will require more than just cursory knowledge of basic legal issues, and with that in mind, a number of resources have been identified that will help; these are listed In Table 57.1.

There are three distinct ways in which England & Wales and EU laws and regulations impact the marketing practitioner.

Legal barriers to market entry

Barriers to market entry such as, for example, the qualifications legally required to practise as a doctor or barrister are useful. Their existence means that the supply of such services is tightly controlled and, as a result, they can command a premium price in the market. Conversely, certain products, such as baby clothing, must comply with fire-retardant regulations, which means that baby clothes that do not comply can't be lawfully sold in the market. A legal barrier to market entry therefore makes it difficult for competitors to enter the market and can help to indirectly protect the market share of existing companies already lawfully trading.

The key legal tools used in marketing to enforce the barrier to market entry are:

- *Trade marks* – legal protection stops other competitors from using the same or similar marks, with protection extending to words (including personal names), designs, letters, numerals and even the shape of goods or their packaging, as is the case for a Coca-Cola bottle.
- *Passing off* – this stops others from producing imitation or fake merchandise, or pretending that their business is in some way linked to your own.
- *Copyright* – a useful legal measure to prevent competitors using someone's material or ideas without permission. This applies to literature, music, and dramatic and artistic works.
- *Personality rights* – important for celebrities whose image may be used in an advertising or marketing campaign as it stops others from using that person's image or endorsement without seeking permission first.

Legal requirements for marketing activities

This is really about staying on the straight and narrow. Failure to comply with certain laws and regulations concerning marketing of products and services can lead to serious consequences; in some cases, non-compliance can even lead to jail.

Laws impact marketing practitioners in three ways

Figure 57.1 Three faces of the law

Laws that place legal requirements on suppliers cover a very wide range of marketing and communications activities, including:

- Advertising, sales promotions and direct marketing – the Committee of Advertising Practice (CAP) provides a body of regulations that organizations must comply with. This includes the requirement that all marketing communications should be legal, decent, honest and truthful.
- E-mail and SMS campaigns – under national and EU laws, spamming is an offence and, subject to a few exceptions, businesses must always get the permission of the recipient to send a marketing e-mail or mobile text message that contains an offer or special promotion.
- Using databases for marketing – the Data Protection Act 1998 is possibly the piece of legislation to have had the greatest impact on marketing in recent times. It gives individuals a legal right to know how a third party has obtained, recorded and holds personal data. The 1998 Act also sets out detailed controls on the transmission, retrieval and protection of such data and makes the staff involved personally liable for any breach of these conditions.

The law as a weapon for competitive advantage

The above presents the law as something that is about limiting or controlling the way organizations conduct their marketing activities. However, there are several areas of marketing practice where knowing how to apply the law will make a difference to the nature and content of a business's marketing and communication efforts. As an example, some laws, such as the EU Directive on Comparative Advertising, have legitimized activities previously illegal in some countries. The Directive allows comparative advertising as being in the interests of competition and public information. However, the law also protects competitors from being undermined by untrue comparisons, but not where comparisons are valid. Thus, when British Airways sued Ryanair for an advert that compared prices under the heading 'Expensive B. . . . . . ds', they were unsuccessful as the core claim within the advert was substantially true. In a different vein, pharmaceutical companies can gain significant competitive advantage from careful manipulation of patent registrations to extend the life of a drug beyond the initial protection period.

The law prevents untrue comparisons being made

58 Marketing Due Diligence

The purpose of 'Marketing Due Diligence' is to assess whether an organization's marketing strategies will create or destroy shareholder value. This is achieved by linking a marketing strategy to the **risks** associated with it, as risk and the corresponding required rate of return are directly linked. The normal financial focus of marketing strategies and plans is on predicting outcomes, not assessing the associated risks. These potential financial outcomes are often presented as single point, apparent certainties, rather than being expressed as a range of the possible outcomes that may result, given the volatility of future business environments.

The Marketing Due Diligence process thus looks at the specific risks associated with each element of a marketing strategy, so that individual **probability assessments** of success/failure and the consequent impact on financial outcomes are identified. This enables predicted financial outcomes to be directly adjusted, where necessary, in the light of identified risks. The level of any adjustment that is required clearly depends on how the forecasts were originally prepared. Plans that include extremely optimistic stretch targets ('best case' plans) will normally need more adjustment than more conservative plans that already allow for expected risks and consequent volatility in financial returns ('most likely' plans).

In order to produce a shareholder value 'figure' from the Marketing Due Diligence diagnostic process, probability adjusted sets of expected **future cash flows** are then compared to the financial return required by the business. This is done by assessing the true capital tied up in implementing the proposed marketing strategy. The true capital includes the critically important, and often highly valuable, intangible marketing assets as well as the more obvious tangible assets of the business.

As the specific risks of the proposed marketing strategy have already been taken into account in the diagnostic review, the return required on this capital employed can be calculated by reference to the company's normal cost of capital. In other words, there is no need arbitrarily to increase the required rate of return to try to take account of the complex myriad of risk factors.

There can be one additional adjustment to the predicted financial return if the proposed marketing strategy places any existing assets at risk. This concept of '**capital at risk**' is used to highlight strategies that leverage existing marketing assets, such as umbrella branding. Often this is done to reduce the required marketing expenditure, but the expected financial returns do not normally include the potentially offsetting decrease in value of the existing asset, if the strategy is not completely successful. This adjustment is made as part of the full Marketing Due Diligence review.

Even if the existing marketing planning information is not sufficient to enable a numerical value to be calculated, the Marketing Due Diligence diagnostic process will still highlight the key risk areas of any proposed strategy and show up the specific deficiencies in the current marketing plan. In many cases these deficiencies can be remedied by applying the therapeutic process within marketing due diligence, which reviews and improves the marketing planning process.

The application of Marketing Due Diligence clearly has significant implications for both internal and external stakeholders in any business. The rigorous review of proposed marketing strategies should be a key element in any sound corporate governance process. Marketing Due Diligence provides a methodology to do this consistently across even a diversified group and through time. Indeed, the knowledge that all marketing plans and strategies will be subjected to this type of analysis will rapidly improve the quality of the processes used internally within the marketing function.

Thus, the critical resource allocation decisions at board level should be based on much better and more validly comparative information. Knowing this should provide great reassurance to external analysts and shareholders, as they can be more confident that future marketing strategies will be shareholder value-enhancing.

There are a number of different sources of risk that need to be taken into consideration in the due diligence process as outlined below.

Market risk

Market risk is the risk that the predicted market size will not be as large as hoped for by the plan. It is distinct from, but aggregates with, (market) share risk and profit risk. Market projections can turn out to be wrong for a number of reasons: the targeted market is very new; the product category is very new; the product enters a new stage in its lifecycle; or the uncertainty arising from this 'newness' is not compensated for by effective research and analysis.

Share risk

Share risk is the risk that the strategy will not create the degree of customer preference or competitive advantage that is needed to create the planned market share and hence fall short of creating shareholder value. It appears when what is offered to customers is not, in their eyes, valuable enough to them. This happens

Marketing Due Diligence provides a methodology for rigorous review

for a number of reasons: the wrong customers are targeted, they are offered the wrong things, or the strategy involves going head-on with a bigger, stronger competitor.

Profit risk

The required contribution to shareholder value can still founder as a result of profit risk, even if the strategy achieves the predicted market share and sales revenue. Profit risk considers the probability of creating the anticipated financial return from the predicted market share of the planned market value. Risks are greatest in relatively mature markets where established competitors are often fighting to obtain a larger share of a static or even declining total profit pool (profit pool risk). Profit sources risk is higher if planned increases in profit come from competitors, and lower if it comes from growth in the total profit pool. Other profit risks include: unusually aggressive competitor reaction; volatile internal costs; or failure to control adequately marketing expenditure.

The process of conducting Marketing Due Diligence assessments starts with identification of the critical market segments for which marketing plans have been prepared. Projections of the future net free cash in-flows from these segments over a period of between three and five years should then be made. These calculations will consist of cost and revenue forecasts for each year, plus net free cash flow for each segment. Key factors that will increase or decrease future cash flows then need to be assessed for risk under the headings: market risk; share risk; and profit risk. The resultant probability factors should then be applied to the forecast revenues, costs and net free cash flows. Having ascertained the organization's cost of capital, the proportional cost of capital from the free cash flow for each segment for each year is deducted. An aggregate positive net present value indicates that the business is creating shareholder value – i.e. achieving overall returns greater than the weighted average cost of capital, having taken into account the risk associated with future cash flow.

59 Marketing Metrics

Traditional fast-moving consumer goods businesses such as household consumables have many tried-and-tested models for measuring the effectiveness of promotional expenditure. Indeed, some of these are quite sophisticated and include mathematical models for promotional campaigns, for determining advertising thresholds and wear-out levels, and so on. Over time, these models have been transferred to business-to-business and service companies, with the result that, today, any organization spending substantial sums of shareholders' money on promotion should be ashamed of themselves if those responsible cannot account for the effectiveness of such expenditure.

Accountability at this level can only be measured in terms of the effects that promotional expenditure can be expected to achieve, such as awareness and attitude change, both of which can be measured quantitatively. However, to extend this and assert that the effect of such expenditure can be measured directly in terms of sales or profits is inappropriate as there are so many other variables that affect sales, such as: product efficacy; packaging; price; sales force activities; competitors; and countless other variables that, like advertising, have an intermediate impact on sales and profits.

The problem with finding metrics that will measure the effectiveness of marketing and making marketing managers accountable has, therefore, never been with how to measure the effectiveness of promotional expenditure. The problem occurs because marketing is a more pervasive discipline than just promotional activity. In world-class organizations, where the customer is at the centre of the business model, marketing as a discipline is responsible for defining and understanding markets; for segmenting these markets; for developing value propositions to meet the researched needs of the customers in the segments; for gaining alignment from all those in the organization responsible for delivering this value; for playing their own part in delivering this value; and for monitoring whether the promised value is being delivered. In many organizations, not all these will be the direct responsibility of a marketing function. However, they do form the **marketing domain** which, when represented as a map, can be used to clarify the problem of how to measure marketing effectiveness.

Activity in the '**Strategic Zone**' is vital because this is what determines whether the strategies developed as a basis for the longer-term competitive positioning (usually three to five years) will destroy or create shareholder value. The main thrust of

Marketing metrics are difficult as marketing is a very pervasive discipline

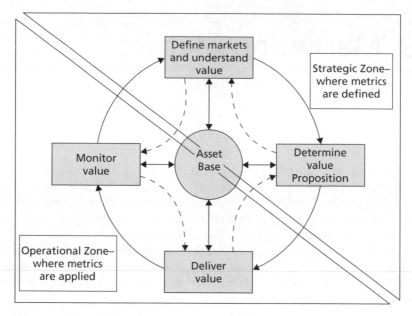

Figure 59.1 Map of the marketing domain

these activities will usually be contained within the strategic plan for the business and should build on the corporate asset base and its associated competences. In a well-balanced organization, they should lead to sustainable competitive advantage. Once established, such strategies can be subjected to a process of **Marketing Due Diligence** to establish the impact on shareholder value (see Topic 58 Marketing Due Diligence).

Effectiveness of promotional activity in the '**Operations Zone**' can be measured by the well-established metrics commonly used in this arena. Metrics for other marketing-based operational activities, however, are only recently beginning to emerge.

Such metrics are moving away from the over-simplistic view of measures of marketing effectiveness based on accounting notions of return on investment, which imply profit divided by investment as a simple input/output relationship. As explained in a recent *Harvard Business Review* article:

> *'Measuring marketing performance isn't like measuring factory output – a fact that many non-marketing executives don't grasp. In the controlled environment of a manufacturing plant, it's simple to account for what goes in one end and what comes out the other and then determine productivity. The output of marketing can be measured only long after it has left the plant.'* [McGovern G., Court D., Quelch A., Crawford B. (Nov. 2004). Harvard Business Review]

One way of developing more sophisticated metrics is to use the powerful Ansoff Matrix as a starting point. As shown in Figure 59.2, each of the cells in the matrix will have a definable set of products that will be offered to specified customers or segments. Each cell therefore becomes a planning unit, in the sense that objectives will be set for volume, value and profit levels over a year's trading.

Figure 59.2 The Ansoff Matrix

The strategies for achieving these objectives will manifest themselves in the form of different activities within the marketing mix, but will be founded on a series of key market needs or critical success factors (CSFs). Once identified, these can be weighted according to their relative importance to the customers in the relevant segment. When an organization's position regarding these CSFs has been determined, it can compare itself to competitors and identify areas where improvements are required to improve market position. An example *pro forma* is shown in Figure 59.3.

It is unlikely that the marketing function will be directly responsible for what needs to be done to improve a CSF. For example, issues like product efficacy, after-sales service, channel management, and sometimes even price and the sales force are often controlled by other functions. Responsibility here reverts to an organization's general or senior management who will be looking to coordinate activities across the business.

The focus for any metrics at this point becomes the CSFs. The improvements in performance required to obtain competitive advantage are easier to measure, and

Sophistication can be achieved by using the Ansoff Matrix

Critical success factors	Weighting factor	Your organization	Competitor A	Competitor B	Competitor C
CSF 1					
CSF 2					
CSF 3					
CSF 4					
Total weighted score (score x weight)	100				

• Strategies to improve competitive position/achieve objectives over time (4Ps)
• Metrics (each CSF) to measure performance over time in achieving goals

Figure 59.3 Critical success factors

will feed directly into the delivery of the marketing objectives set for each segment. Thus, expenditure on marketing and other functional actions to improve CSFs can be linked to marketing objectives and, ultimately, to profitability, and it becomes clear exactly what must be measured and why. It also obviates the assumption that a particular marketing action can be linked directly to profitability. It can only be linked to other weighted CSFs which, if improved, should lead to the achievement of volumes, value and, ultimately, profits.

Index

ACORN, 80
Added value, 114–16, 224, 231
Adoption process, 112–13
Advertising, 3, 4, 7, 12–13, 162–6, 216,
    232, 235, 237, 265, 267, 272, 282
  above-the-line expenditure, 157–8
  AIDA and, 58
  banner, 232
  brand personality, 115
  channel management and, 207–8
  cheap forms of, 162
  cooperative, 55
  definition, 157
  effectiveness, 164–5
  ethical concerns, 20–21
  internet, 59–61
  legal issues, 274–7
  mass, 269
  media, 162–3
  mobile marketing and, 223–5
  objectives, 163–5
  plan for, 165–6
  public relations and, 167–70
  sales promotion and, 157–60
  sponsorship and, 171–4
  types of, 163
Advertising Standards Authority, 274
After-sales service, 7, 11, 17, 73, 115, 157,
    186, 211, 213, 283
AIDA (awareness, interest, desire, action),
  58
Ansoff matrix, 126–30, 283
Audit (market), 25, 28, 97–100, 101–2, 107
  external, 216
  internal, 216

Balanced Scorecard, 24
Barriers to entry, 5, 48, 65, 106, 137
  legal, 275–6
Benchmark product, 143, 154

Benefit (product), 44, 146
  analysis, 47, 190
  differential, 190
  segmentation, 185
Best practice, 56, 274
Biro, 114
BMW, 36, 113
Boston Matrix, 131–4, 135–6, 274
Brand, 70, 82, 113–16, 150, 164, 204, 231
  awareness, 164, 172, 225
  category management and, 226–8
  consumer, 35–6
  differentiation, 55
  ethical issues, 19–20
  franchise, 57, 160
  industrial, 38
  international, 67, 114
  licensing, 64
  lifecycles, 117–21
  management, 7, 17, 35, 24–5, 55, 197,
    226, 267, 269, 271
  mobile marketing and, 220–25
  new, 102, 142
  personality, 35, 115
  positioning, 114–15, 173
  seven enhancements, 220–22
  sponsorship and, 172–4
  value development, 205, 208, 220
  values, 27, 35, 38, 150, 164, 169, 173,
    188
Braun, 202
British Code of Advertising Practice, 21
Brown goods, 33
Budgeting, 155, 252, 270–73
Buy class, 75
Buy centre, 53
Buying signals, 191
Buying behaviour, 80, 81, 145
  consumer, 69–73
  organizational, 74–8

Capital goods, 21, 39, 51–3, 191, 259
Carrefour, 57
Cash cows, 131–4
Cash dogs, 133
Category killers, 56
Category management, 56–7, 226–9, 269, 271
Channel management, 29, 35, 206–9, 283
Channel possibilities, 14
Channel strategy, 202–5, 230
　integrated, 231
　multi, 230
Cluster analysis, 92
Clustering, 81
Coca Cola, 36, 85, 114, 118, 169, 174, 227, 262, 275
Cognitive dissonance, 73
Cognitive stage, 72
Commodity, 27, 34, 38, 113–16, 154, 155, 208
Communication(s), 58, 59, 73, 79, 84, 162–4, 167–8, 173, 199, 245
　channels, 171, 261
　integrated, 13, 235–8
　interactive, 58
　internet, 61
　legal issues, 274–7
　mobile marketing, 220–25
　non-personal, 157
　personal selling, 189–92
　personalization, 214
　strategy, 235, 227
Competitive:
　activities, 133, 157, 164, 209
　advantage, 23, 24, 26, 36, 81, 84, 93, 102, 114, 123, 154, 162, 172, 210, 268, 276, 277, 279, 284
　analysis, 106–10
　environment, 180
　markets, 50, 150, 164
　position, 6, 27, 39, 102, 181, 213, 281
　power, 92
　prices, 208
　strategy, 15
　tendering, 151
　tool, 46
　value, 127
　variable, 98
　weapon, 52

Competitor:
　activities, 164, 237, 261, 280
　advantage, 6, 79, 208
　analysis, 91, 100, 106–10
　information, 89
　positioning, 16, 90, 160
　pricing, 142, 154, 184
　products, 144, 153, 186, 188, 202, 261
　response, 175
Consumer products, 33–6, 127
　branding, 35, 113
　and industrial products, 37–8
　marketing methods, 34–5
　new, 145
Consumerism, 21–2
Cost-benefit analysis, 219
Cost-based pricing, 152
Critical success factors (CSFs), 89, 102, 283–4
Customer:
　defection, 186
　loyalty, 179
　management, 44
　retention, 5, 210
　retention strategies, 184–8
　service, 14, 17, 45, 49, 59, 120, 127, 180–82, 186–7, 195, 230, 236, 267, 272
　service strategies, 210–13
　promiscuous, 185
　value strategy, 231

Database(s), 34, 59, 229
Database marketing, 185, 187, 214–19, 225, 269, 276
Deals, 224, 232
Dealer(s), 70, 203, 205, 208
　loaders, 158–9
Deal-orientation, 207
Decision-making, 48, 89, 121, 165, 208, 247, 258, 265, 279
　processes, 8, 72, 101, 124, 189, 224
　support mechanisms, 92, 195, 216
　trees, 59
Decision-making unit, 38
　for capital goods, 53
　for consumer products, 69–73
　for industrial products, 74–8

Decisions:
  pricing, 153–6, 267
  purchase, 38, 109, 113, 189, 216, 228, 231
Demand, 44, 50, 52, 106, 157, 197, 271
  derived, 39
  excess, 3, 152
  influencing variables, 10, 114
  latent, 50
  managing, 45, 164
  primary, 61
  pull, 50, 54, 204
Demographic, 26, 123, 182, 214, 221
  descriptors, 80
Desk research, 90
DHL, 198
Direct mail, 17, 34, 59, 61, 163, 187, 222, 230, 237, 271
  retailers, 203
Direct response, 164, 221
Directional Policy Matrix, 135–9
Discount(s), 4, 11, 45, 55, 57, 127, 154–6, 207, 226, 234, 272
  loyalty, 187
  structures, 91
  volume, 7
Distress purchase, 123
Distribution, 10–14, 41, 84, 91, 99, 129, 160, 203, 209, 235–7, 271
  channel, 85, 124, 145, 160
  costs, 56, 202
  patterns, 247
  selective, 204
  strategy options, 204
  system, 202, 228
  wide, 24
Dogs, 131–4

Early adopters, 123
Early majority, 123
E-commerce, 55, 221, 230
E-mail, 58–9, 119, 220, 234, 235–7, 276
Efficient Customer Response, 226
Electronic Data Exchange (EDI), 212, 213, 271
Emotional, 115
  appeal, 115
  convictions, 72
  response, 72

End user markets, 204
End users, 46, 54, 56, 65, 76, 114, 204, 207
Enhanced value, 105, 203
Environment(s), 29, 56, 63, 78, 97–8, 220, 247, 251
  competitive, 180
  cultural, 155
  international, 63–4
  market(ing), 4–5, 53, 72, 89, 119, 249
  personal, 220, 223
Environmental:
  change, 252
  conditions, 9, 69
  scanning, 24–5
ERP (Enterprise Resource Planning), 91
Ethics, 19–21
Europe, 84–5, 157, 202, 257
European Union, 84, 274
Experience Curve, 132–3
Expert systems, 92
Exporting, 64–5

Family, 64, 70, 79
Fast moving products, 259
  consumer goods (fmcg), 33, 37, 179, 191, 281
  industrial goods, 54, 191
Field research, 90
Financial orientation, 9
Fisher Price, 22
Five Forces (Porter's), 100, 106
Floor pricing, 151
Ford, 5, 36, 115
Forecast(s), 28, 258, 271, 278
Forecasting:
  sales, 247–50
  for planning, 251–4
Four Ps, 4, 9, 10, 29, 45, 60, 179, 253
Fuji, 170

Gatekeepers, 75, 77
General Electric (GE), 232
General management, 9, 18, 40, 200
Geodemographic, 217
Germany, 56, 84, 202, 262
GKN, 65
Government, 53, 182
  agencies, 149, 162, 218
  activities, 5

Government (*contd*)
 foreign, 65
 procurement, 152
 restrictions on advertising, 169
 statistics, 90
Greece, 84, 102
Guarantees and warranty, 48, 159, 186,
 264

Hedging arrangements, 154
Heinz, 55, 254, 259
High-tech products, 47–50, 85, 169
 features of, 47
 marketing issues, 47–50
 risk, 46
Hoardings, 163
Hoover, 114
Hungary, 84
Hybrid products, 85

IBM, 25, 118
Image, 35, 113, 138, 150, 160, 167–8,
 174
 brand, 113, 115, 121
 corporate, 180
 self, 70, 71, 245
 of sponsor, 171
 statement, 220
Impersonal promotion, 12
Implementation, 6, 21, 197, 200–201,
 212, 255, 256–70
Incentives, 45, 245
Individualization, 59
Industrial products, 33, 37–40, 52, 85, 113
 conceptualizing, 37
 marketing issues, 38–9
Influencer markets, 169, 181–82, 187
Information needs, 38, 77, 89, 120, 217
Information sources, 71, 90, 217
Information systems, 89, 219, 273
 for marketing, 91–3
Informative advertising, 163
Innovation, 9, 11, 36, 52, 144
 diffusion of, 117, 122–5
Institutional changes, 5
Institutions, 180
 financial, 41
 marketing, 21
 media, 43

Intangibility, 42, 113
Intangible, 187, 242
 aspects of marketing, 8
 assets, 17, 278
 attributes, 114
 benefits, 125, 157, 187
 features, 181
 products, 42–4
 relationships, 249
Intangibles, 194
Intel, 37, 56
Intelligence, 16, 60, 91–3, 109, 133, 137,
 215
Intensive distribution, 204
Interest group, 163
Interest rates, 4, 5, 137
Intermediaries, 13, 39, 46, 54–7, 114, 144,
 169, 182, 187
 managing, 206–9
 strategy for, 202–5
Internal customer data, 218
Internal information sources, 91–2
Internal marketing, 101
Internal marketing audit, 98, 216
Internal markets, 45, 169, 181–3, 215
Internal variables, 98, 221
International market segmentation, 84–6
International marketing, 63–6, 261
International product planning, 261–3
International products, 85
Internet, 36, 56, 162, 211, 220, 230
 marketing, 58–62
Interview(s), 89, 92
 sales, 190–91, 206
Interviewing, 168
Invoices(s), 91, 216
 and pricing, 155–6
IT department, 215
Italy, 84

Japanese, 120, 146, 182, 208, 252
Joint ventures, 64, 65, 85

Key Account Management (KAM), 40,
 193–6, 198–200
 and traditional selling, 193
 benefits of, 193–5
 future challenges, 197
 skills, 199–200

Key account relationship types, 193–7
Kodak, 118

Laggards, 123–4
Late majority, 123–4
Lead users, 48, 143
Licensee manufacturers, 65, 203
Licensing, 64–5, 174
Life cycle, 27, 70, 186, 230
  budgeting, 271
  cost, 154
  family, 80
  maturity, 118–21
  product, 53, 117–21, 122, 125, 132,
    150, 208, 247, 279
  technology, 48–9
Long term, 52, 58, 114, 158, 207, 258
  customer retention, 4, 56
  perspective, 53
  profitability, 57, 195, 201, 229, 271
Loyalty, 185, 188, 242
  brand, 114
  cards, 113, 214
  customers, 179
  discounts, 187

McKinsey, 136
Magazine(s), 162–3, 168, 221, 232
  trade, 225
Mail order, 14
Mail shots, 3
Mailings, 163
Malaysia, 151
Market:
  analysis, 5, 263, 267
  attractiveness, 28, 135–9
  life cycle, 27, 118
  maturity, 23–7
  monitoring, 6, 91–2
  orientation, 7–9, 23, 269, 273
  market uncertainty curve, 145
Market research, 7, 17, 18, 39, 63, 89–91,
  94, 145, 207, 250, 267–8
Market segmentation see segment(s) and
  segmentation
Marketing:
  communications, 6, 16, 17, 58, 79, 222,
    235–8
    legal issues, 274–7

concept, 15–18
department, 6, 7, 9, 15–18, 219, 265
information systems, 89, 91–2
management, 4, 7, 47, 208, 216, 217,
  271
mix, 4–6, 10–14, 55, 69, 179, 255,
  267–9
  expanded, 45, 179–80
  strategies, 214, 283
strategy, 35, 48, 58, 60, 100, 120, 149,
  160, 216, 217, 228, 278
  international, 82
world-class, 23–30
Marketing plans, 28, 97, 181, 207, 251–5,
  279
  barriers to implementation, 256–60
  contents, 252–3
  planners, 219
  timetable for, 253
  types, 251
Mass advertising, 201
Mass communications, 118, 171
Mass media, 62, 163, 167, 235
Mazda, 208
Mercedes, 118
Micro-marketing, 36
Micro-segmentation, 214
Microsoft, 61, 113
Mission statement, 28, 252
Mobile:
  3G technology, 46
  marketing, 220–25
    campaigns, 224–5
  telephony, 54, 58, 61, 234
  text messaging, 274
Modified re-buy, 75–6, 189–90

Need recognition, 72
Needs and wants, 3, 5, 8, 19, 143
Netherlands, 84
New buy, 75, 189
New entrants, 100, 106, 150
New products, 21, 72, 119, 122–5, 163,
  212
  adoption, 122
  and marketing departments, 16–17, 267
  and the Ansoff Matrix, 126–30, 283
  awareness, 169
  class, 117

New products (*contd*)
  developing, 142–6
  form, 118, 119
  high tech, 47–8
  revolutionary, 142
  sources of ideas for, 142
Newspaper(s), 12, 79, 90, 91, 105, 162–3
Nielson, 228
Norway, 84

Objectives, 160, 251, 270
  marketing, 152, 241
  research, 94, 95
Off-invoice concessions, 155
One-stop-shopping, 128, 203
Operating:
  budget, 271
  efficiency, 3
  systems, 89, 195
  units, 258, 268
Order-filling, 273
Order-getting, 273
Order-qualifying, 102, 211
Order-winning, 102, 211
Orientation, 77
  customer, 24
  deal, 207
  financial, 9
  market, 7–9, 23, 269, 273
  marketing, 23
  social, 9
  technology, 9
Outsource, 60, 78
Own label, 35, 227, 228

Packaging, 114, 128, 155, 160, 161, 169,
    203, 262, 271, 275, 281
Pareto analysis, 91
Partnership(s), 56, 187, 188, 195, 208
  approach, 128, 197
  demands of, 197
  development, 143
  DHL and, 198
  supply, 137, 152, 227
  with intermediaries, 207–8
Passive:
  distributors, 227
  research, 89–90
  users, 58, 62

Pepsi, 114, 227
Performance monitoring, 91
Perishability of a service, 43, 44
Perrier, 113, 169
Persil, 113, 118
Personal computers, 37, 118
Personal promotion, 12
Personal recommendations, 186
Personal risk, 76
Personal selling, 34, 157, 162, 189–92
Personal service, 12, 41, 59
Personality:
  brand, 25, 115–6
  rights, 275
  sports, 172
Persuasive advertising, 164
PEST analysis, 100
Pilkington Glass, 65
Pilot production stage, 145
Place, 4, 6, 10, 13–14, 29, 45, 121, 180,
    253
Plans *see* marketing plans
Poland, 84
Policy, 89, 101, 173, 185, 211
  defence, 85
  makers, 77
  returns, 211
Politics, 70
  internal, 53, 78
Porter, Michael, 100, 106
Portfolio, 36, 56, 92, 131–3, 135–9, 173,
    227, 269
  management, 27–9
Portugal, 84
Position(ing), 73, 93, 101, 105, 108, 120,
    128, 134, 142, 160, 167, 185, 261
  advertising and, 162–5
  brand and, 113–15
  competitive, 27, 107–9, 213, 281
  competitor, 16, 35, 90, 102, 153
  high-tech products, 49
  internal and KAM, 200–201
  market, 12, 27, 72, 97, 104, 113, 115,
    132–4, 135, 137, 145, 157, 194,
    252, 283
  market segmentation and, 26, 29
  niche, 24
  price, 11, 138, 149–51, 153–4
  product, 27, 117–21, 160, 208, 228, 247

public relations and, 167–70
repositioned new products, 143
sponsorship, 171–4
Post-purchase perceptions, 70, 164
Post-purchase support, 47, 180, 187, 236
Price, 55, 57, 71, 161, 172, 191, 194, 206,
    235, 272, 277
  brand, 113–6
  capital goods, 52–3
  competitor, 149, 184, 228
  continuum, 153
  cost-based, 152
  critical success factors (CSFs) and, 102,
    283
  industrial purchasing and, 76
  marketing mix and, 4, 10–13, 45, 55,
    61, 127, 179–80, 253, 267, 281
  point, 11, 55
  product lifecycle and, 27, 120–1, 124,
    271
  sensitive, 184–5, 230
  setting, 151–4, 236, 261, 275
  strategies, 149–52
  wars, 127, 133
  the Web and, 60, 230–31, 234
Primary research, 90
Problem children, 133
Problem definition, 92
Problem-solving, 98, 128, 157, 195, 199,
    241
Process(es), 14, 15, 45, 80, 150, 169,
    180–81, 211, 226, 237, 238, 262
  redesign, 268
Procter and Gamble, 15, 72
Product:
  capital goods, 51
  consumer, 33–6, 37, 54, 113, 127, 145
  high-tech, 46–50
  industrial, 37–40, 52, 85, 113
  international, 85, 261–4
Product adaptation, 128, 262–4
Product class, 117–18, 124
Product development, 5, 7, 48, 49, 56,
    133, 150, 207, 212, 234, 268, 282
  stages in, 145
Product differentiation, 27, 106, 127
Product failure, 51, 236
Product form, 70, 118–21, 163–4
Product innovation, 9, 36

Product life-cycle, 117–21
  deviant, 119–20
  explanation for shape of, 122–5
  stages, 118–19
Product management, 131–46
Product portfolio, 131, 135
Product performance, 102, 186, 261–2
Profit, 11, 22, 26, 27, 53, 137, 208, 229,
    241, 253, 269, 282–3
  category management and, 226–9
  conscious customers, 158
  customer retention and, 184–6
  KAM and, 195–8, 201
  risk, 279–80
Profitability, 9, 114, 126, 149, 179, 206,
    284
  analysis, 91
  customer, 156, 272
  long-term, 57, 184, 201
  product, 56, 91, 272
  short-term, 11, 109
Promiscuous customers, 185
Promotional mix, 162, 167, 170
Prospective purchasers/prospects, 12, 190,
    217, 237, 242, 244
Pull strategy, 204
Purchase decision, 38, 69–73, 76–8, 109,
    113, 189, 228
  high involvement, 71
  low involvement, 71
Purchasing:
  department, 76, 235
  officers, 77, 189
Push strategy, 204

Qualitative, 217
  methods, 217, 247–50
  objectives, 241–2
Quantitative:
  assessments, 102, 281
  comparison, 136
  methods, 247–50
  objectives, 241–2, 253
Question marks, 131
Questionnaire, 92, 95
Quotas, 64

Rational appeal, 115
Rationality in planning, 251, 259

Rationalized personal preference, 89
Raw materials, 128, 154, 226, 263
Reactive research, 191
Re-buys, 75–6
  modified, 76, 190
  straight, 76
Recruitment:
  customers, 184–5, 184
  markets, 44–5, 181–2
Re-engineer, 104
Reference site, 58
Referral:
  customers, 52, 184, 207
  markets, 43, 45, 77, 169, 181–2, 186
Relationship management, 53, 54, 150, 230
Relationship marketing, 45, 78, 167, 179–83, 193
Repeat business/purchase, 21, 52, 73, 157, 160, 189, 197
Research see market research
Retail, 129,151, 202, 232
  audits, 90
  brands, 35, 269
  category management and, 226–9
  concentration, 84
  loyalty, 80–82
  power, 54, 107, 227
  trade marketing and, 54–7
Retailer(s), 59, 104, 108, 156, 175, 204, 236, 271
  consumer goods, 33–6, 128
  internet, 23, 235
Reverse engineering, 144
Risk, 109, 204, 247, 250, 278
  averse, 124
  business, 278–80
  capital goods purchase, 51–2
  diversification and, 129
  financial, 263
  new channels and, 231
  new products and, 145
  purchaser's, 46–9, 71, 73, 75–7
Rolls-Royce, 85
Root cause analysis, 186

Sales aids, 12, 242, 245
Sales calls, 54, 190
Sales function, 18, 198

Sales force, 12, 54, 138, 169, 191, 204, 230–31, 237–8, 249, 266, 271, 281
  automation, 230, 237–8
  managing, 29, 241–6
  motivation, 13, 35, 159, 245–6, 267, 283
Sales person/people, 4, 12, 34, 59, 91, 189–92, 237, 243, 246, 272
  representative(s), 144, 192, 216, 242–6
Sales message, 12, 192
Sales objectives, 246
Sales orientation, 9
Sales plan(s), 14, 241
Sales process, 34, 189–92, 232, 237–8
Sales promotion(s), 12, 13, 17, 45, 127, 156, 157–61, 169, 185, 227, 267, 269, 272, 276
Sales relationship, 34, 52
Sales targets, 179, 243
Sales volume, 91, 118, 199, 226, 241
Saturation phase, 118–21
Scalloped life-cycle, 119
Secondary research, 90
Segment(s), 14, 35, 91, 101–2, 107, 109, 136, 138, 142, 151, 172, 257, 267
  internet, 60
  in planning, 251–3, 283–4
  pricing, 154
  profitability, 81, 227, 280
  single customer, 39
Segmentation, 47, 93, 174, 212
  benefit, 185
  channel, 231
  international, 84–6
  market, 5, 16, 25–9, 39, 79–83, 109
  micro, 59, 81, 214
  objectives, 81
  process, 26, 79, 215, 231
  variables, 39, 81, 217
Service:
  businesses, 41–5, 181
  customer see customer service
  elements, 4, 13, 41–2, 210, 211
  evaluation, 43
  levels, 61, 211
  organizations, 41, 211
  package, 59, 213
  products, 10, 41–5, 113, 125, 128, 186, 236

programmes, 212
quality, 44, 76, 150
Shell, 136
Six markets model, 181–3
Skimming (price), 121, 149–52, 153
Small-user market, 108
Social, 171
  Affairs Union, 85
  bonds, 194
  consequences, 21, 71
  environment/context, 4, 64, 70, 72, 78,
    99, 125, 195
  needs, 118
  networks, 222
  orientation, 9
  status, 80
  trends, 119
  values, 72, 154
Socio-economic, 70, 80, 185
Sponsorship, 115, 168, 171–5, 224
  processes, 173–5
  types, 171–2
Standard Industrial Classification (SIC), 80
Standards, 48, 64, 119, 133, 137, 262–3
  AIDA, 58
  bodies/institutes, 5, 92, 182
Stars, 131–3
Stock, 7, 51–2, 90, 109, 158, 206, 227,
  234
  holding, 202, 271
  turnover, 103, 157, 206
Strategic, 16–17, 28–9, 51, 65, 127, 129,
  134, 158, 194, 200, 203,
  214, 223
Strategic balance, 106
Strategic business units, 131, 136, 226
Strategic level, 5, 7
Strategic management, 18, 89, 131, 226
Strategic marketing, 100, 198
Strategic marketing plans, 28, 252–5,
  258–9
Strategic direction, 89, 126, 197
Strategic objectives, 184–5, 217
Strategic options, 135–6, 138, 187, 204
Strategic partnerships, 198
Strategic positions, 8
Strategic priorities, 28
Strategic zone, 281
Substitute(s), 5, 25, 44, 106, 107, 269

Supply-chain, 46, 54, 104, 127, 197, 199,
  202, 261
  management, 78
Supply-push, 50
Supplier markets, 181–2
Switzerland, 84
SWOT, 26, 100, 101–5, 138, 253, 255

Tactical marketing plan, 252–4
Tactics, 156, 197, 253
  sales promotion, 160
  trade marketing, 55
Tangible, 42–4, 187, 211, 236
  assets, 17, 278
Tangibility, 41
Technology, 46–50, 61, 85, 106, 128, 129,
  188, 216, 223, 226, 263
  advances, 5, 19, 44, 78, 106, 119
  Bluetooth, 220
  information, 34, 55, 56, 92, 172
  lifecycles, 48–9, 117
  orientation, 9, 123
  positioning, 49
  product(s), 46, 117, 149, 164
  production, 107
  seduction, 47
  transfer, 53
Television, 5, 19, 61, 84, 118–19, 124,
  127, 157
  advertising, 4, 12, 162–3
  coverage, 170
  digital, 19, 58, 62
Territory planning, 190
Tesco, 81, 172, 175, 228
Test market, 145–6
Thompson, J. Walter, 85
Timing, 225
  advertising, 166
  purchase, 70
  sponsorship, 173–4
Toyota, 63, 65, 143
Trade associations, 182, 187
Trade Description Acts, 21
Trade marketing, 35, 54–7, 189, 264, 267
  strategies, 56
Trade-off analysis, 211–12
Trade-offs, 155, 204, 259
Transaction-based relationships, 154, 179,
  193, 207

Transaction costs, 232
Transaction price management, 155
Transactional, 40, 179
  analysis, 245
Transactions, 12, 60, 187, 198, 216
  mobile, 221–3
Transport services, 16, 113, 202
Trial close, 191
Trial purchase, 122, 158, 160, 164
Trust, 43, 48, 195
Turnkey solutions, 78
Turnover, 80, 151, 185, 202
  account, 193
  staff, 193
  stock, 103, 206

Unbundled price, 155
Uncertainty, 47–9, 64, 75, 98, 249, 279
Uncontrollable costs, 272
Uncontrollable variables, 4
Unilever, 61, 170, 224
Unit cost(s), 106, 138, 230
Unique:
  identity/position, 93, 114, 116
  information, 90
  products, 52, 59, 102, 149
United Kingdom (UK), 14, 56, 59, 65, 107,
      114, 169, 172, 175, 208, 209
United States (US/USA), 41, 56, 60, 61, 65,
      107, 124, 141, 174, 226, 257
Unitization, 262
User groups, 207
Users, 58–9, 75, 77, 116, 128, 158, 221,
      224
  active, 58
  internet, 231

passive, 58
regular, 123, 127
small, 108
Utility, 187

Validating/validation, 73, 137, 187,
      224
Value added content, 222
Value added resellers, 203, 231
Value adders, 39, 114, 224
Value chain, 33, 107
  management, 35
Value for money, 11, 194, 198
Value proposition(s), 16–18, 25, 69, 81,
      151, 234, 281
Values, 8, 9, 35, 70, 72, 168, 171, 188
  brand, 27, 35, 38, 164, 173
  family, 70
Vertical marketing, 267
Visual identity, 168
Volkswagen (VW), 115, 143, 202
Voluntary standards, 262

Waitrose, 59
WalMart, 57
Warranty and guarantees, 48, 157, 186,
      264
Western Europe, 26, 54, 84–5
Western European, 70, 124, 263
White goods, 33
Wholesalers, 203, 209
Word of mouth, 43, 125, 222
World class marketing, 23–9
World class organizations, 27, 281
World Cup, 120, 172, 174
World Wide Web, 58